THE NEW MIDDLE AGES

BONNIE WHEELER, *Series Editor*

The New Middle Ages is a series dedicated to transdisciplinary studies of medieval cultures, with particular emphasis on recuperating women's history and on feminist and gender analyses. This peer-reviewed series includes both scholarly monographs and essay collections.

QUEER LOVE IN THE MIDDLE AGES

Anna Kłosowska

QUEER LOVE IN THE MIDDLE AGES
© Anna Kłosowska, 2005.

First published in 2005 by
PALGRAVE MACMILLAN™
175 Fifth Avenue, New York, N.Y. 10010 and
Houndmills, Basingstoke, Hampshire, England RG21 6XS
Companies and representatives throughout the world.

PALGRAVE MACMILLAN is the global academic imprint of the Palgrave Macmillan division of St. Martin's Press, LLC and of Palgrave Macmillan Ltd. Macmillan® is a registered trademark in the United States, United Kingdom and other countries. Palgrave is a registered trademark in the European Union and other countries.

ISBN 1–4039–6342–8

Library of Congress Cataloging-in-Publication Data

Kłosowska, Anna, 1966–
    Queer love in the Middle Ages / Anna Kłosowska.
        p. cm.—(The new Middle Ages)
    Includes bibliographical references and index.
    ISBN 1–4039–6342–8 (cloth)
        1. Literature, Medieval—History and criticism. 2. Homosexuality in literature. I. Title. II. New Middle Ages (Palgrave Macmillan (Firm))

PN682.H65R63 2004
809′.93353—dc22   2003065636

A catalogue record for this book is available from the British Library

Design by Newgen Imaging Systems (P) Ltd., Chennai, India

First edition: January 2005

10 9 8 7 6 5 4 3 2 1

Printed in the United States of America.

Dla Cioci Marysi
and to Professor Jeanette M.A. Beer

CONTENTS

ACKNOWLEDGMENTS

I owe a great debt of gratitude to the editor, Bonnie Wheeler, whose interest has fueled this project since the beginning. I also have the privilege to thank Renate Blumenfeld-Kosinki, Michel-André Bossy, E. Jane Burns, Carolyn Dinshaw, Claire Goldstein, Elisabeth Hodges, Sante Matteo, Nick Nesbitt, Claire Nouvet, William Paden, Joe Pucci, Sven Erik Rose, Randy Runyon, Francesca Canadé Sautman, Judith Zinsser, and the anonymous Press Reader, for detailed and inspiring comments on the manuscript. Adele Parker edited my English. I also want to thank Veena Krishnan, copy editor, Chris Cecot, indexer, and Donna Cherry, Matthew Ashford, and Ian Steinberg, production manager, for the care with which they worked on the manuscript. As a nonnative speaker, I thank them all for the special generosity it takes to read my work. Fundamental concepts of this book benefited from reading Jim Creech's work, published and unpublished, from the intellectual fellowship of my Department colleagues, and from the support of my mentors, Sanda Golopentia, Laurie Finke, and Martin Shichtman.

An earlier version of chapter 1 has appeared in *Arthuriana* 11:3 (2001), pp. 49–88, and I am grateful for the permission to reprint. I am also greatly indebted to the anonymous Reader from *Arthuriana*.

I thank Dr. Maria Letizia Sebastiani, at the Biblioteca Nazionale Universitaria in Turin; Mme Marie-Pierre Lafitte at the Bibliothèque Nationale in Paris; M. Bernard Bousmane at the Bibliothèque Royale Albert Ier in Brussels; and Mr. Ed Via and the staff at Miami University Libraries. Miami University generously awarded research, sabbatical, and travel grants.

This book was inspired by deep friendships and intellectual community created by my colleagues in the Department of French and Italian at Miami University. My other dear friends, Clara Román-Odio, Jean Blacker, Kris Sullivan, Faye Maris, Yvonne Parker, and Judith Zinsser, gave love and support to me and my family. Without them this book would not be written. To my sweet, beautiful, and brilliant daughters, Katherine and Helen, hugs and love—and thanks for their help.

INTRODUCTION

HISTORY OF DESIRE, DESIRE FOR HISTORY:
THE QUEER CRYPTOLOGY PROJECT

Several years ago, I started writing a book on women's friendships. I was interested in the irreconcilable differences between two discourses: medieval theory of friendship versus friendship's fictional *mise en scène* in vernacular romances. Medieval theory of friendship, represented by conduct manuals, moral treatises, and other texts, was influenced by Aristotle and by Cicero's *Laelius de amicitia*, a text that presented multiple, interested, episodic, pleasant friendships as a foil against which it defined a single, permanent, perfect friendship between two equals. French writers from Andreas Capellanus (*De Amore*, book 3) to Montaigne inherited that dichotomy. Women, as social subordinates bound to a tight network of potentially conflicting loyalties, are excluded from the ideal friendship. According to this theory, women's principal contribution with respect to friendship is to ruin friendships between men.

This does not account for fictional situations in medieval romances, saints' lives, or stories of "female worthies." By definition, protagonists are autonomous, even if they are female. Heroes are without means or lose their status, but they emerge unscathed from desperate situations with the assistance of friends. This fictional framework featuring the heroine and her adjuvants is so ubiquitous in romance that it recalls the Proppian structuralist model of the folktale. However, although friendships between women may be explained in terms of the mechanical workings of the elementary structures of narrative, they cannot be reduced to them. Female friendships carry an affective charge that makes them an important part of the romance fantasy. The first exciting thing I noticed was that some medieval manuscripts focus on them. For instance, the early-fourteenth-century *Roman du comte d'Anjou*, a Cinderella-like story that begins with the heroine's flight from incest, depicts almost as many female figures as male in the miniatures. The scenes with women account for a full one-third of the illuminations (MS BnF français 4,531). All but one of the episodes where women interact are illuminated, while other crucial parts of the plot are omitted. Two scenes stand out: women sitting on a bed, forming the resolution to escape; and a repeated image of two women running away (two ladies and a suitcase), transporting us from one episode to the next.[1] The focus of the text of the *Roman du comte d'Anjou* is different. There, men and their actions dominate, although the countess of Anjou is the character that connects the different episodes. As daughter and wife, she gives the two main male characters the opportunity to fall in love, to lose, search, mourn, avenge, and in the end to find her.

The study of the entire manuscript, not the text alone, is necessary to appreciate the importance of bonds between women. Since romance manuscripts were often commissioned as gifts for women and inherited through the female line, the history of production and ownership is also significant. Yet, matters of ownership and art history are a footnote to modern critical editions of medieval texts, if they are mentioned at all. All of this seemed very exciting to me at the time: my research on women forced me to present even well-known texts in a richer context. Friendship between women was a place where two discourses clashed, a promising place for poststructuralist and feminist reflection. I had the sensation of stepping into an unknown world whose existence we have always suspected. Women's networks of patronage and friendship, fictions depicting mutual affection and solidarity, and especially the elusiveness of that depiction (who would count miniatures?), reminded me of the discreet loyalties between women in the traditional, patriarchal societies where I grew up. There, solidarity between women is taken for granted, and it enables women to do more to support each other than men suspect. The mark of true friendship is elusive. Women and men alike show respect to a woman who knows how to use her power discreetly.

In the meantime, Stephen Jaeger published a book on medieval friendship that posited an infinite distance between the bodies of friends, no matter how passionate and lubricious their language.[2] Jaeger's goal was to restore a "lost medieval sensibility," which led him to read passion as friendship and to counteract the tendency to read friendship as passion, a tendency fueled by a veritable explosion of queer studies. Around that same time, I came across a 1926 YMCA pamphlet on mental hygiene that advocated friendships with women as a remedy for "single friendships" between men leading to "blind, muddling infatuation—often mistaken for love." The company of women, "when of the right sort,. . .is the most effective aid to a wise control and refinement of the sex urge. Separation of the sexes does not minimize these impulses; it renders them more insistent—and more subtly so. The World War strikingly revealed this fact. When we took great masses of men out of their normal setting and placed them in military camps. . .sex tension among the men was greatly increased. In the moral conservation program which was developed in the army no measure proved more fruitful than the service of fine women among the troops.. . .their presence helped men to hold on to their ideals and resist the pull towards savagery" (Exner, *The Question of Petting*, pp. 5–6).[3]

Suddenly, writing on women's friendships seemed less like my own project and more like a part of the strategy of diversion from the real issue, same-sex love. As the company of the "right sort" of women was to "blind, muddling infatuation" between men, so my book on friendship would be to love between women—a role I could not allow it to play. It seemed lifted straight from the YMCA plan of social hygiene, which promotes procuring as a "moral conservation program," and aims to eradicate jazz and petting (although, the exasperated author writes, "the young people have kept on petting"). I had to focus my book on same-sex love. At the time, I anticipated that my subject matter would be barely audible. In return, I thought, the pleasure of hearing it was more exclusive. But as the project progressed, I became convinced it was not the volume, but our hearing range, that accounted for near-silence on queer-related topics. The texts brought together here include Arthurian romances, fictions of cross-dressing, short lyric forms, extended allegories, crude fabliaux, nation-building legends, translations from Latin, and others. The task was to separate and amplify the voices, and to connect those that may potentially have to do with same-sex love, to those that speak of it directly.

In some ways, my approach was very traditional: examining "thematic sites," or hotspots, narrative motifs or themes that produce representations of same-sex desire. "Thematic sites" discussed in this book are either under-or overdetermined. One way of solving this paradox is to say that it does not matter, in pragmatic terms, whether a motif is supersaturated or under-determined. Both the supersaturated and underdetermined thematic sites function as a metanarrative device: an index, a cipher that has a phatic role—"something is encrypted here," it says—rather than a sign with a specific content. Such sites may be legible in the context, they may be thematically situated, but because they are over- or underdetermined, they are ultimately indeterminable. In their capacity as indexes, thematic sites are themes or motifs that may seem odd, almost disjointed, and either slightly incomprehensible or excessive in the context of the romance in which they are found. A good example is the wound of the Fisher King. It stimulates a prolific commentary, is vaguely sexual, is central to the narrative, and says something crucial about which we speculate endlessly without arriving at a resolution. Thematic sites are suggestive and striking, but we wonder: suggestive of what?

Another way to describe a thematic site is to distinguish between different levels of meaning, for instance, not only content but also "color" (as in "off-color"). A typology based on rhetoric, reader, or textual semantics would specify the tone, the genre, the horizons of expectations of presumptive author; patron; audience, targeted and presumptive; the register; the deictic; and so on. In that typology, the paradox of equivalence between overassigned and underassigned sites would disappear: they would all be assigned, at some level. The messy category that includes thematic sites—qua—signs and thematic sites—qua—indexes, would be reduced. For example, an underassigned thematic site is an episode in *Cent Nouvelles Nouvelles* where a handsome young man at court repeatedly goes to the outhouse, and there repeatedly has a harrowing encounter with the devil, from which he returns disheveled, half-naked, and tired. Everybody laughs, at what we are not told. Because this episode is unassigned (there is no clear interpretation inscribed), it occurred to me that the encounter is queer—explaining the humor and the color of this enigmatic story. Only in retrospect did I realize that the color ("off-color") of that story has a thematic function that led me to decipher its content. In the more complex system I sketched out above, where "color" is one of the levels of contextualization, this episode no longer would be described as "underdetermined." Instead, it would be determined by its color, or its "off-color" elements (outhouse, chance encounters, being roughed up, disheveled, undressed). In this book, however, I deal mostly with supersaturated thematic sites like the Fisher King episode.

When I examine thematic sites not only as indexes but also for content, I read the themes and motifs that are "unattached," "unassigned," or "overdetermined" in the light of normative, theological, and medical texts, in order to anchor them and limit the play of their signifiers to the queer signified, the one of most interest to me. This is not a revolutionary proposition but an old-fashioned thematic reading. I assume a risk in that I use a thematic reading to establish connections between thematic bundles that only have some elements in common. It works like a syllogism but, unlike in logic, there is an entire context to justify the last term of the operation, and that is why I stand by it.

Another aspect of the thematic site is its capacity to attract seemingly unrelated motifs, whose relatedness only becomes clear in context. To explain this capacity I borrow the Lacanian image of "quilting point"(*point de capiton*), a place on the quilt that allows us to come in one way and immediately come out the other, collapsing layers or stages of reasoning, flattening to nothing the distance in between them. In its capacity as a quilting point, a thematic site is a place, a connection, an interchange. For instance, the discussion of castration in medical texts frequently leads to the discussion of eunuchism which, in turn, leads to the discussion of effeminacy and, sometimes, of same-sex preference. In some theological texts, this connection between castration and same-sex preference is also activated, but without the intermediary stage. It is as if castration, instead of leading to a chain of reasoning that eventually could lead to same-sex preference, delivered an instant connection. For example, in Saint Augustine's *City of God*, the discussion of the Attis myth (genital automutilation) leads directly to the discussion of the rapt of Ganymede and Augustine's own experience of gender bending, same-sex promiscuity, and same-sex preference among males.

What is more, late-fourteenth-century French glosses to Augustine not only grasp but also amplify this connection between castration and same-sex preference. I find it very significant that the gloss to Augustine's discussion of ritual castration in the rites of Cybele does not provide other examples of castration, but rather references to same-sex preference. This suggests that the two, castration and same-sex preference, were closely connected and may have been interchangeable in the mind of the author. I take it further and suppose that the connection existed for other medieval authors and their changing publics across the centuries, in other texts. For instance, I look at the castration of the Fisher King assuming that it may function as a thematic site or a quilting point leading to same-sex matters. In order to substantiate that hypothesis, I look for supporting evidence. In the case of the Fisher King, that evidence exists, because queer themes and motifs attach themselves to the Fisher King story like barnacles to a ship. This is visible in later rewritings of the story, be it the one by Wolfram von Eschenbach (*Parzival*) or Wagner (as to the queerness of *Parsifal*, surely generations of opera-going gay men cannot be wrong). Although the text of Chrétien's *Perceval* must be read in the context of these other texts to assume a queer meaning, such a reading, yet again, is nothing but a traditional thematic reading.

If same-sex couples were as much on the medieval reader's mind as they are on mine, wouldn't it have been more obvious? The voices that articulate medieval queer subjectivity negotiate between need for privacy and desire for representation. Hostile representation of same-sex desire takes on the forms familiar to us: sodomite, heretic, coward, eunuch, molly. Some hints are transplanted from Latin literature, but in the new climate they do not look like their classical avatars. New forms arise, and as they are echoed across centuries, they gain legitimacy. That the examples presented here are not more often discussed, and that their record here may come as a surprise, especially in connection with some of the best-known texts, underscores the usefulness of this book.

Why would anyone *not* want to see same-sex pleasures in medieval texts? I suspect it is because one would like to reserve the Middle Ages for the type of chaste reading that procures no pleasure, or procures the "right kind" of professional pleasure, one that is not embarrassing or personal.

Two years after *The Pleasure of the Text*, where Roland Barthes described the author, the text, and the reader as sharing the same neurosis, he commented in his autobiographical essay, *Roland Barthes by Roland Barthes*: homosexuality and perversion allow ultimate *jouissance*.[4] Homosexuality is a pedagogy—Barthes even personifies homosexuality as the ultimate Muse, "Goddess Homo." His intent is clear: he designates homosexuality as a transcending principle, "an invokable figure," a goddess. A queer reading is a deeply ethical approach to the text, in that it takes the text beyond itself in a necessary way. A personal pleasure in the text implies the reading is not less, but more ethically engaged: "but I can always quote myself to signify an insistence, an obsession, since my own body is in question" (Barthes, *Oeuvres complètes*, vol. 3, p. 153).

At the time the present book was written, not literary or philosophical but rather historical legitimacy was the center of the debate in queer studies. It is as if the question of history became a stand-in for the question of viability, once queer medieval studies imposed themselves as a cutting edge field thanks to the publications in dedicated journals and university press series, colloquia, and an elite of senior scholars with established agendas of research; the question of historicity displaced the debate concerning essentialism versus constructivism. Where there is a heightened awareness of history, literary scholars occupy interesting positions. Fiction not only is not reality, it is an elitist nonreality. In step with a century of historical scholarship, the issues of unequal representation (encompassing all strata of society) push to the forefront of issues of representation in general. Judith Bennett expresses the concerns of many historians when she writes:

> The rich insights brought by intellectual, cultural, and literary studies of same-sex love are invaluable, but I seek to complement these with more complete understandings of the same-sex relations of people who were more real than imagined and more ordinary than extraordinary. For example, I have been delighted to read in recent years about how medieval theologians conceptualized (or failed to conceptualize) same-sex relations between women; about how medieval nuns might have expressed same-sex desire in their kissing of images of Christ's wound; about how a lesbian character might have lurked in the thirteenth-century *Roman de Silence*, a story with a cross-dressed heroine; and about how a fourteenth-century Parisian play explored the meaning of accidental marriage between two women. But I want more. I want to know about actual lives of ordinary women—more than ninety percent of medieval women—who never met a theologian, contemplated a Christ's wound, heard a romance, or even saw a Parisian play. (Bennett, " 'Lesbian-Like,' " pp. 1–2)[5]

Bennett does not discount the apparitional nature of the "ordinary" subjects of historical study. She acknowledges that the "real" is "always a reductionist fantasy." But in the end, historians' reflection on the constructedness of the "real" and the "ordinary" is intended to shield historical study from its inevitable fictionality rather than embrace it. In this case, history is a matter of degree, not of absolutes: of "actuality" versus "plausibility" (Bennett, " 'Lesbian-Like,' " n. 2, pp. 1-2). And it so happens that the approach I adopt completely evacuates the only question that might have directly related my work to that of historians: the degree of plausibility of fiction, the proper domain of new historicism in medieval literary studies. For me, unlike for historians or literary historicists, all fiction corresponds to an absolute reality—not of existence, but of desire that calls fiction into being, performed by the authors and manuscript makers; and continuing desire for it performed by the readers, a desire that sustains the book's material presence across the centuries. That desire is incorporated in an existence. It is the backbone of an identity. It is an essential part of the bundle of motives that lie behind all that the body does. A part essential because it is retrievable, but also because it is privileged: art reveals more of life than life does.

Bennett points out that we are only skimming the surface of medieval society. It happens to be the only activity relevant to me, but I agree it is limited. The contrast between the absolute interest I have in medieval literary texts and the limited relevance literary texts may have had to medieval society is at the root of the pronounced historical anxiety among literature scholars. In the past, this discussion has had a tendency to focus on two issues: the fit between Foucault's work and our readings; and the fit between our readings and our material. Allen J. Frantzen formulates the second point as follows: "As [Bruce W.] Holsinger has observed, queer theory is full of references to desires, fantasies, phantasms, borders, sites, and possibilities; these textual inquiries establish the ingenuity of the critics and the malleability of medieval texts" (Frantzen, *Before the Closet*, p. 19).[6] Frantzen stresses the need to "face. . .historical responsibilities" (Frantzen, *Before the Closet*, p. 25). In his book, Frantzen not only responds to that need, but also criticizes queer theory from an insider standpoint, articulating recommendations for future research. Three main points of his critique guide my thinking. One, queer theory is wrapped up in textual detail; cultural context and historical probabilities need to be brought to the fore: "the most productive investigations will, for some time to come, concentrate on describing and analyzing the primary evidence, not a particularly Foucauldian task, rather than applying poststructuralist or Foucauldian terminology to it" (Frantzen, *Before the Closet*, p. 172). Frantzen's reference to rote Foucauldian readings is in no way intended as a repudiation of theory. Rather, he denounces formalism, and not only calls for, but also formulates theoretical positions. It is in this context that we read his call for groundwork: not as a substitute for, but as a subject of, theory. Indeed, much work remains to be done on the basic level. For instance, the term *mol*, a Middle French designation for men who, among other distinctive traits, are characterized by same-sex preference, has not been properly examined, in spite of the fact that its cognates are signaled in other medieval contexts from Boswell to Frantzen, and there exists an abundant body of research on their classical use (by Williams, Halperin, and Lilja, among others) and on their significance in later periods in English.[7]

Read in an extended mode, Frantzen's call for groundwork also anticipates Carolyn Dinshaw's interest in queer pedagogy.[8] It is important to my argument that, starting with the same perceived need, the two arrive at complementary ways of fulfilling it: Frantzen advocates that queer theory eschew the canon, on political grounds; while Dinshaw appreciates the pedagogical economy of elaborating queer readings, which would allow us to teach canonical works (as illustrated by her discussion of Margery Kempe and the *Pardoner's Tale*). Other texts to discuss with our students include the mainstays of the canon, such as the *Roman de la Rose*. And we need more clarity on basic questions: terminology, historical spread, comparisons between disciplines (e.g., English and French). Frantzen quotes Halperin to remind us that these too are Foucauldian imperatives: "The standard apology for Foucault's antiempirical stance [concerning the Middle Ages] is that his example, in Halperin's words, 'teaches us to analyze discourse strategically, not in terms of what it *says* but in terms of what it *does* and how it *works*.'" Halperin adds, "That does not mean that we learn from Foucault to treat the *content* of particular discourses as uninteresting or irrelevant (after all, one has to understand what discourses say in order to be able to analyze what they do and how they work)" (Frantzen, *Before the Closet*, p. 9).

This leads us to Frantzen's second point: there is a tendency to abduct examples from their context. Frantzen's corrective strategy is to "begin with the most powerful voices of a culture" (Frantzen, *Before the Closet*, p. 12), to distinguish essential from incidental and trivial, to curb "wishful thinking." He sets the standard in the discussion of the term *baedling*, where he gives all available evidence, makes several hypotheses, repeats that "the matter is hardly settled" (Frantzen, *Before the Closet*, p. 164), and emphasizes that "the term was obviously not in wide use in the period, and attaching great significance to it may well exaggerate its relation to the sexual terminology of the Anglo-Saxons" (Frantzen, *Before the Closet*, p. 165). But the objective stated by Frantzen—"beginning with the most powerful voices of a culture"—is also, with very different results, that of Gregory Hutchison and Josiah Blackmore who, in the preface to *Queer Iberia*, articulate the need to pull queer studies "out of the closet and cabinet of curiosities" and into the mainstream, both in terms of the subject matter and the articulations with dominant critical currents, such as postcolonial theory.[9]

In practice that may mean a necessary and, in my view, appropriate inclusion of issues essential to the mainstream and contingent to queer studies. The relative weight in Hutchison's and Blackmore's collection does not, according to some critics, fall squarely in the area of history of sexuality. For these critics, this exemplifies the diffuseness of the term "queer" and its consequent malfunctioning as an operative category. If everything can be described as queer, then nothing is specifically so. In my opinion, however, the diffuseness perceived by some in that pioneering collection does not call for a change in content but rather a change in framework. We need more theory on how to do the groundwork.

For instance: can we legitimately do the history of sexuality in the absence of direct references to sexual acts? It may not be immediately apparent why the differentiation between acts and desires should make a difference. It was not at all apparent to me, and I was very surprised to discover that it structured the field. It seems to me, in strictly historical terms, that there is no difference between desire and acts. Not only is it impossible to measure the amount of genital friction and the decibel level of the cries of passion, but the information so collected would not be particularly helpful. The amount of sex one has is just the tip of the iceberg—most sex through the ages never happened.[10] But can we talk about same-sex preference if sex never happens? The answer to this question continues to divide the field. I want to emphasize that this division is fruitful in that it imposes a tightening of descriptive categories, visible in the preference for specific terms such as "same-sex desire" over "homosexuality."

What of the behavior of people that are same-sex oriented during a stage of their lives, same-sex preference limited to, or concealed behind the pretence of, generational rather than lifelong same-sex preference? The research on generational same-sex cycles of the ancient males (among others, by French classicist Paul Veyne), as well as the research on Renaissance Italy, documents that same-sex acts and relationships were an essential part of the socialization process of the male adolescent. However, past a certain age, social pressures forced the adolescent to pass from the passive to active role in same-sex settings, as well as to exercise his new, active, adult role in marriage. The age at which that passage occurred is subject to debate, and from my point of view—that of an outsider to the discipline—the conclusions are heavily influenced by researchers' personal attitudes toward sexuality. The conservative estimates place it in early adolescence, while those allied with queer studies situate it much later, in the thirties. Moreover, if the social pressures forced the passage from passive to active role in Roman males, they seem to have had little effect on the continuation of same-sex relationships. As classicists point out, Roman poetry and marriage contracts attest to the wives' power struggles with the husbands' male lovers.

In the development of Roman comedy from Plautus to Terence and New Comedy, Saara Lilja notes a shift from same-sex slave/master pairs to freeborn *pueri delicati*. This counters the well-accepted perception that Roman same-sex relations left less room for affect and were increasingly bound by political and hierarchical prerogatives. Rather than institutionalizing the power differential by attributing a wide difference in status to the partners, the later Roman comedy seems to blur that distance. Another example quoted by Lilja is consonant with that. An orator from the Augustan period, Haterius, is credited with a *dictum* that by Seneca's time became a joke, although Haterius reputedly used it in all seriousness to defend his client. The case Haterius worked on was much like others Lilja quotes from Cicero, where having granted same-sex favors in the past casts a negative light on the client's *virtus*, his "worth" or standing as a citizen, and consequently influences the outcome of the trial. Haterius's *dictum* reads: "impudicitia in ingenuo crimen est, in servo necessitas, in liberto officium" (sexual favors are a disgrace in a freeborn, an expression of gratitude in the freedman, and a duty for a slave) (Lilja, *Homosexuality*, pp. 96–97). That this dictum became current is consistent with an intense fascination with sexual passivity in Roman poetry and historiography (Suetonius), where passivity functions as an insult or a threat. Yet, as Lilja points out, the fact that this dictum is passed on to us as an amusing anecdote signals a discrepancy between the ways Roman society conceptualized passivity versus the ways it enacted it. While passivity may have been construed as negative, it was obviously not always performed as such. Between men of equal rank, it was not an act of submission but a freely chosen relationship intended to give and receive pleasure. If the pressures were great, they were not overwhelming. Roman texts portray freeborn same-sex couples, and couples where the lover of higher status was seen as more submissive, or otherwise overstepped the prescribed bounds of a homoerotic relationship. Such couples included very famous ones. Cesar and Nicomedes, king of Bithynia, were a transgressive couple since Nicomedes "conquered Cesar"; Lilja quotes Suetonius who says Dolabella called Cesar "the queen of Bithynia." The relationship between Mecenas and the actor Bathyllus also transgressed "conventional" bounds: Mecenas was so invested in it that he postponed marriage. A remarkable intensity also characterized the relationship between Hadrian and Antinous, becoming especially prominent in Hadrian's mourning of Antinous. The same social context that relies on sexual passivity to mark subordination, elevates examples of a powerful individual's devotion to his lover to the status of legend. Clearly, that is not a society where same-sex relationships can be fully explained as direct or reliable application of the mechanics of privilege, power, and hierarchy.

The relationship of the structures of affect to the structures of power is foregrounded by Jonathan Goldberg's study of English Renaissance.[11]

Focusing on relationships characterized by a sharp power differential, Goldberg analyzes friendships between literary men and courtiers. Just as the same-sex apprenticeship of the male adolescent, these literary and political friendships, and the shared beds in which they were enacted, remained invisible on the Renaissance gaydar. Goldberg concludes that they were invisible because they contributed to, rather than undermined, the bonds of homosocial, familial, political, and other alliances defined as acceptable. Same-sex relations only caused a scandal, becoming intolerable and visible, if they cut across class structures or other hierarchies; if they became the center of, rather than the means to, power. This visibility is at work in the punishment of royal favorites by political rivals. One can extrapolate that a similar principle is actuated in very rare instances where a powerful personage, perhaps a nobleman or an important church official, is brought to justice on charges of same-sex acts.[12] I understand from Herrup that such charges could be used as means to discredit a high-ranking official or head of family, and from Bray that the reluctance to use them contributed to the perception as asexual of same-sex behaviors that we may today characterize as sexual.[13] The charges were the instrument rather than the target of a prosecution aimed at the power base. This is very similar to the use made of charges of passive sexual conduct in the Roman legal system, described by Lilja and others: they served the lawyer of the opposing party to erode the *virtue* of the targeted person, to undermine his social credibility. It is as if the boundary of acceptance were the same as the boundary of power. And, says Goldberg, for theoretical reasons and for reasons of strategy and sound research, relations that were then not categorized as transgressive, should not now be categorized as homosexual. Thanks to Goldberg's nuanced analysis of the practices and the potential of male friendships and homosocial bonds, his book constitutes a new step in the discussion of passionate friendships begun by Carrol Smith-Rosenberg and Eve Kosofsky Sedgwick.

It is instructive to compare Goldberg's resolution not to cloud Renaissance discursive structures by use of contemporary concepts with Judith Bennett's work. Bennett strictly follows the same principle as Goldberg (not to occlude the historical object of study by inappropriate structures of inquiry), but she starts from a dramatically different position, including a terminology that is not only modern but also controversial. Bennett created a stir when, some years ago, she began to advocate the use of the term "lesbian-like" in research on "singlewomen," the latter being a Middle English term that she had adopted to describe the population she researched. Bennett's approach, quite radical at the time, is commonsensical. If, in a given community, there exist women who never marry, who provide for themselves economically, and about whose sex life we know nothing, what else can we call them but lesbian-like? This elicited criticism similar to the critique of diffuseness in the use of the term "queer": one should not use the word lesbian in vain.[14] Some historians maintain that we should not use it unless we have evidence of same-sex acts. As for Bennett, she attempts to define the proportion of lifelong singlewomen versus generational singlewomen. There was at any given time a large proportion of singlewomen in all premodern communities, fluctuating but always present. That presence is well accepted, and was already problematized in medieval historical studies as *Frauenfrage*, essentially the question of the surplus of women available on the marriage market. The length of time during which women remained single was longer at some periods, and in some socioeconomic circumstances. The number of episodic singlewomen was at any given time likely more significant than the number of terminal singlewomen. That is, if we look at all singlewomen in a given community across time, more of them end up as generational singlewomen, and only a fraction remains single for life. Among these, only some were single as a matter of choice. What Bennett attempts to do is to correct the prevalent understanding that the presence of singlewomen was due exclusively to a generational, episodical singlehood, and that marriage was always the preferred outcome. The principal correction that she asks for, the principal work that the term "lesbian-like" is supposed to do, is to recognize the presence and cultural importance of lifelong singlewomen, and of their sexual choices or desires. I like the term "lesbian-like" because it allows us to use the word *lesbian* in a medieval context, just as the term "proto-feminist," applied to Christine de Pizan, allowed us to use *feminist* in a medieval context. And it is for the same reason that I use the term *queer*.

Research on the medieval period is frequently prefaced by the statement that whatever we know about sodomy, or about male same-sex love, affection, friendship, sex, and identity does not apply to women. However little we can learn from medieval texts about men, we learn less about women—and we cannot extrapolate from one to the other. Simon Gaunt was among the first to retrieve elements of homosexual male identity formation in medieval French texts (*Roman d'Eneas*).[15] Reading between the lines of his discussion on women (the French life of Sainte Euphrosyne) I came to the conclusion that, although there are elements of male homosexual identity in the Middle Ages, in the case of women conceptualization of same-sex acts and gender bending corresponds to the Foucauldian definition of premodern, disallowing the use of such categories as sexuality and homosexuality.[16] In her reading of the Lollard Conclusions and other materials, including court records, legal compilations, and literary texts, Dinshaw notes a similar phenomenon: the conceptualization of male sodomy anticipates on some points the homosexual category elaborated by nineteenth-century sexology, but the discursive strategies used to describe sex between women do not follow that pattern. We can even say: the discursive strategies were calculated not to describe sex between women. For instance, there is a certain rudimentary visualization of genital acts between men, and not only of genital, but also erotic topology of the male, but when the texts, or laws, get to women, the image abruptly fades. Finding out about women in texts written by men presupposes an inherent loss. Yet, descriptions of sexual acts and organs, of erotic topologies and affective geographies of women continue to emerge, for instance, from Etienne de Fougères's *Livre de Manières* (Sahar Amer).[17] Continued interest brings these texts to our attention.

Why need we be so prompt to examine our right to queer readings, and precisely what entitles us to take for granted the legitimacy of heteronormative readings? Bennett denounces the involvement of history as a field in preempting the research on queer topics:

> I seek ways better to resist the heterosexist bias of history-writing, especially as seen in the history of women. This queering, if you like, of women's history is essential and long overdue. In recent years, one feminist historian has bewailed the "distorted and unhappy life" of medieval nuns, seen by her as forced to choose between the joys of heterosexual sex and motherhood, on the one hand, and a life of learning and contemplation, on the other. For Gerda Lerner, both heterosexual intercourse and childbearing were (and presumably still are) normal and desirable for women, and medieval nuns— as well as many early feminists—are to be pitied for having had to do without these purported joys. Another feminist historian has produced an impassioned history of female monasticism, a history that nowhere notes the evidence—as discussed by Ann Matter and others—of intense emotional and homoerotic relations between medieval nuns. For Jo Ann McNamara, the celibacy of medieval nuns seems to have been threatened only by men. And a third feminist historian has written about ordinary women in the medieval countryside in ways that normalize the heterosexual lifestyle. For myself, when I studied peasant women in the 1980s, the marriage-defined roles of not-yet-wed daughter, married wife, and bereaved widow loomed deceptively large. Women's history must not continue along this road, simply must not continue to view women—from whatever time or place—through such a distorting heteronormative lens. (Bennett, " 'Lesbian-Like,' " pp. 4–5)[18]

It is not sufficient to rely on general rules of scholarly practice, on one's right to a reading—this would result in making queer readings an issue of contention or competition with women's studies, or medieval studies. Instead, there is a need for a collective theoretical consensus legitimizing queer readings in relationship to their disciplinary matrix. As Bennett suggests, that consensus can start from examining basic categories and research agendas.

In *Sodometries*, Goldberg defines configurations of power and sexuality through a cohesive analysis of cultural evidence ranging from private letters to courtly portraits and literary works. Included in the discussion is the articulation between power and masculinity in the case of Elizabeth I, and in Shakespeare's historical plays. In that equivalence, the personage in power occupied the position of the male, and the others —irrespective of gender—assumed the position of the female. As a result, the relationship of male courtiers to Elizabeth I looked like a same-sex relationship, producing, in Goldberg terms, "same-sex effects." In the evolving relationship between Falstaff and Henry, the elaboration of a power base followed the same pattern, the establishment of a position in which the personage in power was the focus of a heteroerotic desire on the part of his subjects. However, this elaboration had the opposite result in terms of same-sex effects. The social ascendance of males follows the Greek and Roman paradigm of generational same-sex passivity. Prior to constituting themselves as powerful, males are, as part of their "apprenticeship," objects of homoerotic desire. The next stage requires the rejection and closeting of homoeroticism. In order to become a ruler, Henry renounces Falstaff's company, precisely the opposite of the opportunities for homoeroticism created by Elizabeth's access to power. Goldberg insists that the dichotomy homosexual/heterosexual is anachronistic for the premodern period not just on principle, because he believes in a disciplined adoption of Foucault, but rather because it enables him to precisely think through the relationship of heteronormativity to power during the Renaissance. Goldberg's insistence that there is no homosexual/heterosexual dichotomy in these relations is necessary for him, in that the identity between the two patterns (powerful male, powerful female in relationship to courtiers) would be erased by that dichotomy.

That is a major point of Goldberg's study, but I want to emphasize something else instead: the results of Goldberg's project differ in a significant way from its premises. These results complicate the bracketing necessary to initiate the process that leads to them. This, I believe, is of paramount importance. If erasing the homosexual/heterosexual dichotomy is the prerequisite for showing how heteronormativity was related to power during the Renaissance, Goldberg's project ends up reinstating a link between early modern and modern categories (a goal that is wholly anticipated in his introduction). In tracing the roots of the dichotomy he bracketed out, Goldberg positions the early modern period as a participant in the elaboration of these categories. Consider what then happens to the epistemic break: it is not necessarily blurred or erased, but it is justified in terms of preexisting structures on which it draws in ways that were not anticipated, producing results that were not anticipated either. The surplus

of Goldberg's project vis à vis its premise fulfills a very important function
in our collective enterprise, that of creating a history of sexuality, mapping
its manifestations in time. And that is crucial. A structural property of a
Foucauldian approach, that surplus corrects the fallacy identified by
Carolyn Dinshaw in studies of post-, early-, and modern sexuality inspired
by Foucault's work, studies that exhibit a common tendency to shift the
epistemic break and to reassign it to a *terra incognita*, a nebulous originary
past, usually premodern:

> We should be concerned about nuanced accounts of premodernity and the
> creeping implication that theoretical interventions are only made in relation
> to modernity or contemporaneity. . . . In some very influential theoretical
> and critical work developing out of postmodernism, the Middle Ages is still
> made the dense, unvarying, and eminently obvious monolith against which
> modernity and postmodernity groovily emerge. It is important to assert
> medieval indeterminacy because such postmodern interventions are ham-
> pered by their binary blind spots; the point is not simply to claim that the
> medieval is postmodern *avant la lettre* but to argue that a more patient con-
> sideration of the Middle Ages would extend the range of their interventions
> and. . .clarify their politics. (Dinshaw, *Getting Medieval*, pp. 15–16)

I do not mean to say that the mechanism to which I have just referred
is a structural property that will always be borne out. That whenever we
study a historical moment, we will always be met by the conditions that
allow us to find the epistemic break precisely in the slice of time we're
looking at, in a series of predictable epiphanies. Instead, I want to refer to
the consensus that arose in the discussion on the current status of queer
theory.[19] We have independently identified and differently labeled a
common phenomenon: the rootedness of homophobia in the past (that
Goldberg denounced in the introduction to *Sodometries*), but also the rootedness of the category "homosexual" in the past. Judith Butler's related
notion of sedimentation in *Bodies That Matter* has been exploited by Robert
Sturges in *Chaucer's Pardoner* (there exists a large body of articles that address
the question of layering of traits, focused on the Pardoner, including
Dinshaw, Burger, Bullough, Calabrese).[20] Mark Jordan mentioned that our
study of the medieval period is tragically facilitated by the fact that we are
still living in it, and Glenn Burger gave it the name I borrow, the *rootedness*
of discursive structures of homophobia. The discourse that configures the
world in terms of sodomy rather than, or parallel to, homosexuality is not
contained in the historical past, but rather it continues to configure modern social phenomena, including the phobias that homophobia stands for,
such as nationalism, the grim, merciless fight for so-called family values, and
so on. We denounce the residual operation of sodomy, that more than

premodern category, in the present—residual not in the sense of scale or impact, but time. This concerns us for the present, but gives us hope for the future, as the generational gap widens between the supporters and the detractors of same-sex marriage. Mark Jordan and Carolyn Dinshaw alike recognize a fragmentary presence of elements of homosexual identity in the premodern period.[21] David M. Halperin makes a point in his new book to remind his readers that, while he has always "made a rigorous distinction between a sexual orientation in the modern sense and the kinds of sexual identity current in the ancient Greek world," he has also always asserted that "it was possible for sexual acts to be linked in various ways with a sexual disposition or sexual subjectivity before the nineteenth century" (Halperin, "How to Do the History of Homosexuality," n. 33, p. 167). Without trying to erase differences that separate literary criticism from the work of historians like Mark Jordan, or appearing to have received an endorsement or a mandate from those I cite, I believe this "transition theory," the awareness of our rootedness in the past and of the past's cohabitation with the present, is a significant development that marks a new stage in queer theory. It is a collective and successful attempt to deal with Foucault's periodization and with the issue of historicity in queer theory. As Halperin observes:

> It is a matter of considerable irony that Foucault's influential distinction between the discursive construction of the sodomite and the discursive construction of the homosexual, which had originally been intended to open up a domain of historical inquiry, has now become a major obstacle blocking further research into the rudiments of sexual identity-formation in pre-modern and early modern European societies. Foucault himself would surely have been astonished. Not only was he much too good a historian ever to have authorized the incautious and implausible claim that no one had ever had a sexual subjectivity, a sexual morphology, or a sexual identity of any kind before the nineteenth century (even if he painstakingly demonstrated that the conditions necessary for having a *sexuality*, a psychosexual orientation in the modern sense, did not in fact obtain until then). His approach to what he called "the history of the present" was also too searching, too experimental, and too open-ended to tolerate converting a heuristic analytic distinction into an ill-founded historical dogma, as his more forgetful epigones have not hesitated to do. (Halperin, "How to Do the History of Homosexuality," p. 44)

In the years when I worked on the roots of the category "homosexual" and the representation of the then-current state of queer theory as "transition theory," the relationship of my research to that of the authors mentioned was not as simple as saying "I am quite seduced by Goldberg's demonstration, and if the price I have to pay is to be reminded every five pages that the dichotomy homosexual/heterosexual is an anachronism, I am willing to pay that price." The relationship was not that of complementary opposites. Instead, my readings directly benefited from theirs. In Goldberg's case, what I retained was not only his examples, but the principle: the economy of power is described by structures and equations blind to bodily gender. That is, the persons in power, whatever their genital sex, are always desired, and the equation of power with masculinity may produce effects of same-sex desire and effects of gender bending, which we would be mistaken in classifying as homosexual, transvestite, or transgendered.

But that leaves us with a theory that cannot account for a possible presence, in the premodern period, of a desire for same-sex acts, gender bending, and affection that is not reducible to the grid of the distribution of power. That would be simply wrong, and I doubt Goldberg's analysis allows this. The medieval period is rich in examples of affects that transcend the power grid. Parents' love for their children is one of them—we see its operation principally in the texts that document the excessive mourning of a parent for a child. Another example: the deliberate divestment of power on behalf of the beloved. We see it in literary texts, for instance, in Galehot who loses his kingdom and his life to Lancelot (in *Lancelot en prose*), and in historical figures, for instance, Edward II and Piers Gaveston. Finally, and most importantly, it appears to me on the basis of my research on women in French romance that same-sex configurations in premodern texts encompass a greater range of positions of hierarchical differential than do heteroerotic relationships. I see an erasure of social hierarchies in some fictional relationships between women that I read as homoerotic (*Yde et Olive*). I find that idyllic erasure very significant. I don't sense a similar utopian potential in medieval heteroerotic texts where there is no erasure but rather a reversal of power positions: subordination of the man to the lady ("la belle dame sans merci") in courtly love. This reversal also operates in texts that portray same-sex male pairs. Galehot sacrificing to Lancelot reenacts the scenario of opposite-sex courtly love on which their same-sex relationship is modeled.

Hierarchical differential, perhaps fully explained by the operations of the passive/active dichotomy, is for Goldberg the underlying principle of political and erotic desire. In turn, that explains the participation of homophobia in the establishment of claims to power, and in the maintenance of power regimes. That maintenance works in two directions: constituting the heterodox norm, national and individual, and destroying the alternatives, for instance through the exclusion of the same-sex alternative in building a national dynastic legend. Noah D. Guynn analyzes that exclusion in his work on the *Roman d'Eneas*, and I describe it as the collateral of the functioning of the Grail romances and French translations of Augustine's *City of God* as symbolic capital in the service of dynastic legitimacy.[22]

Homophobic slander in political tracts, religious reform and inquisition, and fiction, are also in this category.

Considering that the field's momentum now comes from postcolonial studies, the question of hierarchical differential or simply power, is one of the crucial areas that queer theory will address in the next few years. Halperin made the question of power, what he called "sex as hierarchy," the focus of his manifesto article, "How to Do the History of Male Homosexuality."[23] But there is an absence in premodern studies of a clearly articulated prerogative to look at power, compared to the work done on the eighteenth century and later periods, particularly in French studies (e.g., the relationship of the individual to the state, and universalism). What is power and why do we take it for granted? Why is power considered more palpable than desire or affect? Why do we have to prove the existence of same-sex preference by acts, but no acts are required to assume the existence of power? In our society, power is maintained by institutions, by procedures and technologies that communicate them. Do we not still find myriad informal ways to circumvent it? What was the status of power in a despotic society much less structured and centralized than ours? I would go so far as to say that, in premodern societies, but also in ours, power is to a large extent an affect.[24]

I now return to Frantzen's third point, the need to elaborate a tight theoretical framing that springs from the texts (as opposed to mechanical "processing" in a theoretical grinder that delivers monotone conclusion patties no matter what texts we put into it). Frantzen's study is centered on the concept of the shadow, a term he traces to Foucault, Sedgwick, Bray, and others, "doing more than substituting a Foucault-derived figure [the shadow] for one that is not [the closet]" (p. 15). I want to focus on the work that Frantzen wants "shadow" to perform. He emphasizes: "I am also seeking to differentiate my approach to the same-sex economies of medieval texts from critical practices of queer theory as it has come to be known in medieval studies" (p. 15). With the exception of Karma Lochrie and Dinshaw, he says, the field offers "glancing references" to theory elaborated by Foucault, Butler, and Sedgwick—a formalism, not a theoretical endeavor (p. 16). Now that the discipline has elaborated a new, binding paradigm in its relationship to Foucault, among others, the terms of that engagement are clear.

Halperin says: "Those historians of sexuality who redescribe in modern conceptual terms the culturally specific phenomena they observe in the distant historical record behave, in effect, like tourists in the archives: they misrecognize the sexual features of the period they study as exotic versions of the already familiar" (Halperin, "How to Do the History of Homosexuality," p. 60). The "already familiar" is not self-evident either, and itself in search of definitions: "a notion of modernity that relegates to pre-modernity all contemporary subjects whose desires do not conform to established definitions of sexual modernity has already confessed its own inability to capture the experience of modernity as such" (p. 19). A postcolonial critique alert to totalizing applies to the present as it does to the past. In that, Halperin's critique is an invaluable pedagogy. Only time and dialogue can result in a full unfurling of consequences derived from theoretical positions. I believe recent work shows just such a ripening. For instance, when Judith Bennett shows David Halperin's refining of his position on the existence of sexual identity in the premodern period, we anticipate the tonality of Halperin's latest book, where he repeats that Foucault never authorized "the incautious and implausible claim that no one ever had a sexual subjectivity, a sexual morphology, or a sexual identity of any kind before the nineteenth century (even if he painstakingly demonstrated that the conditions necessary for having a *sexuality*, a psychosexual orientation in the modern sense, did not in fact obtain until then)" (p. 44), and continues to define his own project ("history of homosexuality") as a reading of the past in the fullness of its historical specificity.[25] For me, queer theory is a dialogue that allows for the confrontation between multiple points of departure, conclusions, and radically different models, resulting in a tempering and refining of theoretical positions.

CHAPTER 1

GRAIL NARRATIVES: CASTRATION AS
A THEMATIC SITE

The episode of the Fisher King is one of the defining moments of *Perceval*, leading the hero to finally say his own name (ll.3575–77).[1] In that episode, Perceval encounters men in a fishing boat, who direct him to a mysterious Grail Castle. His host is an exquisitely dressed, invalid man. Seated by his side, Perceval witnesses a candle-lit procession with a bleeding lance, a magnificent *grail* or cup, and a *tailleoir* (platter):

> Uns vaslez d'une chanbre vint,
> Qui une blanche lance tint
> Anpoigniee par le mileu. . .
> Un graal antre ses deus mains
> Une dameisele tenoit. . .
> Aprés celi an revint une
> Qui tint un tailleor d'argent. . .
> Tot autresi com de la lance
> Par de devant lui trespasserent
> Et d'une chanbre en autre alerent. (ll.3,191–243)
>
> [From a room came a young man holding a white lance by the middle. . .a young woman was holding a cup in both hands. . .after her came another holding a silver platter. . .just as with the lance, they walked in front of him, and went from one room to another.]

The man's dress, the castle's luxuries, and the precious vessels, minutely described, fuel our curiosity about the story behind the scene. Although tempted to ask, Perceval remembers the precepts of his most recent mentor and forces himself to remain silent. In the following episode, he learns that the fisher in the boat was none other than his host at the Castle—the Fisher King:

> Rois est il, bien le vos os dire,
> Mes il fu an une bataille
> Navrez et mahaignez sanz faille
> Si que il aidier ne se pot.
> Il fu feruz d'un javelot
> Par mi les hanches amedos,
> S'an est aüz si angoissos
> Qu'il ne puet a cheval monter.
> Mes quant il se vialt deporter
> Ou d'aucun deduit antremetre,
> Si se fet a une nef metre
> Et vet peschant a l'ameçon:
> Por ce li Rois Peschierre a non (ll. 3,508–520)

[. . .he is a king, I can vouch for it, but he was hurt and maimed in battle and cannot move. He was struck by a javelin between the hips and he is in such pain that he cannot ride. When he wants to amuse himself and have some sport, he has himself carried into a boat and goes fishing with a hook: that is why his name is Fisher King.]

Perceval also learns that, by failing to ask about the significance of the procession, he missed the chance to cure the ailing King. The unsolved mystery is a tantalizing device: since the question was never asked, its answer remains unknown; but we learn, as does Perceval, that the enigma could have been solved. The phatic dimension is highlighted, not by presenting a solution to the riddle, but by expressing grief over a missed opportunity. Later in the romance, the Hermit gives another explanation of the scene, where a *grail* becomes *the Grail*, the fulcrum of a Christian spiritual recuperation of *Perceval*, expanded in later rewritings of the romance by Robert de Boron and others.

The inevitable recuperations feed on, but do not erase, the ambiguity of the Grail scene. The Grail Castle episode is a narrative space that carries a negative charge, a melancholy space of regret. It is not a void, but a definite absence, not a staid silence, but a vibrant, unsettling "un-said"—a screen onto which all readers can project notions crucial to their understanding of the romance. In the corpus of readings, beginning with the first recorded readers of *Perceval*, its continuators, and ending with contemporary medievalists, that enigmatic space has been invested in a variety of ways, often spiritual; still, as Daniel Poirion put it, "the Grail scene is. . .at the heart of an anxiety produced by an obscure feeling of guilt" (*Perceval*, p. 1312).

I think this episode participates in the queer subtext of *Perceval*. Whether explicitly connected to same-sex preference or not, a fiction of castration acts like a Lacanian "point de capiton" (quilting point), a thematic site that connects two areas—castration and queer concerns—and transports us from one to the other with no intermediate steps in the logic, no narrative thread, no justification provided by a heading ("genitalia and sex") as in a medical text. A quilting point works as an interchange between two topics. It allows for one of them to be articulated (genital wounding) and the other implied (same-sex preference). In setting up these thematic sites, romance authors and their public implicitly evoke queer interests, which are explicitly stated in other texts. It helps that effeminacy and castration are connected to same-sex preference in three different systems relevant to us: the heteronormative framework of the nineteenth-century sexual hygienist; Roman poets who privilege the penetrative role; medieval theologians who privilege reproductive sex performed by married couples. These three systems have different and partly incompatible ideals of male sex—heterosexual, penetrative, married/reproductive—but they are all phallocentric, and their definitions of castration and effeminacy are markedly similar. They all have a place for castration, preferably an inaccessible one: in the psychoanalytic context, fear of castration is the chief incentive for a young male to participate in the socialization process. In Rome, the Galli, or the priests of Cybele, goddess of war and cities, castrated themselves in reenactment of Attis's original, mythical mutilation. Although the cult of Cybele was central to Rome's state religion, ritual castration was downplayed by the cult's association with the foreign cities of Carthagina and Troy.[2] In the Christian tradition, moral bestiaries, some of them contemporary with Chrétien's *Perceval*, include the story of the beaver, whose association with castration derives from his Latin name, *castor*. The animal, hunted for his genitals, bites them off, leaves them to the hunters, and escapes with his life. The moral: a monk pursued by carnal desires should castrate himself—but only figuratively, the Church having condemned automutilation. Origen is the early Church writer who supposedly castrated himself.[3]

In Saint Augustine's *City of God*, castration and the rites of Cybele count among the most blatant examples of pagan atrocities, and the discussion of Attis, the Galli, and same-sex male prostitution is followed by the story of Jupiter and Ganymede. Thus, *City of God* presents many elements of the association between same-sex preference, castration, and effeminacy that were articulated in nineteenth-century sexology. In the nineteenth century, effeminacy reveals same-sex preference: a homosexual is an individual whose body has the characteristics of his type. In Saint Augustine and *Perceval*, there is no explicit operator that connects these elements, castration and same-sex preference; and yet, the elements coexist and are consecutive. Without being connected, these elements are associated, and their association survives the transfer to a different context. From Augustine's *City of God* in the fourth century to his French translator Raoul de Presles in the fourteenth, a reference to castration is tied to a reference to same-sex acts.[4]

Before turning to Raoul de Presles's commentary, I want to briefly point out the interest of the French translation as a resource for the vocabulary on sexual matters and a witness to fourteenth-century French usage. The translation departs from the text at times. For instance, in chapter 24, Raoul de Presles renders Augustine's *Galli* as *les chastres* [the castrates], and *Galli abscisi* [mutilated Galli] as *galles chastres* [castrated Galli], while he conserves *abscision* [mutilation] in the chapter title in reference to Attis. From that, we could deduce that *galles* as a word was not part of French usage, and the Galli as a cultural reference were not familiar to Raoul de Presles's public, but that *les chastres* were understood. This is confirmed by the commentary on chapter 24, where the translator elucidates the reference to the Galli. He refers the reader to Augustine's chapter 4 of book 2, an earlier mention of the Galli accompanying Cybele when she appears during her festival:

> Et apres ce char aloyent les prestres de celle grant mere et les ministres tous armez les quelz se chastroient eulx mesmes ou estoient chastres [the writer repeats twice "castres," with h added in superscript] Lesquelz estoient appelez galles ou coribans. (fol. 336v col. b)
>
> [The chariot was followed by the priests and ministers of the Great Mother, all armed, who castrated themselves or were castrated. They were called Galli or corybants.]

In another instance of cultural translation, Latin "sterile" is translated as *brehain* (used of farm animals routinely castrated to render them more useful), a French word derived from a pre-Latin root. *Brehaigne* is attested in the *Bestiaire* of Philippe de Thaun, 1119, with variants *baraine* and *brehaigne*. A close relative, *mehaigner* "to maim"—is frequently encountered in the description of the wounded Fisher King and Perceval's father in Chrétien de Troyes (*mahaigna*, l. 437; *mahaignez*, l. 3,510) and in Manessier's *Perceval* continuation.[5] Elsewhere, Raoul de Presles uses *steriles* in the French. This last example shows a tendency to "undertranslate": sometimes a French homonym or related word is used although it is not a frequent word in French or it lacks the full range of the Latin meaning. For example, when translating the distinction Augustine makes at the end of chapter 24 between a castrate, a man, and a woman, the translator renders *amputatur virilitas* [the man's virility is cut away] as *la vertu de l'homme est trenchie*, although the word *vertu* means virtue rather than virility in French.

Although I have only begun work on Saint Augustine's translation as part of my next project, for the purpose of the current discussion, I will quote an interesting mistranslation of the beginning of chapter 26. When the commentary is checked against its predecessors (the standard Latin commentaries of Thomas Walleys and François de Meyronnes), I expect that my attribution of the mistranslations to Raoul de Presles may be revised and redistributed. Augustine's text in the Loeb edition is followed by a modern English translation, then Presles's fourteenth-century translation and my translation of Presles, and finally Presles's commentary followed by my translation:

> Itemque de mollibus eidem Matri Magnae contra omnem virorum mulierumque verecundiam consecratis, qui usque in hesternum diem madidis capillis facie dealbata, fluentibus membris incessu femineo per plateas vicosque Carthaginis etiam a propolis unde turpiter viverent exigebant, nihil Varro dicere voluit nec uspiam me legisse commemini. Defecit interpretatio, erubuit ratio, conticuit oratio. (book 7, chapter 26, vol. 2, pp. 466–68)
>
> [Varro was likewise unwilling to speak of the effeminate persons consecrated to the same Great Mother in defiance of all male and female modesty. Even till yesterday you could still see them, with oily hair and whitened faces and soft limbs, passing with feminine gait through the squares and streets of Carthage, demanding even from hucksters the means to continue their shameful life. Varro chose to say nothing of these people, nor do I recall reading about them elsewhere. Interpretation failed, reason blushed and eloquence fell silent.] (book 7, chapter 26, vol. 2, pp. 466–69)

> Et de rechief ycelui varro ne voult riens dire ne Je ne me recorde mye que je laye leu quelque part des molz consacres A ycelle mesmes grant (fol. 338r col. a) mere cest assavoir La dieuesse tellus contre toutes verguongnes dhommes et de femmes Lesquelz molz Jusques au jour de hyer alans en manieres de femmes par les places et rues de la cite de carthage Les cheveux moittes ou moulies la face blance les membres degouttans pourchassoient des pueples dont ilz peussent vivre laidement (par mark) ya falli interpretacion Raison y ot honte et biau parler se teut (fol. 338r col. b)
>
> [Varro did not choose to say anything, neither do I recall having read anywhere, about the *molz* [Lat. *mollibus*] consecrated to the Great Mother, that is the goddess Tellus, against all dictates of masculine or feminine shame. No longer than yesterday, these *molz* walked in a woman's fashion about the squares and the streets of the city of Carthagina, with wet or doused hair, white face, dripping members, chasing after people by whom they could make a filthy living.
> Interpretation failed, Reason was ashamed, and eloquence was mute.][6]

I explore the Roman and medieval stereotypes of same-sex–oriented men in chapter 3, and make only a few observations here. It seems quite clear that the fourteenth-century translator was not familiar with Roman stereotypes connoting same-sex preference or effeminacy when he translated Augustine's passage on the *molz*. What we see in French are men who walked around dripping wet from head to toe. Nor did he translate them into any contemporary image of same-sex–oriented or effeminate men— although such images were available, and he does not rule out a contemporary translation in other cases, taking liberties to render more legible the culturally and linguistically foreign text, as we have seen in the examples above (*sterilis* translated as *brehaing*, *Galli* translated as *chastres* when the word first appears in the text, and so on). He renders *madidis capillis* as "humid or wet"—the wet-hair look achieved with too much hair pomade, in Rome proverbially connoting same-sex–oriented men, as well as those who were perceived as too interested in women, or dandified. More interestingly, he renders the Roman (and modern) stereotype of overly flexible joints—in Augustine, *fluentibus membris*—as "dripping members," *membres degouttans*. The verb *degoutter* is first attested in the early-twelfth-century Cambridge Psalter (1120), and means to drip fluid drop by drop; it is also used by Chrétien de Troyes, for example to describe Perceval weeping as he first approaches the Hermit.[7] This is an altogether obvious mistranslation, producing an idiosyncratic image that has nothing to do with what Augustine intended. The phrase associating the two collocutions: "*facie dealbata, fluentibus membris*," translated as "white face and members dripping with drops" (in Augustine, "bewhitened" face, powdered or pomaded, calling on another Roman stereotype: use of cosmetics), produces an inexplicable association with the lance in the Fisher King episode:

> La lance blanche et le fer blanc;
> S'issoit une gote de sanc
> Del fer de la lance an somet
> Et jusqu'a la main au vaslet
> Coloit cele gote vermoille. (ll. 3,197–201)

> [. . .the white lance and the white iron. A drop of blood was coming out of the iron at the tip, and this red drop flowed all the way to the youth's hand.]

I want to emphasize that, although Presles mistranslated Augustine's vignette of the *molz*, he was not ignorant or uninterested. Perhaps the mistranslation originates in the association of same-sex desire with castration that interfered with the translator's understanding of Augustine's passage— an association that is also a key feature of the Fisher King episode. Given the way these texts seem to think about acts, which for us are same-sex acts, something must have been feminine about one of these individuals for the sex act to make sense. For the medieval translator and the romance poet, same-sex acts were not homosexual. They were not even same-sex, in the sense that they did not involve two individuals of the same sex, but rather one passive and one active, or one receptive and one insertive. This does not mean that the same-sex acts were heterosexual, either: that much is obvious as well. These were "sodomitical" acts, weighted with obscure but terrifying consequences. The participant in "sodomitical" acts, not man and not woman, is Wolfram von Eschenbach's Fisher King—I discuss later the female characteristics of his genital wound, and also the masculine spear thrust into that wound to cure it. For now, I would like to note the essential points that echo in Wolfram and Raoul de Presles. In Wolfram, the wound is feminine, and masculine elements are applied to cure it, producing the ultimate paradox: the effeminate man is cured by contact with the masculine element, or (if one were willing to read the cure of Anfortas as a sexual metaphor), by having sex with a man. This is consistent with what Raoul de Presles imagines about the *molz*: they are castrated (emasculated) in such a way as to be sexually available to men. Castration appears in these texts as an inherently necessary element that makes a "sodomitical" coupling imaginable. These were the historical origins of the discourse producing the effeminate homosexual subject of the nineteenth century, defined by his morphology rather than his acts.

Raoul de Presles was not unaware of the sexual behavior Augustine was describing, although he thoroughly mistranslated the standard Latin array of metaphors attached to that description. The fact that this particular passage was thoughtfully analyzed is revealed in the commentary, in a critique of those commentators who did not distinguish between the *molz* and the priests of Cybele. Raoul de Presles's understanding of the sexual activities of *molz* is spelled out in medieval terms: he says that "men had relations with *molz* as *sodomittes*." He makes sense of Augustine's passage describing the *molz* by misinterpreting the phrase "*molz* walk about town in the manner of women" as a description of prostitutes. This is apparent from the commentary, not from the translation itself. The commentary's reference to prostitution makes us realize that when *incessu femineo*, "with feminine gait," was translated as *en manieres de femmes*, it was meant as streetwalking, not catwalk-like gait. This confirms that Raoul de Presles was unaware of Roman stereotypes concerning the *molz*, but familiar with male same-sex acts, and perhaps also with male same-sex prostitution, modeled on female prostitution.

Another characteristic of Raoul de Presles commentary on the *molz* is the connection he makes between a specific form of castration and same-sex receptiveness:

En ce xxvie chapitre monseigneur Saint Augustin denoustre la laidure du service qui se faisoit a celle grant mere des dieux Especialement dun service

que len luy faisoit duquel varro ne aultre ne rent aucune raison Et fait en ce
chapitre ii choses Premierement il repreuve la laidure de ce service ou de
celle maniere de aourer en especial Secondement il prent aucuns conclusions
de ces dieux superesleux en general (fol. 338v col. b) (. . .) Quant du pre-
mier Il est assavoir que aucuns se chastroient eulx mesmes en lhonneur de
celle mere des dieux Les quelz monseigneur Saint Augustin apelle molz Et
croient aucuns que ce furrent les prestres de celle dieuesse qui aussi sont
apellez galles Mais il nest pas ainsy si comme Il apert par le texte de monseigneur Saint Augustin Car du chastrement de ces Galles est rendue la raison cy dessus ou xxiiiie et xxve chapitres Mais de ces molz Il dit quil not
oncques raison de varro Ne il ne se recorde que il ayt ailleurs leue si comme il
apert par le commencement de ce chapitre Et pour ce ces molz estoient con-
sacres a aultres choses par especial que nestoient les galles Et estoient chastres par telle maniere que Ilz souffroient que les hommes eussent a faire a
eulx comme sodomittes Aussi comme en lhonneur de venus pluseurs
femmes estoient prostitueez si comme il a este dit ou xi chapitre du quart
livre (par mark) (. . .) Secondement il la compare a la laidure de iupiter et
preuve encores quelle fut plus laide que celle de iupiter Car combien que ce
Jupiter violast pluseurs femmes toutesvoyes Il ne abusa oncques que dun tout
seul enfant cest assavoir de ganimedes qui fust fil de tros qui fut fil des dar-
daniens Les quelz furent depuis apellez troyens De tros Lequel enfant tantalus roy de frige ravy treslaidement pour acomplir la luxure de Jupiter pour
le ravissement du quel grant batalle sourdy sicomme dit orose en son pre-
mier livre ou vii chapitre Et celle dieuesse en fist abuser pluseurs Tiercement il
compare ceste laidure aux laidures de saturne (fo. 339r col. a) auxquelles elle
est mieux comparee et les seurmonte quant aux aultres choses Car jasoit ce
que len faigne que sa(b)turne chastra son pere toutesvoyes nul ne se chastra
en son temple ja soit ce que len y en (en in superscript) ocie aucuns pour
luy faire sacrefice si comme nous avons touchie au xix chapitre de ce livre.
(fol. 339r col. b)

[Commentary on this chapter:

In the 26th chapter, lord Saint Augustine shows how disgusting were the
rites of the great Mother of Gods, especially one of her rituals which Varro
and the others do not describe. He does two things in this chapter: first, he
denounces the abomination of that ritual or that type of devotion in particular. Second, he presents conclusions concerning the principal deities in general (. . .) (fol. 339r col. a). Concerning the first: some men would castrate
themselves in honor of the Mother of Gods. Lord Saint Augustine calls them
the *molz*. Some [commentators] believe that these were the priests of the
goddess, also called the Galli, but lord Saint Augustine's text makes clear that
this is not the case. Castration of the Galli is described in chapters 28 and 25,
but he says there is nothing about the *molz* in Varro and he does not remem-
ber having read about them elsewhere, as the beginning of this chapter
shows. That being the case, the *molz* must have served a particular purpose,

different from the Galli. They [the *molz*] were castrated in such a manner that
they allowed other men to have relations with them like sodomites, just as
many women were prostituted to honor Venus, as described in chapter 11,
book 4. (new paragraph) (. . .) Second, Saint Augustine compares them [the
rites of Cybele involving castration] to Jupiter's abominations and proves that
they were even more disgusting than Jupiter's. Because, although Jupiter
raped many women, he nonetheless only abused one single child:
Ganymedes, son of Tros, descended from Dardanians [i.e., descendants of
Dardanos, the founder of Troy], later called Trojans after Tros. The king of
Phrygia, Tantalus, shamelessly ravished that child to fulfill Jupiter's lust. That
ravishment led to a great battle, described in Orosius, book 1, chapter 7. [If
Jupiter abused just one—Ganymede,] that goddess [Cybele] abused many.
Third, he compares this filth to abominations of Saturn —a better compar-
ison, but it is still a greater abomination. Because, in spite of the fable about
Saturn castrating his father, no one castrated himself in his temple, although
some were sacrificially killed, as mentioned in chapter 19, book 7.]

To sum up: Saint Augustine's reference to the rites of Cybele clearly
interested the fourteenth-century translator. Differentiation between the
Galli and the *molz* is of prime importance because through that distinction,
the fourteenth-century commentator described eunuchism, same-sex
prostitution, ritual castration and same-sex receptiveness not as a single
undifferentiated category (luxury, sodomy, heresy, etc.), but as a number of
understandable and identifiable practices. At the same time, castration was
so fascinating for the medieval writer that it hijacked his translation of
Augustine's passage. I have suggested that this happened because, for the
translator, the idea of castration was strongly associated with same-sex acts.
He even created a specific articulation between castration and same-sex
acts that is absent from Augustine: the *molz* are "castrated in such fashion"
that they are receptive to other men. The translator used different frames of
reference to describe the less well-known *molz*, some from classical sources
(*molz* are like female ritual prostitutes in the rites of Venus), some contemporary (*molz* allow men to have the same relations with them that men
have with *sodomittes*, a medieval term whose tradition has been traced by
Mark Jordan).[8] The next topic discussed by Saint Augustine and the
glossator is the rapt of Ganymede, another thematic site that attracts references to same-sex desire throughout the Middle Ages; and the third,
castration of Saturn's father imputed to Saturn, and sacrificial murder in
Saturnine rites.

Unlike in nineteenth-century fiction, to read castration in medieval
romance as an implied reference to same-sex preference is to take a big
risk. Supporting evidence is crucial, and that is why the French translation
of *City of God* and other texts mentioned here are so important. If the

genital wound of the Fisher King has been interpreted in many mutually exclusive ways, *City of God* was accompanied in the Middle Ages by a commentary in which the association between the discussion of castration and same-sex preference, present in the original text, was confirmed and developed into an articulation. And, if the episode of the Fisher King in Chrétien's *Perceval* is brief and completely enigmatic, Wolfram von Eschenbach's *Parzival* fleshes out this episode in a way that further invites a queer reading. But if there is, without any doubt, a relation of filiation between Chrétien's *Perceval* and Wolfram, any other images of castration that may have been on the horizon of readings of the authors and public of the Grail fictions are a matter of speculation, including those of Saint Augustine. Among other Latin texts current in the Middle Ages, Ovid seldom mentions castration. *Metamorphoses* does not expand on Attis, and neither do its medieval glosses. Catullus's masterpiece, *Attis*, was probably lost until the humanistic rediscovery of a manuscript in Verona in 1314; although if Catullus were available, it would have also been present in northern France: enough traces point in that direction. In his gloss to Saint Augustine, Raoul de Presles only mentions Ovid, Isidore (*Etymologies*, book 8) and Fulgentius as resources on Attis (fol. 47 r–48r). If there are other likely texts, I am unaware of them; that is why I dwell on Augustine and Catullus, not obvious choices for the discussion of *Perceval*.

Wolfram von Eschenbach's *Parzival* is of all rewritings the one closest in time, if not in language and geography, to Chrétien's. Wolfram seems to have rewritten and divided Chrétien's maimed Fisher King into two punished philanderers—Clinschor and Anfortas. The *dédoublement*, doubling of characters, allows for differentiation between castration whose meaning is limited to punishment for adultery (Clinschor), and Anfortas's "wounding" whose narrative significance includes, but is not limited to, that causality (philandering): Anfortas's wound is interesting in itself. The treatment of the wound and its link to the macrocosm of Anfortas's kingdom are described at length. One could almost say that while Clinschor's castration functions as a result, Anfortas's is a process; and it is to that process that the narrator devotes his attention, while Clinschor's is one of the lesser "adventures." Arthur Groos differentiates between the two figures along the same lines ("the wounded Anfortas and the castrated Clinschor," Groos, *Romancing the Grail*, p. 148), and focuses on Anfortas's wound, without discussing Clinschor.[9] Given the nature of the treatment of Anfortas's wound— repeated penetration, intense and prolonged attention from the male entourage—this figure bridges seemingly opposed characteristics: uxoriousness, philandering, and homoeroticism. While the reason for the wound is an excess of heterosexual activity, the treatment requires male-to-male genital manipulation.

Not much about Anfortas is learned in the Fisher King castle episode in chapter 5—and the narrator explains the reasons for this strategy: "'if one were to shoot a tale at people that is bound to weary them—for it finds no lodgment there but follows a broad path, in one ear and out the other" (chapter 5, p. 128).[10] The narrative of Anfortas's sorrows is part of chapter 9, the meeting between Perceval and his uncle, the hermit:

> Jousting, he was wounded by a poisoned lance. . .through the scrotum. . .he carried the lance–head away with him in his body. . .
>
> When the King returned to us so pale, and drained of all his strength, a physician probed his wound till he found the lance–head and a length of bamboo shaft which was also buried there. . .
>
> The King's wound had festered. None of the various books of medicine we consulted furnished a remedy to reward our trouble. All that was known by way of antidotes. . .were of no avail. (chapter 9, pp. 244–45)

All fails: herbs from the vicinity of Paradise, the twig recommended by Sibyl in the *Eneiad*, pelican's blood, dragon-wort, a unicorn's stone (chapter 9, pp. 245–46). The story of Anfortas's cure is so long, it has to be interrupted for dinner and taken up again the next day:

> Now tell me, did you see the Lance at Castle Munsalvaesche? We knew from the wound and the summer snow that the planet Saturn had returned to its mark. Never before had the frost caused your dear uncle such pain as then. They had to place the Lance in the wound—one pain relieved the other— and so it was reddened with blood. The advent of certain planets which stand so high one above the other and which return at different speeds, gives the denizens here great sorrow: and the change of the moon, too, is bad for the wound. At these times which I have named, the King can find no peace. The intense frost torments him, his flesh grows colder than snow. Since the venom on the spear-head is known to be hot, it is laid on the wound at those times. It draws the frost from his body and round the Lance . . .
>
> There is a lake called Brumbane onto which he is taken so that the stench from his gaping wound shall be quelled by the fragrant breezes . . . From this a rumor went the rounds that he was a fisherman. He had to endure this story, though, sad, unhappy man, he had no salmon or lamprey for sale. (chapter 9, pp. 249–50)

Wolfram's expansive version invites us, in retrospect, to read Chrétien's brief formulation as the source of two distinct traditions represented by two "branches" of *Perceval* translations and continuations. In the majority of later rewritings, the castration of the Fisher King is a punishment for his heterosexual transgressions. In others, for example in Manessier's version, no such causality is expressed. I suggest that this ambivalence makes it more likely that castration serves as a cipher for queerness—including Wolfram's Anfortas, in spite of the heterosexual causality expressed there (castration as punishment for philandering). This is consistent with the indeterminate meaning of effeminacy, of which Halperin reminds us: while it has "traditionally functioned as a marker of heterosexual excess in men," it is also one of the main "pre-homosexual" categories (Halperin, "How to Do The History," p. 93).

These texts invite us to see the Fisher King, depicted in terms of suffering, pathology, and inversion, in a way that is in keeping with our expectations of how the dominant medieval culture would perceive a queer character. Anfortas is scripted so as to inspire pity and abjection. This may well be the dominant mode of representation of queer characters in romance, but a less tortured queer representation can be seen in the figure of Perceval himself—a possibility explored in modern gay appropriations of Grail fictions.

If Wagner calls his *Parsifal* "a sacred dramatic festival," Richard Mohr points out that the drama concerns men, not gods. Today, the Grail is for and about men—"Knights, Young Men, and Boys"—both as a text and as a cultural institution. Wagnerian opera "outs" its public, as Terence McNally's characters observe in *The Lisbon Traviata*: "it was kind of obvious: two grown men at the performance of *Parsifal*."[11] In that performance, Mohr notes the "necessary absence" of women. He reads Kundry's "vanishing" death, unadorned by musical flourishes, as the ultimate exclusion: "Parsifal. . .successfully resists Kundry because, well, he is in the end not interested." Instead, the Spear and bodily fluids form the dramatic nexus: "For Parsifal and the other Grail knights, *the* Spear, unlike *a* spear but like a cock, ejaculates male bodily fluids worthy of worshipful adoration." Mohr reads Parsifal's pose, "reverently lifting his eyes to the spear-head," as a glory hole scene:

> This reverence—which one critic calls "one of the famous imponderables of *Parsifal*"—while in the same breath admitting that the Spear is "indisputably a phallic symbol"—is obviously a homoerotic act. And it bestirs the opera's most famous musical passage, the Good Friday Spell, with its wondrous depiction of spring's unfurling and of birth in nature, for which various types of asexual, vegetal reproduction provide the models of splendor. The day on which Christ is penetrated is the day in sacred time on which not even Mary is needed for procreation. (Mohr, *Gay Ideas*, p. 138)

I want to focus on what Mohr points out as the essential feature of Christian symbolic genealogy: its exclusive masculinity. It is, I believe, the key to the versatility of *Perceval*. The story can be read as a spiritual quest, or a knight's apprenticeship, or male homoerotic fantasy, precisely because all three—Christianity, chivalry, and male homoeroticism—are principally for and about men. To discuss the relationship between masculine symbolic genealogy, castration, and eroticism, I reach for a text that, I am fully aware, is not directly related to *Perceval* or male homoeroticism: Kristeva's essay on *Stabat Mater*. I need Kristeva's text, first, because it is a close reading of a spiritual text inspired by Christian mythology—the Passion of Christ—that focuses on the erotic. Kristeva's text is a pattern for my own: an erotic (homoerotic) reading of *Perceval*—a narrative that only a generation after Chrétien assumes full spiritual potential in French verse and especially prose continuations. Second, I need Kristeva because she dissects masculine symbolic genealogy and finds a repressed feminine element at the center, revealing the paradox of an ideology that simultaneously incorporates and rejects, and the paradox of an expression that simultaneously reveals and hides. Third, Lacanian and structuralist approaches enable her to create an articulation between art, language, and the pre-linguistic: the pre-linguistic union with the mother as a model that incest, love, and art simulate. This theoretical position and the articulation that derives from it are central to my project.

Stabat Mater, the Marian hymn attributed to Iacopone da Todi, is a short text describing the Mother of God at the foot of the Cross.[12] The brevity of the poem is in such contrast to *Perceval* that its use here may raise legitimate questions, and to answer these questions satisfactorily it is necessary to recall that the title *Stabat Mater* refers not only specifically to the poem, but also to the musical envelope and visual representations of the scene. The references condensed under this title are the iconographic, musical, and textual tradition of the poem. The text itself does not matter for my argument, except as the refraction point of these references and the origin of Kristeva's article: it is not as it was then, but in the context accumulated throughout the centuries, that *Stabat Mater* is discussed by Kristeva. Then as now, *Stabat Mater* functions not only as the title of a specific representation but, like the Man of Sorrows, it refers to the human condition for which Christianity and its art found an adequate expression. It seems to me that the force of this representation and, indeed, the force of Christianity as a system of thought and a religion derives from the fact that this condition is not local. Even though it evokes a specific moment in the essential rite of Christianity—Christ's Passion—that moment, embodied (as opposed to: articulated) by the figure of the Mother at the Cross, takes on a collective and individual significance that makes it relevant to all mothers, and beyond them, to all suffering. For instance, in the work of the Polish composer Krzysztof Penderecki, *Stabat Mater* encrypted the senseless suffering of a subject dignified rather than diminished by his participation in a collective tragedy, a suffering whose public acknowledgment was disallowed when the work was created, both with respect to the present and to large swaths of the past. *Stabat Mater* stood for the Holocaust, for the past, for the present, and because it was so pathetic and yet so abstract, it worked for everyone: to the government, it was about the war; to the opposition—about the government; to the man in the street, it was resistance the more precious because, being so elusive in its precise meaning, it went unpunished. But it is only with Kristeva that we can uncover the inherent paradoxes of that figure, and begin to ask what is silenced in *Stabat Mater*, before we go on to acknowledge what suffering silenced elsewhere can find its powerful expression through her.

In comparing the Fisher King to *Stabat Mater*, I reflect on the contradictions inherent in the repression of desire and on other resonances underscored by Kristeva's essay: the pain of the mourner, the sublimation of grief, the cosmic dimension of loss. The comparison with *Stabat Mater* allows me to focus on the latitude and indeterminacy gained by a silent, bodily expression of pain; on gender reversals; and on the "paranoid logic" (Kristeva's term) of a sacrificial figure torn between competing orders of transcendence: for *Stabat Mater*, feminine and bodily (genealogy) versus paternal and symbolic (theology); for the Fisher King, queer desire versus queer anxiety.

Kristeva refers to the same scene Mohr observes—the death of Christ— but she complicates the picture, pointing out the "paradoxical logic" of Mary who embodies the principle of life (mother) and death (mourner), the feminine principle (the three Parks) repressed by an exclusively masculine Christian transcendence. In Wagner's opera, Mohr studies the extension of that masculine symbolic order from God's genealogy to priesthood: "the equality between persons, for which institutionalized homoerotic attraction between males serves as the sign"; an order where "the 'pure' replace heterosexuals in a social form in which knights become priests" (Mohr, *Gay Ideas*, pp. 137–39). Mohr shows that the homoerotic hero of Wagnerian opera is Parsifal the priest. I argue that in medieval romance, the homoerotic hero is not only Perceval, the youth transfixed with longing when he first sees knights in shiny armor, but also the Fisher King, the wounded man. The one makes the other possible:[13]

Et quant il les vit en apert. . .
Lors dist: "Ha! Sire Dex, merci!
Ce sont ange que je voi ci. . .
Ne me dist pas ma mere fable,
Qui me dist que li ange estoient
Les plus beles choses qui soient

Fors Deu, qui est plus biax que tuit.
Ci voi ge Damedeu, ce cuit,
Car un si bel an i esgart
Que li autre, se Dex me gart,
N'ont mie de biauté le disme. . ." (ll. 127–49)

[When he saw them clearly. . .he said: "Thank you, Lord God! I see angels. . .My mother did not exaggerate: she told me angels are the most beautiful thing ever, except God, who is more beautiful than anything. I think I am seeing Lord God here, because that one I see is so beautiful, that the others, God help me, don't have one-tenth of his looks. . ."]

Mohr sees the drama of Christianity as profoundly homoerotic; with Kristeva, I focus on that drama's apposite, mastered and repressed; on sacrifices that, unlike the triumphant sacrifice of the Son, seem unredeemably tragic. Leaving the discussion of Perceval aside, I focus on the Fisher King. That figure, with its alternating feminine and masculine traits, its transgressive sexuality, embodies the conflict immanent in the representation of homoeroticism in the hostile, heteronormative economy of medieval romance, just as the Mother embodies the conflict immanent in the hostile economy of a patriarchal symbolic system; the conflict that Wagnerian *Parsifal*, in Mohr's interpretation, temporarily erases. If Perceval stands for the triumphant aspect of the homoerotic gaze, love at first sight, in his encounter with the knights, the Fisher King could stand for its tortured obverse, homoerotic anxiety, riddled with distortions inflicted by a heteronormative optic. In my reading, the homoerotic hero is not posed like Christ or a priest, but rather like Mary in *Stabat Mater*, Mary who embodies irredeemable suffering, but who also articulates that which is repressed, while leaving it thinly veiled.

Reading the Fisher King as a coded queer figure depends on finding parallels between the Fisher King's wounding and other inscriptions of suffering in medieval texts. I find in *Stabat Mater* a more developed context for concerns that the Fisher King episode elliptically posits. The comparison between the Fisher King and Jesus appears in previous scholarship on Perceval.[14] My choice of parallel, not with the Man of Sorrows but with *Stabat Mater*, is best explained as a narrowing of the field of comparison to one affect that the two figures embody: suffering without transcendence. Unlike the suffering of the Man of Sorrows, part of the heroic narrative of redemption, the pain of Mary at the Cross is its own finality, her body—an organic text. Another reason is the paradoxical position of Mary and the Fisher King in terms of gender and power. Finally, the two figures are posed in a similar way: silent mouths, loud bodies, in a landscape of massive desolation. In *Stabat Mater*, *Dei genitrix* incorporates cosmic suffering at the death of God. Like the castration of Perceval's father in Chrétien's *Perceval*, and Anfortas's wound in Wolfram's *Parzival*, Mary focuses and reflects the macrocosm of the Wasting Kingdom.

According to Kristeva, *Stabat Mater* both stages and attempts to suppress the feminine principle: the maiden, the mother, and the ritual mourner, ruling the three realms of sex, birth, and death, the principle of transcendence evacuated by the symbolic genealogy of the Christian dogma in which Son descends from Father. As Kristeva points out, this citation is further erased from the seventeenth century on, smothered by the lachrymose sweetness of the accepted, Counter-Reformation forms of Marian piety (litanies, rosaries), and by the baroque excesses of the musical envelope of *Stabat Mater* in Pergolesi's and other orchestrations. The Fisher King narrative meets a similar fate. In most later versions, as the Fisher King episode was rewritten and expanded, the subversive potential present in Chrétien's brief treatment was repressed by a heteronormative causality: the Fisher King's wound was identified as a punishment for philandering. In Wolfram's *Parzival*, and later in Wagner, however, the queer potential of Chrétien's *Perceval* becomes clear. That capacity for suppression is another reason for comparing the Fisher King episode to *Stabat Mater*.

Supposing that the Fisher King is queer—that the incoherences of this episode can be explained thus—what work is this episode doing? To what feelings of queerness in the medieval audience does it give voice?[15] According to Kristeva, the figure of *Mater dolorosa* allows for the emergence of the repressed feminine principle—a biological, reproductive continuity—as opposed to the exclusively masculine, Christian continuity of resurrection and redemption. The tradition of ritual mourners accounts, for Kristeva, for the popularity of Mary as *Stabat Mater*—that is, the popularity of the hymn is based in equal measure on the resurgence and on the mutation that the feminine principle undergoes in the Christian context. This dialectic of resurgence and mutation is a model for the functioning of queer desires and anxieties in a heteronormative text.

I want to acknowledge a debt to Sanda Golopentia, whose remark on Mary's silence in the "score" of *Stabat Mater* led me to the distinction between organic text and giving voice. Mary has no "lines" in the hymn, but her body is described in detail. The very grammar bespeaks passivity by the preference for the gerund (standing, dying, suffering, trembling, seeing) and the past participle or adjective (pained, crying, saddened, suffering, sad, afflicted):

Stabat mater dolorosa
Juxta crucem lacrimosa
Dum pendebat Filius.

Cuius animan gementem
Contristatam et dolentem
Pertransivit gladius. . .
Quae marebat et dolebat
Pia mater, dum videbat
Nati poenas inclyti. . .
Eia, Mater, fons amoris
Me sentire vim doloris
Fac, ut tecum lugeam (ll. 1–27)

[The suffering mother stood crying at the foot of the Cross from which hung the Son. The sword pierced her soul, pained, suffering, and mourning. . .How the pious mother mourned and despaired, from where she saw the son doubled in pain. . .Mother, spring of love, make me feel your pain, so I can mourn with you.]

The narrator asks to share in Mary's suffering just as she shares in Christ's, but he is the one who speaks, describing and imploring. Her pain is evoked in the opening strophe as a sword piercing her soul, a metaphor so strikingly visual that one readily recalls its iconography, in the portrayals of the Virgin skewered by one or multiple blades: "*cuius animam. . .pertransivit gladius*" [whose soul. . .pierced the sword] (ll. 4–6; the image, as the hymn, refers to a passage in the New Testament). A vehicle of pain, the Virgin is allowed none but bodily expression, although that expression is ample and intense. I argue that the Fisher King, whose wound is made to play such an important role, can likewise be read as an organic subject.

The narratives of *Stabat Mater* and Chrétien's Fisher King differ greatly. If Wolfram dwells on his torment, in Chrétien's version the words "mourning" and "suffering" are never applied to the King; rather, Perceval uses them to describe his regret at his own failure at the castle of the Fisher King (ll. 6,381–82: S'an ai puis eü si grant duel / Que morz eüsse esté mon vuel [I mourned [my failure to ask questions] so much / That, if I had my way, I would have died]). The King refers to his condition as an indisposition (l. 3,109: je n'en sui pas aeisiez [I am unable to]) or in terms of power (Je n'ai nul pooir de mon cors, / Si covandra que l'an m'en port [I have no power over my body, so I will have to be carried, ll. 3,342–43]). If Perceval, his mother, the hermit, and innumerable other characters in the romance faint from pain, weep, and writhe in agony, the Damsel alone speaks of the King's suffering (ll. 3,510–11: navrez et mahaignez. . ./ Si que il aidier ne se pot [struck and wounded. . .so that he cannot move]); (ll. 3,513–14:. . .si angoissos / Qu'il ne puet a cheval monter [in such suffering that he cannot mount a horse]); (ll. 3,522–23: Qu'il ne porroit autre deduit / Por rien soffrir ne andurer [because he could not suffer or even endure any other pleasure]). However understated it may be, the image of the King barely lifting himself up, carried into a boat, or carried out of the great hall in a sheet, has great significance. Other than death, only love so stills a man in romance; we may think of Lancelot, slowly drowning as his horse moves forward into the river, lost in the contemplation of Guinevere, in *Lancelot en prose*; or Troilus who loses the use of his limbs at the thought of Criseyde, an episode studied by Christopher Baswell. Powerful, bodily expression of subjectivity is incomplete, easily manipulated and discounted. These weaknesses are compensated by an advantage, since an organic text can express (somaticize) anxieties and desires that are not permitted to be articulated openly. Vulnerability to manipulation, but heightened opportunity for expression: the organic text—a fictional character's body—resembles iconography in that respect.

In *Stabat Mater*, Mary "speaks" as a mother, her body transformed by grief at the death of her son, fruit of her womb. According to Kristeva, *Mater dolorosa* is a sum of contradictions: women's bodily participation in divine genealogy versus Christian patriarchal marking of the female body and sexuality as unholy. This paradoxical figure reveals the traces of the matriarchal symbolic order erased by Christianity's patriarchal insistence on the Name of the Father:

> La figure magistrale de cette torsade entre un désir pour le cadavre masculin et une dénégation de la mort, torsade dont on ne saurait passer sous silence la logique paranoïde, est magistralement posée par le fameux *Stabat Mater*. Il est probable que toutes les croyances de résurrections s'enracinent dans des mythologies à forte prédominance de déesse mère. Le christianisme, il est vrai, trouve sa vocation dans le déplacement de ce déterminisme bio-maternel par le postulat que l'immortalité est principalement celle du Nom du Père. Mais il n'arrive pas à imposer *sa* révolution symbolique sans s'appuyer sur la représentation féminine d'une biologie immortelle. N'est-ce pas Marie bravant la mort que nous transmettent les nombreuses variations du *Stabat Mater* qui, dans le texte attribué à Jacopone da Todi, nous enivre aujourd'hui en musique, de Palestrina à Pergolèse, Haydn et Rossini? (Kristeva, *Histoires d'amour*, pp. 238–39)

> [The brilliant illustration of the wrenching between desire for the masculine corpse and negation of death, a wrenching whose paranoid logic cannot be overlooked, is masterfully presented by the famous *Stabat Mater*. It is likely that all beliefs in resurrection are rooted in mythologies marked by the strong dominance of a mother goddess. Christianity, it is true, finds its calling in the displacement of that bio-maternal determinism through the postulate that immortality is mainly that of the name of the Father. But it does not succeed in imposing *its* symbolic revolution without relying on the feminine representation of an immortal biology. Mary defying death is the theme that has been conveyed to us by the numerous variations of the *Stabat Mater*, which, in the

text attributed to Jacopone da Todi, enthralls us today through the music of Palestrina, Pergolesi, Haydn, and Rossini.] (Kristeva, *Tales of Love*, p. 251)

This paradox, according to Kristeva, is the inevitable corollary of the equation between sexuality and death in the ascetic tradition, an equation that relegates women's bodies and their generative powers to the side of death. The equation between sexuality and death justifies Kristeva's interest in the erotic aspects of the *Mater dolorosa* theme. She recounts its visual and musical representations, emphasizing the connection between the ecstasy of sexual fulfillment and Mary's spasmodic contemplation of the naked, youthful, male body in her lap. Trancelike behavior is the gender exclusive prerogative of female mourners, who ceremonially possess the corpse (Kristeva implies erotic possession) and mutilate their own bodies in funerary rites. Female mourners alone, orgiastic and Maenad-like, have access to male *jouissance* which is also death, *la petite mort*—"the longing to experience the wholly masculine pain of a man who expires at every moment on account of jouissance due to obsession with his own death" [L'aspiration d'éprouver la douleur toute masculine d'un homme expirant à chaque instant de jouissance par l'obsession de la mort] (Kristeva, *Histoires d'amour*, p. 238; *Tales of Love*, p. 251).

What other forms does the sexual desire of the mother take in a masculine tradition? Peggy McCracken, who establishes a typology of maternal sexuality in romance, especially Arthurian, and in Christian devotional texts, speaks of "the uneasy association of desire, pleasure, sin, and conception in the representation of maternal sexuality." This association is always already uneasy because it is "part of the 'ambivalent project' of including a discourse of sin and redemption into the romance world of chivalric values" (McCracken, "Mothers in the Grail Quest," p. 45). Romance narratives use a number of strategies to efface the "mother as a subject of desire." Three strategies are particularly visible in Grail romances: "mother's sexual desire is negated (mother is ignorant), displaced (she desires a child), or redeemed (desire becomes friendship)." McCracken's "contested representation of maternal sexuality in medieval culture" and Kristeva's "paranoid logic" are expressions of a shared paradox. For McCracken, romance simultaneously shows and denies maternal sexuality, just as Jacopone da Todi's hymn does for Kristeva. The means are genre-specific—romance strategies are different from those of a popular devotional text. However, as McCracken also notes, the two genres—romance and "discourse of piety"—intersect in the "ambivalent project" of later romance fictions. *Perceval* and its continuations are a fine example of such an intersection, where we can speak of a double ambivalence: (1) intrinsic to the contested, "paranoid" expression of queer sexuality (that resembles what McCracken has outlined as the contested representation of maternal sexuality), and (2) intrinsic to the "ambivalent project" of infusing romance with spirituality.

Kristeva points out that Mary combines sexual fixation on the corpse and denial of death. She suggests that the incoherence of grief in *Stabat Mater* (both pleasure in death and negation of death) reveals a paranoid logic. The incoherence and paranoia stem from the binding together of irreconcilable, competing orders of transcendence. *Stabat Mater* displays the contamination of the Christian postulate that immortality is primarily "of the Name of the Father," by the "intoxicating expression of immortality as the maternal, or the feminine." Biological immortality is ensured by giving birth, not by symbolic order. These two contradictory orders of immortality are also at the core of *Perceval*. The aristocratic or knightly lineage as a structure of the Symbolic Order, as a form of collective existence with its sequence of heroes defying mortality, is at odds with the mother's plan to protect Perceval precisely by never allowing him to participate in the order of chivalry where he, like his maimed and dead father and brothers, would have to risk death to earn immortality. Although the mother's logic is rather more convincing than the logic of chivalry, it is the mother who appears to us as a freak, a monster even, as she raises Perceval in an artificial world from which chivalry has been deleted. Thus begun, the story has only one place to go: the forbidden chivalry—a simple narrative device well known from fairy tale or myth, but *Perceval* enriches it with a circular logic that recalls the paradox Kristeva discusses in *Stabat Mater*. The story of Perceval is indeed the separation from his mother and his apprenticeship as a knight, but the mother's death is, as we learn much later, what keeps Perceval from becoming the perfect knight—causing his failure in the Fisher King episode. One of the lessons of Perceval is that the father and his Order (the order of chivalry) only allow access to immortality through risking death. The other lesson is that, abstracted from paternal symbolic economy, as long as he remains with his mother, Perceval is not self-aware. He only begins to know himself through encounters with the members of his family. When he finally articulates his name, we learn that his mother has died of grief. Up to this point, the narrative of Perceval's apprenticeship as a knight progresses in a predictable fashion, filling in the father's genealogy that the mother had erased; as he sets out, the mother passes on. But the next, paradoxical lesson is that Perceval fails in his quest because he has left his mother.

How essential is to romance the contest between symbolic and maternal order? Perhaps primordial: romance is, to a great extent, a narrative that legitimates a symbolic order, a narrative that (to recall Foucault) legitimizes institutions. The later function of the Grail romances as part of the nation-founding myth of the French dynasty relies on the importance of lineage in the narrative, as it creates the appearance that there is a genealogical link between the Arthurian world and the French ruling family.[16] This at the level of its reception, duration, and manuscript transmission; but an argument can be made that the two orders of desire—maternal and symbolic—are also in play intrinsically, in the text itself. A school of reading represented by R. Howard Bloch makes a conjunction between genealogy and etymology, or making sense of lineage and making sense. Bloch's reading shows that not only is genealogy thematized in romance—most romance fictions can be defined as a quest for lineage—but it is also formalized: the crisis of lineage affects the meaning. Let us first take care of the first proposition: that the need to create fiction is thematized as a genealogy crisis in medieval romance. In his study of "matrimonial romance" (late-twelfth- and thirteenth-century fictions that typically begin by a failure in arranging marriage), Bloch defines the quest for lineage as "narrative confusion:" "implicating the *estoire* both as story and as lineage, [narrative confusion] is sometimes thematized as a failure to recognize true genealogy, and sometimes as a search for paternity" (*Etymologies*, p. 195).[17] This observation is made specifically in the context of *Perceval* and its continuations. Of course, Bloch does *not* evoke *Perceval* as an example of "matrimonial romance," rather as a salient example of the equation that defines the quest for lineage as thematized confusion, and, one assumes, a thematized instance of a more general and universal impulse: the necessity to write.

That is where we arrive at the second proposition: that the meaning in romance is in crisis, and there exists a formal (in addition to the thematic) relationship between genealogy and "supersaturation of the signifying system" in the economy of romance. The narrative "bears an asymptotic relation to the process of search," be it the search for genealogy, origins, conclusion, solution, or sense: "Chrétien, like Perceval, himself seeks a poetic rectitude that is, in the telling of the tale, constantly disseminated—scattered and partial; and that accounts, ultimately, for the increasing incoherence of a bifurcated romance which cannot end." For Bloch, the unfinished state of Chrétien's text is not an accident of the author's biography, but rather "the logical consequence of an unresolvable drama of language, lineage, and literary form" (Bloch, *Etymologies*, pp. 206–207). Again, specifically speaking of *Perceval*: "the dispersal of his lineage, its loss of property, and of intelligibility. . .serve to inform the text to such a degree that there is, finally, no adequate means of differentiating the hero's *estoire*—his genealogy—from Chrétien's *estoire,* or tale." The quest for lineage is no longer an excuse for the narrative, rather the problematic nature of language as a pattern of all symbolic orders calls into question the status of the author and of meaning.

Bloch speaks of "thematized confusion," and Kristeva is struck by the
excess of the musical partition as she ponders the paranoid logic of *Stabat
Mater*—an excess that, she notes, translates into musical terms the paradox of
bringing together the irreconcilable principles of Mother and Father.
According to Kristeva, the myth of immortality incorporated in *Mater
dolorosa* and in the tradition of female mourners is of an unorthodox, genital,
female nature. She describes this feminine variation of the immortality myth
as an intoxicating departure from the Symbolic Order in Lacanian terms,
akin to what she called *le sémiotique* in her earlier *Révolution du langage poétique*.[18] Kristeva never mentions *le sémiotique* in "*Stabat Mater*," but the concept obviously sustains the very structure of her piece, which alternates
between standard graphic form (page-wide blocks of text) and disposition in
two columns. There is a tension, a dialogue between the associative left column, in bold print, where Kristeva evokes the physiology of motherhood in
floating lists of nouns, and ponders its linguistic repercussions; and the right
column, in standard print, reasoned, essay like, and centered on ideology.
Rather than referring to *le sémiotique*, Kristeva attributes to Christianity the
unveiling of the "bipolar structure of belief." She then remarks that there is
an "artistic" language characterized by a "supersaturation of sign systems,"
serving the two poles—the Father who deals in the Word *and* an attempt to
recreate the pre-linguistic fusion with the mother. Artistic language is a
response to the irremediable poverty of language, experienced as panic:

> Le christianisme est peut–être aussi la dernière des religions pour avoir
> exhibé en pleine lumière cette structure bipolaire de la croyance: d'un côté,
> la difficile aventure du Verbe: une passion; de l'autre—le rassurant enrobe-
> ment dans le mirage préverbial de la mère: un amour. C'est pourquoi il ne
> semble exister qu'une seule façon de traverser la religion du Verbe comme
> son pendant, le culte plus ou moins discret de la Mère: la façon des "artistes,"
> ceux qui compensent le vertige de la pauvreté langagière par la sursaturation
> des systèmes des signes.
>
> [Christianity is perhaps also the last of the religions to have displayed in
> broad daylight the bipolar structure of belief: on the one hand, the difficult
> experience of the Word—a passion; on the other, the reassuring wrapping in
> the proverbial [mistranslation; should be: pre-verbal] mirage of the mother—
> a love. For that reason, it seems to me that there is only one way to go
> through the religion of the Word, or its counterpart, the more or less discreet
> cult of the Mother; it is the "artists" way, those who make up for the vertigo
> of language weakness with the oversaturation of sign systems.] (Kristeva,
> *Histoires d'amour*, bold, p. 239; *Tales of Love*, bold, pp. 252–53).

Stabat Mater richly stimulates the "artistic" with its multiple musical and
visual versions of the theme, and given the popularity of the hymn's rewritings by Palestrina, Pergolesi, Haydn, and Rossini. But it is in an aside on

modern art that Kristeva makes the essential point concerning love, the subject of her essay. She says that the defining characteristic of modern art is the absence of a totalizing stylistic profile. Instead, there is a cacophony of multiple and mutually exclusive (or mutually indecipherable) simultaneous discourses. Kristeva relates this to incest, in the sense of a belated, impossible return to the pre-linguistic fusion with the mother. In modern art, the "sublimated celebration of incest" pushes beyond representation. Kristeva then returns to medieval iconography, and uses modern art and its defining inchoate stylistics as a parallel explaining the emergence of the iconographic tradition of "fire of tongues" (*feu de langues*)—a flame-like index appearing over the apostles' heads as they "speak in tongues." For Kristeva, love, or its language, may be just such a "fire of tongues"—a "language" whose existence is not predicated on any communal synchronicity or even on reciprocity—no constrictive matrix limiting the "play" of signifieds and signifiers. This language of love recreates the fusion with the mother and "naturally" (Kristeva's term) constitutes mother's love as both the first and the ultimate configuration of love proper. *Stabat Mater* is a crucial example: it combines thematics of love, specifically its original formulation, maternal love, with music, a "language of love" that is a system at the same time more elusive and more expressive than language (Kristeva, *Histoires d'amour*, pp. 239–40; *Tales of Love*, pp. 252–53). When *Perceval* breaks away from the maternal, agrarian, "chtonic" project and embraces the paternal, knightly order, it remains seductively indeterminate: it does not foreclose, but remains open as a supersaturated system.

Kristeva's text is in some sense celebratory—in the fragment quoted above she speaks of "exhibiting in broad daylight the bipolar structure of belief"—suggesting that *Stabat Mater* is a symptom so flagrant it functions as the indictment of the paternal order. On the other hand, she leads us to acknowledge the erasure of the feminine principle: in Pergolesi's score, through baroque supersaturation, "an overabundance of discourse" converting the stark hymn into a pretext for auditory pleasure; in the Counter-Reformation's devotional practice, imprisoning violent mourners in a vast, impassable, tepid matrix of approved litanies and rosaries; in the courtly love paradigm, combining woman-object of desire and woman-saint "in a totality as accomplished as it was inaccessible. Enough to make any woman suffer, any man dream."[19] The mother is lost in the attempt at "passing through" the bipolar structure of belief just as she is lost in *Perceval*. But *Perceval* does not make explicit the necessity of that loss: on the contrary, it seems preventable, a missed opportunity like curing the Fisher King. Still, the mother is dead, and the King maimed:

Ce est li dix que ta mere ot
De toi quant tu partis de li,

Que pasmee a terre cheï
Au chief del pont, delez la porte,
Et de ce duel fu ele morte. (ll. 6394–98)

[It's the grief of your mother at your departure from her, for she fell to the
ground in a faint, at the head of the bridge, next to the door, and she died
of that grief.]

Pain constitutes a fundamental link between *Stabat Mater* and the Fisher
King. As I noted, Jesus is an obvious parallel. Yet, the suffering of Jesus is, in
pragmatic terms, a means to an end, setting off the pivotal events: his death
and, most importantly, his resurrection. Far from designating the Fisher King
as a lyrical figure of queer *jouissance*, we are forced to acknowledge the negative value of automutilation and castration as characteristic forms of representation of male homoeroticism in a heteronormative framework. Suffering
from extreme pain, implicating the whole kingdom in his illness, the Fisher
King is far from the ideal human androgyne imagined by modern theorists
of gender, such as Elizabeth Badinter, via Jung's archetypal coexistence of the
fundamental masculine and feminine principles.[20] If for Kristeva *Stabat
Mater* is the representation of female *jouissance* canceled out by various male-
normative strategies, the Fisher King episode configures queer *jouissance* within
the hostile framework of heteronormativity: repression of same-sex desire.

The parallel between *Stabat Mater* and the Fisher King goes beyond
pragmatics (pain as a finality) and logic (techniques of simultaneous representation and erasure, paranoia that both represses and expresses), to include
gender play.[21] The Fisher King is cast as queer, genitally transgendered, an
"emotive transvestite" who accesses male *jouissance* through a *Mater dolorosa*
script. Let me explain: this is not the same as the positioning of the speaking subject in Marian devotion, for instance. Jacopone da Todi asks for the
gift of the Mother's pain, he asks to be like a woman in grief, who is herself a gender impostor: as Kristeva points out, the mourner longs to experience a masculine *jouissance*. Still, the hymn subject's intention to
experience Mary's pain seems less queer than male confraternities singing
their joy at suckling Jesus (an aspect of popular piety explored by Louise
Fradenburg). However, Kristeva does not focus on the lyric "I" of the
hymn, but rather on gender reversal in Mary. This reversal recalls the feminine attributes of the Fisher King—cold, moon phases, genital inversion—
a condition of queer *jouissance* in the economy of heteronormative
discourse. Medieval heteronormative imagination can conceive of queerness through the figures of the effeminate and the castrate; it veils the queer
by substituting a cipher (castrate).

Thus, three elements of Kristeva's reading of *Stabat Mater* are relevant to
my interpretation of the Fisher King episode: grief, gender reversal, and

supersaturation of signifying systems resulting in (or attempting to recreate) *le sémiotique* (writing beyond representation, *une sortie de la représentation*; Kristeva, *Histoires d'amour*, p. 240). The "fire of tongues" could well serve as an emblem of Chrétien's text, with its longstanding reputation of hermeticism. Contrasted with the symbolic, paternal-order reorganization for French dynastic or Christian spiritual needs in later Graal continuations, the hermeticism of Chrétien's unfinished poem helps support a queer reading of the Fisher King episode in *Perceval*. It is also relevant that this very episode became the crux of controversy over *Perceval's* meaning—a controversy I shall now recall in some detail.

During the 1980s, discussions of Chrétien were dominated by poststructuralism and reader-oriented criticism, developing the concept of play between the hermeneutics of the romance and the audience.[22] For instance, R. Howard Bloch imagined an "exchange between Lévi-Strauss and Derrida, mediated by Merlin," while Robert Sturges focused on the notion of ambiguity, derived from Jaussian "alterity," or otherness ("essential difference of mentalities historically distant from ours," which "means that we can never experience medieval literature as its original audience did") (Bloch, *Etymologies*, pp. 1–17; Sturges, *Medieval Interpretation*, p. 176). Sharing Bloch's interest in the romance's self-awareness as a signifying system, if not his methodology, Sturges also proposed a "metonymic rather than metaphorical interpretation," and, like Bloch, showed how Chrétien's works "thematize indeterminacy" (Sturges, *Medieval Interpretation*, p. 33).

Two approaches may illustrate an earlier interpretive bent: while L. T. Topsfield saw Christ in the wounded Fisher King, and God the Father in the Grail King, Urban T. Holmes identified the Fisher King with Jacob and Oedipus.[23] Earlier still, Jessie L. Weston's 1920 study of the archaic mythical origins of the Grail legend gave a prominent place to Attis.[24] In a *tour de force* opening of a chapter, Bloch listed no fewer than thirteen esoteric explanations of the Grail in one sentence, discounting them as "attempts to explain the *obscurus per obscuriorem*," either too general or too idiosyncratic: "they tend either to universalize their object to such an extent that, within the context of assumed thematic archetypes, everything is to be found everywhere and meaningful difference vanishes; or, they tend to be overly genetic, to seek the positive traces of tradition where no evidence exists—to mistake analogy for influence." For Bloch, a common fallacy of these explanations is that they posit an unverifiable cultural context: "we are asked by the workers at this building site of Babel to believe that all of the above sources of Chrétien's tale reached the medieval poet without leaving any visible trace" (Bloch, *Etymologies*, p. 199).

Interpreting Chrétien's unfinished *Perceval* in a spiritual fashion is, of course, nothing new—it has been a national literary pastime in France since the late twelfth century. Within a half-century after Chrétien, there were no fewer than four verse continuations of *Perceval* inspired by Christian themes. The earliest chronologically was the most spiritually oriented: Robert de Boron's *Roman de l'estoire dou Graal*, or *Joseph d'Arimathie* (before 1215). Each decade produced a new text: an anonymous continuation, followed by Wauchier de Dedain; Gerbert (de Montreuil?) (1225–30); and Manessier (1233–37). Already in the first half of the thirteenth century, these verse continuations were giving way to ever longer and more spiritual prose narratives, which fall into three families: first, a prose trilogy (ca. 1220) close to Robert de Boron, containing *Roman de l'estoire dou Graal, Merlin*, and *Didot-Perceval* (also called *Perceval de Modène*). Second, *Lancelot-Graal* (or Vulgate) cycle (between 1225 and 1230), which changed focus to Lancelot and added Chrétien's *Chevalier de la charette*. The core of this version, and its most substantive part, was *Lancelot Proper*, followed by the more spiritual *Queste del saint Graal* and *Mort le roi Artu*. This cycle later also included *Histoire du Graal* and *Merlin*. The *Haut livre du Graal* or *Perlesvaus* (date uncertain, possibly beginning or second half of the thirteenth century) form the third family.

The prose continuations soon surpassed in popularity Chrétien's text, which was apparently no longer copied after 1367, the date of the most recent manuscript. *In toto*, there remain forty-five manuscripts and fragments of Chrétien's works, indicating a relative lack of popularity in the fourteenth century and later, compared to such bestsellers as the *Roman de la rose* or, indeed, the *Lancelot-Graal* continuations themselves, whose copies are numbered in the hundreds. Sandra Hindman makes a compelling argument that Chrétien's version was no longer as satisfactory for the French audience as were the new, especially prose, rewritings, with their clearly articulated spiritual or dynastic agendas. Sturges too emphasizes the difference between Chrétien's and later versions. He contrasts Chrétien's text, which "has provoked many allegorical readings but has just as often been read as a straight romance" because it "invites its readers to refuse allegory," with the later rewritings, especially *Queste del saint Graal*. "Clearly allegorical and. . .almost universally accepted as such," that later version of the Grail story "thematizes signification in order to encourage allegorical reading" (Sturges, *Medieval Interpretation*, p. 34).

Despite the long-standing prefernce for allegoresis, the indeterminacy of *Perceval* was not a new concern in the 1980s. When Sturges set out to show how the "atmosphere of mystery is created [in Chrétien]. . .how it affects the reader's response to the romance," he acknowledged an antecedent in Jean Frappier's willingness to appreciate indeterminacy (a "sense of mystery") as Chrétien's goal, as opposed to a stand-in for a further, determined, allegorical meaning; so that Frappier appears as the precursor of the anti-allegory *débacle* of the 1980s. However, if esoteric allegoresis was one wing of pre-1980s criticism, Frappier was the center, the other wing being Maurice Delbouille who read Chrétien more literally and criticized Frappier for undue emphasis on ambiguity and mystery.

Such latitude of interpretations is not only invited by the text's self-conscious gesturing (Bloch's thematized confusion, Sturges's thematized signification), but also by ellipses, incoherences, "blanks," and silences. Among these, the ambiguities of the Fisher King episode are considered prominent. First it is unclear how many maimed kings there are. In Chrétien's version, three characters converse with Perceval about his visit to the Grail Castle and the Fisher King: Perceval's cousin, the Hideous Damsel, and the hermit. The women (the cousin and the damsel) refer to a single king—the maimed Fisher King. The hermit refers to two persons—mirroring two figures fishing in the boat that Perceval sees at the opening of the episode. One of them would be the Fisher King (the son), and the other the wounded king (the father) who is fed from the Grail, making him the Grail King. Second, different manuscript variants of Chrétien's *Perceval* create a blurry picture of the Fisher King's wound. Strictly within the bounds of Chrétien's narrative, the manuscript tradition produces what I would call an "ambulatory wound" (to be explained shortly). Third, the presence and location of the Castle is unclear to Perceval, and to the reader who follows his frustrated gaze. Perceval is directed to it, but at first he cannot see it; even as he curses his guide, the castle's tower suddenly appears. Finally, the psychological incoherence of this and satellite episodes reaches the level of alien and uncanny. When Perceval meets his cousin (in the episode directly following his visit to the Grail Castle), she interrupts mourning the dead lover who lies in her lap to ask Perceval where he stayed the previous night, with no castles nearby. The incongruous change of topos, from *pietà* to apparently idle curiosity, introduces an explanation of the mysteries of the Grail Castle. It is interesting that the mourning woman's question in this episode is redeemable (seemly and coherent) in the context of *Perceval's* continuations, where the Grail becomes the vehicle of eternal life. The Grail symbolizes the promise of transcendence (healing in Chrétien, eternal life in Robert de Boron's version), confirming the association between the female mourner and Mary's *pietà*—making it another instance of the *Stabat Mater* theme, "the wrenching between desire for the masculine corpse and negation of death, a wrenching whose paranoid logic cannot be overlooked" (Kristeva, *Tales of Love*, p. 321).

Overall, characters, locations, and moods are highly unstable in Chrétien's deceptively simple formulation of the Fisher King and satellite episodes. The result is not only plain confusion but also a marked "overbooking" of the signifying system in Chrétien's text (Kristeva's "sursaturation des systèmes des signes"). This gave a pretext to a surprisingly hostile argument between Frappier and Delbouille, quoted here at some length, partly because it is an entertaining page in Percevalian scholarship, but mostly because the disagreement between two such scholars is among the more convincing proofs one might adduce of the systemic incongruities ("paranoid logic") of the Fisher King episode. The Frappier–Delbouille exchange connects two crucial, unstable locations in *Perceval's* system of signs: the Grail Castle and the Fisher King's wound.

Frappier elaborated, in his Sorbonne lectures and other publications, a certain vision of *Perceval* that dealt, among other things, with the question of Celtic origins, and that interpreted the Grail castle episode as a fairylike, transcendental fantasy. In articles written in the late 1960s, Maurice Delbouille offered another alternative to the spiritual reading of *Perceval*. The Fisher King, maintained Delbouille, was wounded in the hips, not in his manhood, making it a less symbolically charged wound, one that, according to Delbouille, occurred not infrequently in battle.[25] The Grail castle did not appear and disappear into thin air in a supernatural fashion, rather it was revealed and hidden by natural bends in the road, much like the towers of Cambray in a well-known descriptive passage by Proust, which Delbouille quoted to illustrate his argument.[26] Delbouille was obviously going against the grain of accepted readings. Among those interpreting the wound of the Fisher King as genital mutilation on the basis of detailed philological study were at the time Frappier, Marx, Brunel, and perhaps Fourquet (although Delbouille calls on Fourquet's philological argument to support his own).[27]

Frappier retorted to Delbouille in two articles, of 1969 and 1977. The second article was edited by Philippe Ménard, as Frappier died without completing it. I quote only a few instances that mark Frappier's resentment of Delbouille's thesis: "this argumentation is ingenious but, it seems to me, not devoid of some artifice," or prevarication [non dépourvue de quelque artifice].[28] "It is curious that quoting lines 3044–49. . .Maurice Delbouille had not noticed [the expression] *ça amont* of the line 3046, which would have spared him a hypothesis devoid of any foundation in fact" ("qui lui aurait permis de faire l'économie d'une hypothèse dénuée de tout fondement"; Frappier, "Féerie," p. 106). "What is this posturing supposed to prove? [Que vaut au juste cette parade?] Surely, the medieval poets had not a precise and thorough knowledge of human anatomy. However, it behooves us not to exaggerate their ignorance or their poetic license, at will, and unto absurdity."[29] "Maurice Delbouille appears extraordinarily impressionable or overly optimistic when he renames 'laconism, abbreviation and concision' what is in fact absolute muteness and total silence. If, in order to say that Perceval continued to advance, Chrétien had truly not deigned to say or write one single word concerning that movement, his record conciseness would be impossible to beat and, faced with such a feat, the Lacedemonians should hand him their weapons"—the weapons in question being, naturally, Spartan brevity (Frappier, "Féerie," p. 106).

One may say, to vindicate both Frappier and Delbouille, that Chrétien achieves with his muteness very much the same effect as Proust with his detailed description: that is, ambiguity and indeterminacy, a surfeit of meaning that destabilizes the signifying system. In *Perceval*, this effect is compounded by play (in the linguistic and Lacanian sense) between different manuscript versions. For instance, the majority of the manuscripts identify the *locus* of the wound as "between the two hips" [*hanches*], while H, L, and R give "between the legs" [*jambes*], and T—"between the thighs" [*cuisses*] (Frappier, "La blessure," p. 184). The genital wound of Perceval's father is just as unstable: "between the legs" [*par mi les janbes*] in P; "between the hips" [*par mi les hanches*] in P6, P8, P13, M1; "through the hip" [*par mi la hanche*] in B, Cl, L1, L2. In focusing on the linguistic stratum alone, Frappier and Delbouille are both right and wrong, each of them claiming victory when they find philological arguments in support of one hypothesis, while the ambiguous text makes both equally plausible. As Delbouille, Brunel, Frappier, and Fourquet show, the semantic field of the Old French *hanche* generously accommodates a number of body parts, and further scrutiny of one fragment of that field, according to one's interpretive preference, only reinforces the stalemate. The solution of the riddle is not in further researching that side of the semantic field of the Old French *hanche*, which seems more promising to one's argument—to Delbouille, "hip," to Frappier, "testicles." Rather, the solution is in examining the semantic value of ambiguity itself. The very presence of play, in the semantic field as in the manuscript tradition, points to the genitals as the most likely locus of the wound. Incoherence is a device commonly used to this day to represent an unnamable object. What is unnamable is, of course, a question of register and convention, subject to cultural paradigm shifts, but the procedure itself remains unchanged.

The number of kings, the uncertainty in locating the Fisher King's castle, and the incoherencies in describing his wound do not exhaust the list of ambiguities in that episode. Among them is also the King's epithet, variously translated as the "sinner king" and the "fisher king," from the homonym *pescheor* in Old French. Even if we opt for one of these meanings, stopping the possible play between "fisher" and "sinner" by choosing the more pedestrian "fisher" as the signified, the figure remains ambiguous, now in terms of social hierarchy: unlike hunting, fishing was not a royal sport.[30] A wound to the leg need not have prevented the king from hunting and reduced him to fishing.[31] Wolfram supplies a practical reason: Anfortas enjoys the sport because it allows him to breathe fresh air—the breeze over the water clears the foul stench of his wound. As usual, Wolfram's account is detailed, making it one of the earliest medieval references to hook and fly fishing (the other occurs in his *Titurel*). Because of the social status of fishing, both are usually interpreted as a negative hint, as in Hatto's translation. A redeeming, spiritual reading of "fisher," connected to the Christian symbolism of fish as a Greek anagram for Christ, and St. Peter as fisher of souls, has been proposed by Michèle Vauthier.[32] I believe that in this instance, as in the previous one, to stop the play of meaning at one end of the symbolic field may be reductionist and unjustified. Rather than help eliminate elements, I add a new one to the spectrum of interpretations of "fisher." This discussion is in support of my argument that the Fisher King figure represents a particular configuration of sex and gender, a figure that could participate, along with Raoul de Presles's commentary on the *City of God*, in this strain of medieval discourse where castration and effeminacy played the key role in making same-sex acts imaginable. I think that the Fisher King's inability to hunt and mount, mentioned in both Chrétien and Wolfram, may be intended to define not so much the extent of his handicap, but rather the sexual and gender characteristics of the castrated King. Hunting and mounting, typically masculine activities and sexual metaphors, can be used to describe the active/insertive male role—they serve that purpose already in Greek texts.[33] A study of medieval examples would be necessary to support this; at present, I focus on the possible feminine characteristics imparted by the astrological and Galenic associations with fishing.

The social incoherence of the Fisher King figure is compounded by the ambiguity, partly sexual in nature, generated by another symbolism of fish—the calendrical. The Fisher King has been repeatedly interpreted with respect to his Saturnine characteristics—the chill that invades his body and spreads through his land—but not with respect to Pisces. This is a curious oversight, which may perhaps be explained by the incompatibility of Pisces with other astrological explanations (e.g., in Groos, *Romancing the Grail*, pp. 131–32). The iconographic association between fish and warming by the fire, linking the Fisher King to the calendrical and the Books of Hours traditions, is hyperbolically emphasized in Chrétien's version, where the king sits by a fire large enough to accommodate four hundred:

> S'ot devant lui un fu molt grant
> De busche seche cler ardant,
> Qui fu entre quatre colommes.
> Bien poïst l'en quatre cens homes
> Asseoir environ le feu

[There was in front of him a very large fire of dry logs burning bright, which was between four columns. Four hundred men could easily be seated around the fire] (ll. 3,092–3,097).

The clear-burning fire is mentioned again later (l. 3,181). The two elements united in the figure of the Fisher King in *Perceval*—the fish and the warming fire—are obligatory in the illuminations of the month of February in the major Books of Hours. In one instance, these two elements are even combined in a genre scene: the Berry Hours portray an old man at the fire, cooking fish. It is interesting that while the fourteenth-century Parisian illumination in *Le conte del Graal* (Paris Bibliothèque Nationale MS fr. 12,577) does not feature one part of this iconographic and symbolic combination—the fish—it nonetheless includes the fire. I believe that this element is purposeful and emphatic, since fire is a rather unconventional element in the representations of aristocratic interiors in similar romance miniatures of that period.

Of course, Chrétien's formulation historically precedes the large-scale production of Books of Hours, which dominated the septentrional book market from the fourteenth century on. However, the zodiacal symbolism was readily available both in iconography (tympans, mosaics) and practice (medical) before calendars in Books of Hours rendered it visually ubiquitous in book form. I believe that the similarity between the attributes of February and the attributes of the Fisher King can justify further association between the Fisher King and the symbolism of the astrological Fish. I am particularly interested in pursuing that association because it carries an implication of sexual ambiguity. In the Galenic theory of humors, the Fish are of feminine nature, cold and wet, and the masculine nature is hot and dry. While Chrétien does not give us any details that could support the claim of sexual ambiguity, his near-contemporary, Wolfram, in the extensive account of the Fisher King in *Parzival* IX, most emphatically tropes the king's wound as an orifice. The wound is inflicted by "a spear thrust through the testicles" (l. 479.12) (Groos, *Romancing the Grail*, pp. 131–32), penetrated with hands (ll. 480.5–9), and in a final attempt, after several remedies fail to cure the King, a hot and dry, that is masculine, stone—the carbuncle—is rubbed against the edges of the wound and then inserted into it (ll. 483.2–5). Phallus-like objects—lance shaft and tip—are repeatedly removed from it, placed on it, and thrust into it (ll. 489.24–490.2). All these attempts fail to warm the King's wound, whose coldness, we are told, is killing him.

Medieval texts on sex change sometimes assume that feminine organs are an inverted version of the masculine, and that women's genitals can change into men's much like one would straighten out an inverted glove, under the influence of a sudden movement, for instance, jumping over a ditch, or from intense sexual pleasure.[34] Inversely, Anfortas's *genitoire* is now a *mehaing*, a wound that the physician's actions never heal but only maintain in its pathological state. Inverted into a hole, the genitals are a place that is no longer one of engendering—it is missing the generative parts, *genitoires* or *genotes* (in the plural, a frequent term for testicles).

In Chrétien, the Fisher King's hunting lodge has no equal in riches and comfort, but Perceval's father's domain is called Gaste Forest (that is where he fled, or rather was carried in a litter, after the fall of Utherpendragon): by extension, the lands in his possession become sterile.[35] The castration of Perceval's father entails the ruin of his realm:

> Vostre peres, si nel savez,
> Fu par mi les janbes navrez
> Si que il mahaigna del cors.
> Sa granz terre, ses granz tresors,
> Que il avoit come prodom,
> Ala tot a perdicion,
> Si cheï an grant povreté. (*Perceval*, ll. 435–41)

[In case you did not know, your father was struck between the legs so that his body was wounded. His great land, his great treasure which his prowess earned him, all went to waste, and fell into great poverty.]

Only if he recovers the power over his body will Chrétien's Fisher King have power over his lands:

> Que tant eüsses amandé
> Le boen roi qui est maheignez
> Que toz eüst regaaignez
> Ses manbres et terre tenist. (*Perceval*, ll. 3,586–89)

[Because you would have cured the good king who is ailing so that he would soon have recovered the use of his limbs and held his land.]

In Wolfram, the Fisher King, his lands, and the planets are bound to suffering together. Anfortas's severe remission precedes snowfall "in Summer's unabated splendour" (ll. 489.24–490.2):

> We knew from the wound and the summer snow that the planet Saturn had returned to its mark. (chapter 9, p. 249)

> . . .never before or since has the King been in such pain as when the planet Saturn thus announced its advent, for it is its nature to bring great frost. Laying the Lance on the wound as had been done before failed to help us, so this time it was thrust into the wound. Saturn mounts so high that the wound sensed it before the other frost had followed: for the snow, however

easily, fell only on the second night in Summer's unabated splendour. While the King's frost was being warded off in this way his people were in depths of misery. (chapter 9, p. 250)

It is not unusual to see a shift in focus from genitals as a site of sexual acts to genitals as a source of heat or cold of universal proportions. A well-known thirteenth-century *Lai de Virgile* accomplishes such a shift. Because of *Perceval's* popularity, length, and the number of continuations, the temptation is considerable to find all medieval texts connected to it in some significant way. The *Lai de Virgile* is no exception: the first half of its plot corresponds to a portion of the thirteenth-century prose continuation of *Perceval* entitled *L'Estoire del Saint Graal*. In *L'Estoire*, that portion, a story of love and revenge, features a lady and Hippocrates. Our *lai* attributes the adventure not to Hippocrates but to Virgil, traditionally credited in the Middle Ages with various feats of magic as well as with *pius Aeneas*. There is another connection, with *Parzival*: Wolfram's Arnive, in telling Gavain of Clinschor's castration, mentions "Virgil of Naples" among Clinschor's ancestors (l. 655.17). The main events of the *Lai de Virgile* are portrayed on the fourteenth-century ivory backing of a mirror, reproduced by Mary Frances Wack who mentions the *lai* in the context of medieval medical texts on lovesickness.[36] On the left, the woman Virgil woos tricks him and shames him publicly. She agrees to hoist him to her chamber in a basket under the cover of darkness, only to have him suspended midway and left hanging in broad daylight. Virgil repays her in kind. He magically extinguishes all fires in the city of Naples. When desperate citizens beg him to relent, he informs them that the only source of fire is his beloved's backside. The citizenry accordingly dip their wicks in her—the scene is portrayed on the right, with the woman bare-backed and radiant. This plot depends on the articulation between the private use of the body (which the woman refuses) and the public one (to which she is consequently submitted), and on the audience's recognition that both events are sexually charged, and thus equivalent in the economy of sexual revenge. Chrétien's and Wolfram's narratives omit the rationale of the *lai*, but they do rely on the articulation between the private and the public body.

In the ivory relief of the *lai*, we interpret the second scene as rape—sexual revenge. The effect of the *lai* depends precisely on that identification, procuring enjoyment mixed with horror. The woman's bare buttocks prodded by the men's candles are more than displayed *pudenda*. The scene carries a surplus of meaning, pointing to a repressed and unnamable truth: this culture encourages rape. The scene is pleasant to behold, making the rape palatable, even desirable. To a modern observer, this is a "terrifying bodily mark which is merely a mute attestation bearing witness to a disgusting enjoyment."[37] The cure proceedings in Wolfram are troped not as rape but as a friendly life-saving effort by a community of physicians, philosophers, and learned men.[38] In parallel with the *lai*, this does not prevent the reader from interpreting their actions as sexual—and, since only men are involved, as male homoeroticism. The equation between desire, power, and coercion, the active/passive polarization are as muddled here as in the *lai*. The king's genital wound is represented as an orifice. Since the healing procedure undertaken in all seriousness, by royal permission, in a company of friendly men, takes forms highly reminiscent of sexual acts, this episode can justifiably be seen as queer, with respect to the king, the company, and the reader.

Two aspects need to be distinguished: the Fisher King's *wound* (in Chrétien, "ambulatory"; in Wolfram, represented as an orifice, penetrated, and cold—in all, "effeminate"); and the *rationale* for wounding (none in Chrétien; madness in Manessier; in Wolfram and most French continuations, punishment for philandering). The implication of queerness cannot be derived simply from Chrétien's "ambulatory wound"—incoherent discourse that represents the unnamable. Rather, this implication is based on Wolfram's poem, which portrays the wound as a "black hole." This creates a certain difficulty since Wolfram's and Chrétien's versions differ on one of the essential points—in Wolfram, the wound is a punishment for philandering; Chrétien's version does not mention a cause. In bridging the two texts, Manessier's version is essential to my argument. It presents the wound as genital automutilation, inflicted in a fit of excessive grief: "je, qui de duel me desvoie" [I, who was mad with grief,] (l. 32,910).[39] The Fisher King's niece brings him the broken fragments of the sword that killed her father (his brother), and the king castrates himself: "parmi les cuises [MP variant: 'jambes'] an [U variant: 'de'] travers / M'an feri, si que toz les ners / An tranchai" (ll. 32,913–15) [I struck myself between the thighs crosswise so that I cut off all the nerves]. In combining these three aspects—automutilation, castration, and excessive grief—Manessier also provides a link to *Stabat Mater*, and to Attis. In these formulations, pity and abjection are the hostile, heteronormative readings inscribed in the text. The causal connection between automutilation and madness or grief overdetermines castration as both the figure and the punishment of same-sex desire. It reconciles the breach of logic that at the same time represents and disallows the existence of same-sex desires and anxieties. It also foreshadows "the articulation of madness with the 'sins' linked to sexuality," and therefore can serve as another point of reference to Foucault's central project: the history of exclusion and its double, the organization of the outlawed elements into a taxonomy of "pathologies" (Eribon, "Michel Foucault's Histories," p. 36).

In Wolfram, and in several French texts, castration is a punishment for philandering—or, to engage theoretical discourse, for the improper citation

of the heterosexual norm. It is important to note that castration is not exclusively or even predominantly associated with punishment for same-sex acts.
If, in his now venerable work on Christianity and homosexuality, Boswell
notes historical cases of such punishment, two from Byzantium and one from
thirteenth-century Castillia, more frequent examples of castration as punishment for heterosexual transgressions may be found—the most famous in the
French context is of course Peter Abelard.[40] A literary parallel is Chrétien's
Constantinopolitan romance, *Cligès*, which ends with an explanation of
eunuchism as a remedy against rampant, transgressive heterosexuality in
the Byzantine imperial household. In Wolfram's *Parzival* (p. 13), Clinschor the
magician is Gawan's opponent, and Gawan laughs "loud and long" when he
is told how Clinschor acquired his magical powers—he was castrated by his
lover's husband (ll. 657.8–11). Mirroring the distribution of castration as punishment for heterosexual versus same-sex offenses in other contexts, in the
textual tradition of *Perceval* castration is usually configured as a punishment
for philandering, and the possibility that it represents anxiety about same-sex
desire emerges in only a few cases, and only in the sense that in these cases,
castration is *not* specifically assigned to philandering. If castration is the threat
that ensures the proper functioning of a particular formulation of heteronormativity (one that centers on marriage, legitimacy, and reproduction), this
threat covers all sorts of transgressions, not exclusively homosexual ones.
Nonetheless, we know from other contexts that castration does play a crucial role in constituting the repressive, heteronormative order *specifically* with
respect to same-sex desire—for instance, in Saint Augustine's *City of God*.

In addition to the homo/hetero polarity, castration had a bipolar value
in the moral sense, within the bounds mentioned at the beginning of this
chapter: positive in asceticism, and negative as a punishment for improper
sexual acts. Yet, it seems that at least in Wolfram and Chrétien, if not
in romance as a genre, more often the second, negative pole is activated.
Wolfram's Clinschor the magician is, in my view, no exception: rather than
representing the positive value of castration, he belongs to two well-
established traditions: (1) gender-shifting prophet or magician (Tiresias,
Merlin) and (2) mutilation as a price for supernatural gifts—a tradition peo-
pled by Oedipus at Colonus, the sightless prophet; biblical Jacob who wrestles
God, wins a blessing, but loses a leg; or one-eyed Odin who knows bird lore.

What other literary echoes resonated with the castrated Fisher King?
The obvious answer is the ritual castration of the priests of Cybele, and its
original mythical performance, Attis's automutilation. Two sources are most
likely, although they provide only brief references: Ovid and (somewhat
more amply) Augustine. I assume that the medieval reception of Ovid's
Metamorphoses was quite standard from the twelfth century on concerning
the relatively minor myth of Attis, and that a good approximation of

previous centuries' practice can be found in Pierre Bersuire's (d. 1362) well-known commentary *Ovidus Moralizatus*, where Ovid's two-line reference to Attis in *Metamorphoses* is annotated with a laconic reference to *Fasti*. A sign of the stability of that tradition is its continuance into the Renaissance—including the edition of *Metamorphoses* with Bersuire's gloss, by Lyons printer Jacques Huguetan (d. 1518). Following a long-standing tradition, Bersuire's gloss was attributed to the Welsh Dominican Thomas Waleys, author of a commentary to Saint Augustine's *City of God* (completed ca. 1332)—forging an illusory link between Ovid and Augustine on Attis. There also exists a real connection between the two authors: Ovid and Augustine, in some respects so different, had a similar role in the medieval tradition as sourcebooks of classical mythology.

In Ovid's *Fasti* IV, lines 221–46 (to which we are referred by Bersuire), Attis's self-castrating frenzy is the punishment for his infidelity—breaking his chastity vow to Cybele with the nymph Sagaritis. We infer from the prologue to *Cligès* that Chrétien may have translated Ovid's *Ars Amatoria*, and his familiarity with Ovid's mythography is usually accepted. Yet, in the figure of the Fisher King, Chrétien skips Ovidian causality. The majority of Grail versions after Chrétien supply, or restore it: the Fisher King's wound, like that of Ovid's Attis, becomes punishment for a breach of chastity. Chrétien's and Manessier's *différance* is more significant. My primary argument is that it enhances the possibility of a queer reading of the Fisher King, but I also would like to entertain a hypothesis of a more antiquarian nature—a relationship between France and the Catulline tradition.

If Augustine's, and especially Ovid's, references to Attis are sparse, Catullus devotes his most celebrated poem to Attis. A manuscript of Catullus reemerged in Verona at the end of the thirteenth century, and it is commonly assumed that Catullus was not available during the Middle Ages. The references to his writing in Martianus Capella, Boethius, and Isidore of Seville are so limited as to imply that they refer only to citations of Catullus circulated in Priscian and other grammarians. On the background of complete silence, the few feeble medieval echoes of Catullus point to France.[41] There is also a Catulline collocation in *De gestis regum Anglorum* (ii. 159) by Chrétien's near-contemporary, William of Malmesbury: "virginem sane nec inelegantem nec illepidam" [fine girl, smart dresser, and not dim], recalling Catullus 6.2 and 10.3.[42] Catullus's version of the myth describes Attis's automutilation as an act of madness, anticipating Manessier:

> stimulatus ibi furenti rabie, uagus animi,
> deuolsit ili acuto sibi pondera silice,
> itaque ut relicta sensit sibi membra sine uiro,

etiam recente terrae sola sanguine maculans,
niueis citata cepit manibus leue tympanum (ll. 4–8)

[There, by raving madness goaded, his wits astray,
He tore off with a sharp flint the burden of his groin.
Then, conscious that the members left him were now unmanned,
Still with fresh blood spotting the surface of the ground,
In snow-white hand she swiftly seized the light tambourine]

Catullus's two lines (63. ll. 7–8), moving from bloody stain to snowy hands, are also reminiscent of Chrétien's most celebrated image, three drops of blood on the snow that transport Perceval into the recollection of his beloved Blancheflor (ll. 4,216–17). Later in Catullus 63, contemplation of the surroundings and the wound has a similar effect, transporting Attis into an anguished recollection of his forsaken country and youthful masculinity (63. ll. 45–68).

If supposing the influence of Catullus is a risky, unverifiable intuition, Augustine's discussion of Attis in *City of God* was among the principal medieval citations of male genital automutilation, both in Latin and (after 1375) in French, on par with Ovid and the bestiary tradition. Raoul de Presles began the work on the French commentary and translation of *City of God* around 1370–71—almost precisely the date of Chrétien's last copied manuscript (1367). That translation may be considered anachronistic in the context of *Perceval*. I think instead that the two texts complete and succeed each other. In Presles's translation, for the first time, castration and other rites were presented in a rich context, in the French language, making *Perceval*'s vague and brief presentation outdated and outmoded. Texts such as the French *City of God* continue the work of *Perceval* in depicting castration. Although neither of these works was produced by an imperative, self-conscious, subject-building longing to represent same-sex desire, these texts document that representing same-sex desire is impossible to avoid in a project that articulates a dynastic, heteronormative ideology.

The first ten books of *City of God* were mined throughout the Middle Ages as a rich depository of classical culture—poetry's vengeance on Augustine's anti-pagan goal. This use intensified in the twelfth century, with the renewal of interest in the classics in the Chartres School tradition, and the use of Augustine's classical references can be detected in such works as John of Salisbury's *Policraticus*. A new wave of interest begun in the first quarter of the fourteenth century, producing popular Latin commentaries by François de Meyronnes, Nicolas Trevet, and Thomas Waleys. Fifty years later, Presles's French translation and *exposicion* [commentary] of 1375 drew on these three standard Latin glosses. The commentary proceeded by accretion. Waleys emphasized that his own commentary was more thorough, because he had access to some classical works that Trevet lacked: five books of Apuleius to Trevet's three, Cicero's *De fato*, and the fourth decade of Livy added to Trevet's first and third.[43]

There are local variations in reception: while English manuscripts mostly preserve the complete Trevet, continental ones use Waleys for the first volume, Trevet for the second, even though his comments in that part are only fragmentary (Smith, *Illustrations,* n.25 p. 17). Unsurprisingly, as Bossuat notes, Presles's commentary reflects the continental preference. Presles also uses François de Meyronnes (in the second part), as well as Bersuire's commentary on Ovid's *Metamorphoses*, mentioned above (Bossuat, *Raoul de Presles*, pp. 50–56). The question of sources should probably be reexamined. For instance, in an oft-cited passage of the first volume (book 3, chapter 1), on the prohibition of inheritance by women (Augustine's *lex Voconia*), where Presles finds himself in the difficult position of having to reconcile a major disagreement between Saint Augustine and French dynastic policy (*lex Salica*), he quotes both Waleys and Meyronnes as his sources.[44] In any event, French commentary on Augustine, tributary to Latin tradition, is an agglomerate of earlier texts, in a new linguistic and material envelope. *City of God* participates in the late-fourteenth-century vogue among aristocratic patrons for exquisite illuminated manuscripts of philosophical and theological texts, formerly produced more modestly for a clerical audience. Some fifty parchment and paper manuscripts, as well as two printed editions, are extant. Most, including the printed versions, are illustrated.[45]

Our relative ignorance of the manuscript variations in Presles's text reinforces an appearance of homogeneity. In the absence of a modern edition or a detailed study, the copy cited here (Brussels, Bibliothèque Royale MS 9,015–16) is considered identical with Presles's translation and commentary presented to Charles V in 1375 (Paris, Bibliothèque Nationale MS fr. 22,912–13). The manuscript I cite, one of the treasures of the Bibliothèque Royale Albert Ier in Brussels, MS 9015 has the content characteristic of all French commentaries: "discours de présentation," prologues, fragment of "Retractions," and the first ten books of *City of God*. The second volume, MS 9016, contains the remaining twelve books. The text follows the usual disposition: Augustine's chapter in Latin, followed by its French translation, followed by French gloss to the chapter (*exposicion*), making it a very ample book. According to Frédéric Lyna, MS 9015 was executed in Tournai ca. 1445 under the care of the preaching friar Nicolas Cotin, for Jean Chevrot of Poligny, archdeacon of Rouen. Thanks to the influence of the duke of Burgundy, Philip the Good, Jean Chevrot was created the first bishop of Tournai by the papal bull of 1436, replacing Jehan d'Harcourt. Close counselor to the duke, Chevrot died on September 22, 1460. His arms appear in the initial of the frontispiece. The manuscript is first mentioned in the inventory of Philip the Good.[46]

As Charity Cannon Willard pointed out, this particular manuscript is unusual in the manuscript tradition of Presles's translation because it was commissioned for an ecclesiastic, while the French commentary was most in demand by aristocrats (Jean de Berry alone is linked to six copies).[47] Second, the illumination programme of the Chevrot manuscript does not reflect the pre-1420 Parisian traditions, rather it represents a different family, originating in the 1430s under the patronage of Philip the Good and in the circle of Master Guillebert de Metz. This manuscript is witness to the appropriation of the symbolic values of the French court by Burgundian aristocracy, and to the reappropriation of the secularized Augustinian tradition by an ecclesiastic patron (one need not overly emphasize the latter: the manuscript may have been intended for the duke). Since the manuscript is indistinguishable from others produced for aristocratic French circles (text) and for the Burgundian audience (illuminations), it testifies to the overlap between different patrons, geographies, and chronologies: lay and ecclesiastic elite, French and Burgundian, late fourteenth- to mid-fifteenth century.

Presles's *exposicion* reiterates earlier medieval commentaries. A cultural continuity exists, therefore, in which French *Perceval* and annotated Latin *City of God* coexist, from the twelfth to the late fourteenth century and beyond. Both participate in the elaboration of French national and dynastic identity—the translation into French was commissioned by Charles V and its frontispieces, including the one in the Chevrot manuscript, are amalgams of French dynastic symbols. Sandra Hindman shows that Chrétien's work also played a role as symbolic capital of the French dynasty. I am interested in one specific aspect of this national identity: its investment in a heteronormative sexuality. In both texts (*Perceval* and *Cité de Dieu*), the castrated male figure is associated with same-sex anxiety. The fear of castration functions as a repressive, punitive device, simultaneously a means of representation and a tool in the establishment and maintenance of the homophobic regime.

In his translation of Augustine, Presles expresses anxiety about same-sex desire by infantilizing the castration victim. In this, he demonizes same-sex preference by casting it as a transgressor of a basic social contract (responsibility for children). This move, which is not found in Augustine, but is based on material he provides, prefigures the homophobic exclusion of same-sex preference from the institution of "family," an exclusion against which our society fights a painfully slow battle. The infantilization of Attis proceeds in two stages. First, instead of the mythology (original automutilation of Attis), Augustine's text focuses on ritual castration, which repeats this originary occurrence for the purpose of organized religion. This practice Augustine finds reprehensible not only in itself but, it appears to me, chiefly because it fosters effeminacy (specifically, mannerisms of dress, hairstyle, and demeanor) and same-sex promiscuity: not exactly the focus of the translator's anxiety. That is why the latter performs a mutation: in French translation and illuminations, castration is performed on a child, not on an adult. The mad youth Attis of classical tradition (Catulline, Ovidian, Augustinian) becomes "child Attis" in French. A close reading reveals that this intervention of the translator is based on a move that Augustine performs in order to erase the responsibility he may have had as a participant in the rite when he witnessed castration. This preoccupation is also present in *Confessions*, in the context of Augustine's relationships with other men. Augustine presents his witness-account of the reenactment of castration as childhood memories, collected "before the age of reason":

> Quant nous estions Joesnes enfans ainsi comme en laage de xiiii ans nous venions en leurs temples et regardions la maniere de leurs Jeux de leurs moqueries et de leurs sacrileges sacrefices Nous regardions. . .nous oyons. . .(fol. 46 v)
>
> [When we were a small child, for instance fourteen years of age, we would come into their temples and see their various Plays their moqueries and their sacrilegious sacrifices. We saw. . .heard. . .]

The infantilization of Attis in French translation is thematically related to this infantilization of Augustine as a witness, but it operates to very different ends.

In the French manuscript, the illumination preceding book 7 occupies the upper half of the column b on fol. 306v (not 346 as in Lyna's index). It represents four men sitting in a semicircle in a rounded chapel, with a child lying on the floor before them, fully excised and bleeding, his testicles and penis to the right. Thin ribbons of blood recall *taena*, red string used to mark a sacrificial animal. The child figure is annotated ("Attis"), revealing the necessity to reaffirm the link between the classical Attis, lover of the Goddess, youthful, passionate, beautiful, and this fifteenth-century representation of a pale, bleeding child, abandoned to the cold contemplation of Greek philosophers: tragic youth versus pitiful child. More importantly, the label reflects the lack of currency of the myth, and it testifies to a fundamental event in the history of art, the creation of illustration programmes for French translation of major theological and philosophical texts such as the Bible or Aristotle, including the representation of abstracts concepts such as nothingness.

The rubric of the corresponding chapter is to the left of the illumination: "Quelle interpretacion ait trouve la doctrine des sages grieux del absasion de cel enfant aatis cest assavoir de ce q[ue] ot coupe ses genitores xxvie chapitre" [What interpretation has found the doctrine of the wise Greeks concerning the abscision of this child Attis, that is to say, that he cut his genitals, twenty-sixth chapter] (fol. 306v. ll. 7–12, col. a). Presles's rendering of Augustine in this rubric, making a child of Attis ("cel enfant aatis"), is the possible source of the iconography. Infantilization makes Attis into a poster child for the crimes of classical gods. Recalling the commonplace image of the Adoration, the miniature taps into a bottomless reservoir of meaning. For instance, the difference between the adoring Mother of God and the useless philosophical fathers marks the superiority of Mary over Varro, true faith over pagan philosophy—Augustine's project in a nutshell.

The discussion of castration is one among myriad arguments against the state religion of pre-Christian Rome summoned by Augustine in *City of God*. Yet, he highlights its particular abjective value. That exception is further emphasized by the illumination programme, which singles out Attis's castration as the illustration of the entire book. The text of the French commentary not only expands Augustine's references to castration, effeminacy, and same-sex promiscuity, but also weaves a network of references to ritual and theatrical reenactment of the myth, directing the reader back to book 3 where Augustine discussed same-sex promiscuity, again connecting it to elaborate clothing and other traits, in the context of theatrical performance and of Carthage:

> Se faisoient des jeux sceniques es theatres ou ils contrefaisoient comment cel athis se chastra et pour quelle cose et de telles ordures sans nombre Et avoient la personnes desfigurees en habit de hommes et de femmes a faulx visages qui contrefaisoient les personnages de celui qui lisoit en la scene Quelle chose est scene theatre ou amphyteatre nous Lartios [sic] declara ou xxxe chapitre chapitre du premier livre (fol. 48r col. b)
>
> [In theaters, scenic plays would be performed where they would represent how this Attis castrated himself and why, and innumerable other filthy things like that. And there were disguised (*desfigurees*) people there in men and women's clothing with masks (*a faulx visages*) who pretended to be (*contrefaisoient*) the characters [in plays] which were read on the scene. What is scene, theater, and amphitheater, Laertios tells us in the first book, chapter 30.]

The commentator's cross-references to "effeminate" dress and demeanor, and to same-sex male promiscuity, reinforce their visibility in the French version. In order to discredit the classical Pantheon, Augustine and the glossator weave a network of narratives that resonate not only with their own overarching objective, but also with my interest in medieval discourse on same-sex desire.

Augustine and the commentator establish a set of parallels between the rites of the Great Mother, Jupiter, and Saturn. Attis's castration becomes a catalyst for the discussion of a wider spectrum of sexual anxieties, expressed by references to phallic rites at weddings, the ravishment of Ganymede, male prostitution, and the evil eye. Attis's castration is also firmly set in the context of fertility rites. Although Cybele's roles as protector of cities and war goddess are also mentioned, these connotations are marginal in comparison with the agrarian themes. Augustine and the commentator evoke the full spectrum of predictable dichotomies: seed/semen (Lat. *semina*) and castration, life- and death-giving seed, cultivation and savagery, nearness and distance, fertility and sterility/infertility. Here, I do not cite Augustine's text but only its modern English translation, with select Latin terms in parentheses. With the exception of the last paragraph followed by my translation, I also omit Presles's translation, except for one expression quoted in square brackets in the body of the modern English. In book 7, chapter 24, Augustine quotes Varro:

> . . .They have created emasculate Galli to serve this goddess, meaning that those who lack seed should follow after the earth, for in her all things are found. They leap about before her, teaching those who till the earth not to sit idle, says he, for there is always something for them to do. The sound of the cymbals signifies the movement of iron tools in men's hands and the clatter produced by all the work done in agriculture. The cymbals are of bronze because the ancients tilled the earth with bronze before the use of iron was invented. She is accompanied by lions, which are unleashed and tame, to show that there is no kind of land so remote or so exceedingly wild that it is not suitable for subduing and cultivating. (p. 461)
> . . .

> These are the famous mysteries of Tellus and the Great Mother, in which everything relates to perishable seeds and the work of agriculture [aux semences mortelles et a lexercice des labourages]. . .They say that the mutilated Galli serve this great goddess to indicate that those who lack seeds should follow after the earth—as if it were not rather their own slavery that caused them to be without seed! (p. 463)
> . . .

> If the earth were not a goddess, men would lay hands on her in toil to obtain seeds by means of her. They would not go mad with violence [*saeviendo*; this expression is missing from Presles] also lay hands on themselves in order to lose their seed for her sake. If the earth were not a goddess, she would become fruitful by the hands of others (*manibus alienis*), without compelling a man to become sterile by his own hands. (p. 465)

> Se la terre ne feust dieuesse (over erasure:) les hommes neissent les mains (end of text over erasure) en elle en labourant affin quilz eussent semence

par elle non mye en faisant cruaulte en eulx mesmes a ce quilz perdeissent
semence pour elle Selle ne fut dieuesse elle seroit faicte si pleintureuse par
mains estranges A ce quelle ne contraignist mye homme estre fait brehaing
De ses propres mains pour elle. (fol. 336v col. a)

[If the earth were not a goddess, men would not have hands in her in culti-
vating in order to get seed from her, instead of being cruel to themselves so
that they lose the seed because of her. If she were not a goddess she would
have been made so plentiful by others' hands, and she would not condemn
a man to be made a eunuch by his own hands for her.]

In the context of Augustine's protracted discussion of fertility, one must
recall the emphasis on seed/ing in the opening of Chrétien's *Perceval*. The
words *semer, semance*, repeated six times in lines 1–9, lead directly to the
panegyric for Phillip of Flanders "the Roman" (l. 12), a purified, Christian
Alexander (ll. 11–68).

Qui petit seme petit quialt,
Et qui auques recoillir vialt,
An tel leu sa semance espande
Que fruit a cent dobles li rande,
Car an terre qui rien ne vaut
Bone semance i seche et faut.
Crestïens seme et fet semance
D'un romans que il ancomance,
Et si le seme an si bon leu
Qu'il ne puet estre sanz grant preu,
Qu'il le fet por le plus prodome
Qui soit an l'empire de Rome:
C'est li cuens Phelipes de Flandres,
Qui mialx valt ne fist Alixandres. (ll. 1–14)

[He who sows little reaps little. Who wants to reap something, let him spread
his seed in a place where the fruit will give back twice a hundred, because
in worthless earth, good seed dries and withers. Chrétien sows and spreads
the seed of a romance that he begins, and he sows it in a place so good that
he cannot help making a great profit, because he does it for the man who
has more prowess than any in the empire of Rome: it is the count Philip of
Flanders, more worthy than Alexander.]

When the story begins in earnest, we see Perceval depart to check on
the laborers harrowing his mother's oat fields. If not a link, I want to fore-
ground at least a similarity in the preoccupation with fertility, *translatio
studii, translatio imperii*, and other dynastic concerns in Chrétien, Augustine,
and Raoul de Presles.

In the opening of the chapter devoted to *Perceval*, Bloch shows how the three *seme* of *Perceval*'s prologue—to sow, to beget, to signify—are seamlessly connected, forming the multifaceted aesthetic object that Bloch is particularly able to describe (pp. 198–203). Still, these well-known lines on *semence* that open *Perceval* should not sound sexless. Once we assume that the sexual context is also intended, and considering the prominence of the passage—the very opening of the narrative—may not further allusions to Perceval's father and the Fisher King struck "between" (*parmi, enmi*) rather than "in" the legs or hips, quoted in the text as the cause for their "*mehaing*" and "*perdition*," be perceived less as a case of poetically confused anatomy (as in Delbouille), or even closeted preference for confusion as suggested earlier in this chapter, than as a conscious and accurate reference to same-sex acts?

A narrative that constitutes an ideology, a nation, and a dynasty borrows a biological, feminine version of immortality (fertility) not to reaffirm the fundamental importance of the feminine principle, but only to repudiate male same-sex desires. The corollary of the relation between agrarian and sexual economy (fertility/sterility, seed/semen) is the equation between the sexual body and the body politic. This produces the equation between the wasting of the land and the castration of the king, between the macrocosm of the realm and the microcosm of the king's body, exemplified by the fate of Perceval's father, and by Anfortas in Wolfram. To "throw the seed in such a place as can give back twice a hundred," instead of "on the worthless ground where good seed dries and withers" [En tel liu sa semence espand / Que Diex a cen doubles li rande; / Car en terre qui riens ne valt, / Bonne semence seche et faut] (*Perceval*, ll. 3–6) is a duality that was activated in medieval French texts to connote same-sex acts as the negative opposite of reproductive sex, for example, in the episode of Agriano in *Bérinus* discussed below in chapter 2 and the monologue of Lavinia's mother in *Enéas*, discussed in chapter 3. It is part of a set of polarized dichotomies: vaginal versus anal and oral; reproductive versus nonreproductive.

Marginal annotations in the French *City of God* MS 9015, whether they record how the manuscript was used, or emphasize the way it was intended to be used, further amplify that multilayered resonance. The placement of pointers appears consistent with the tradition that treated Augustine as a mother lode of classical references. In the part of book 7 on which I focus, marginal annotations refer to the commentary, and never to the Latin text or its French translation, showing that the gloss was the primary object of the annotator's interest in this tripartite text—a fact interesting in itself, considering that the gloss amplifies Augustine's references to homophilia. I use this term, for lack of a better one, to refer to Augustine's description of "effeminate" dress and same-sex promiscuity associated with theatrical representations and rites, presumably of Cybele, and with the Carthage of his adolescence—or childhood, as he would have us believe; instead of homophilia, I would have preferred "same-sex lifestyle," but I shied away from it because rather than define its object in itself it seemed to imply a modern comparison between same-sex and heterosexual lifestyle primarily predicated on the sex of one's partner. Read in sequence, the annotations lead from "*significacions des sacres*" [meaning of the rites] (MS 9015, fol. 330r), to Virgil and the Psalms (fols. 330v–331r), to Attis as victim [*de victima*] (fol. 331r), to "holocaust" and "libations" (fol. 331v), to "monstrous women" in Virgil's *Bucolics*, Pliny, Lucan, and Guillaume de Paris (fol. 332r), ending in the explanation of the classical Pantheon as history that became mythology: "cest chose plus acroire que ce furrent ho[m]mes qui co[m]misrent telz crismes q[ue] dieux" [it is a more believable thing that those who committed these crimes were men rather than gods] (fol. 339v). The aim of Augustine's argument—examination of religious practices of the classical world (including sacrifice, Holocaust, libations)—is maintained in this string of pointers, as well as in the conclusion: classical gods were men transformed into divinities by poets who translated history into mythology. That conclusion derives directly from Augustine's hypothesis concerning the relationship between the epic, mythography, and history. But if we read the content of the marginal annotations, we can speak of another set of issues that emerges somewhat independently of Saint Augustine: issues that, I would think, reflect the annotator's specific, localized concerns. Thematically, the marginal annotations lead from the mysteries of the Great Mother (fol. 330r) to Attis's automutilation (fol. 331r) to the discussion of stone phalluses immediately followed by that of *fascinum*, the evil eye (fol. 332r). This sequence places the closure, the waning of the classical gods, in a context of interest in ritual practices associated with sexuality and with the elaboration of a homophobic Christian identity—an inalienable though closeted part of Augustine's story.

Sexually charged examples, as well as a focus on women, men's experience of women, and male homosexuality, already present in Augustine, are amplified by the commentary that not only recapitulates and references, but also independently develops two themes in particular: *fascinum* and homophilia. The commentary refers to passages on castration and phallic rites in Augustine's first two books, imposing a self-referential reading at the level of book structure as well as through thematics of specularity (references to theater, Augustine as the model reader/spectator). Circular patterns of cross-reference and specular themes of theater seem to me to forecast the theme of the eye and the mirror—interactive elements of *fascinum*. The site of readers' interests in MS 9015, mapped out by the pointers within the Augustinian matrix—Great Mother, Attis, phallic effigies, *fascinum*, and the *clef-de-voûte*: the waning of the gods—is for me a classic site of the crystallization of a discourse on homophilia in a homophobic regime. Why would *City of God* be a privileged site where homophobic discourse would precipitate, achieving a distinguishable and recognizable form? In answering, I must acknowledge my debt to Jim Creech, who commented on the distinction between the ritual and the abstract, a difference constitutive of Foucault's chronology. Through the manipulation of objects, the ritual enacts and embodies the abstract relationships between castration complex and phallocentrism. The abstract relationship cannot emerge unless the ritual relationship loses its performative value. No longer a religious practice, it becomes a superstition. Foucault identifies the French Revolution as the constitutive moment when the ritual identity lost its innocence—when regicide opened the possibility, and simultaneously created the necessity, of an abstract, interiorized regime of castration. The corollary of this shift was the emergence of technologies of the psyche as a means of scientific management of the interiorized regimes. The waning of the ritual and its replacement by modern technologies—in the *cabinet* of a doctor or that of a technocrat—marks the beginning of an era. The treatise of the sexual hygienist and, later, the couch of the psychoanalyst, replaced the ostentatious parades of the court in the maintenance of the *status quo*.

My answer is that a similar event occurred as the nation-founding myths of the Roman Empire (of which Cybele and her castrate priests are a prime example) succumbed, not to poets' wit as Augustus and other censors feared, but to the onslaught of monotheism. That historical moment of change is fixed in Augustine's *City of God*, not only because monotheism is its explicit, defining ideology, but also because that historical moment defines the author's conflicted identity, a lifelong experience of the classical tradition he rejected and the Christian identity he espoused. The prevalent medieval use of Augustine worked toward the erasure of his project—it focused on the juicy literary and cultural detail, not on theology. Still, until the humanist revival of the fourteenth century, Augustine's digest, and not the pagan sources, were preferred. This points to the importance of the framing effected by Augustine: classical myths were safely handled in Augustine's repressive framework. The myth was accessible but sterile. The sterilization of the myth—its translation into fiction—accompanied the sterilization of the religious ritual and its translation into a pathological symptom. Of course, Augustine does not initiate, but rather documents the sterilization of the myth. Deplored by moralists, halfheartedly arrested by compulsory exercises of national religion, the loss of the myths' performative value was not due to Augustine, but rather recorded by him. When Augustine was translated into French, however, the epistemic break (sterilization) was not only displayed, but also adopted for current purposes. And that is the second part of my answer: the epistemic episode narrated in *City of God* was replayed in the late fourteenth century not as a thing of the past, but of the present.

The seemingly arbitrary choice of subject for the frontispieces to Raoul de Presles's translation—a panoply of French dynastic symbols, including *fleur de lys*, the sacred *ampoule* carried by a dove, and other elements of French coronation rite—emphasizes that the symbolic function was the primary goal of the translation. The frontispiece leaves no doubt that French national identity was to be shaped by Augustine's project. A part—how essential a part may be subject to discussion—of this project was the reinscription of castration as a symptom of anxiety concerning same-sex desire, leading to the repression of homoeroticism. In the establishment of a homophobic regime, Presles's translation of Augustine fills the functional niche left empty by the phasing out of *Perceval* (in Chrétien's formulation) as one of the dynastic romances of the French monarchy. It seems no coincidence that the translation of Augustine into French is contemporary with the humanist revival and the rediscovery of pagan sources. A new balance was established between further interiorization of Augustine's homophobic use of castration, through translation into French, even as the previous arrangement was being threatened by the return of the repressed—the return of Catullus, for instance, and of the texts sterilized by Augustine, in their threatening autonomy.

CHAPTER 2

DISSECTION AND DESIRE: CROSS-DRESSING AND THE FASHIONING OF LESBIAN IDENTITY

If later authors' autographs also carry shreds of life attached to writing, reading medieval manuscripts is the most sensual of literary experiences.[1] It begins with the noise of the cover opening, depending on how tight and in what (boards, leather, velvet) the volume is bound, and with the dry sound of leather leaves touching each other. Light diffuses in opaque, milky, soft vellum but glances off stiffer, buttery parchment. The pigments capture and imprison the light, but even a hairline of gold sharply ricochets it back. Larger pools of gold, especially on raised ground, have a hypnotic quality, like shimmering heat waves. The slope of the ground is almost imperceptible to the fingertips, but the eye recognizes it as a miniature landscape. There is a vanity in it, like in a *tournure* that puffs out the croup, or a padded brassière, or a codpiece. There is also a soft irregularity, as in a dollop of cream—although the ground is usually tinted red with minium, giving the somewhat translucent gold its characteristic warmth. In comparison, gold applied directly to the page as dust or leaf looks somehow modern, like a house with a flat roof. Plants, seeds, slugs, trellises are painted directly over the gold ground, wasting swaths of it, except for a brief period after the gilder applied it and before the painter got his hands on it, a period confined to the workshop. Painful, obvious waste of gold, paid but inaccessible, ostentatiously invisible like a cult object. Next to the excesses of gilt, the nervures in pastel grays, pinks, and malachite greens seem almost disappointing.

Then, there are the cuts and the holes. Small slits allow the sinews of the binding to slide through. Regularly spaced pockmarks set the grid for the ruling or, far less frequently, mark a pattern copied from the master. Ink, if incompetently prepared, eats into the page. Lacy holes open up where letters used to be, like precursors of an Anne Hamilton installation. There are also intentionally decorative cutouts. Doily-like margins favored by some modern collectors. Pop-up prayer books of Christ's passion, allowing us to put our fingers through Christ's bleeding heart, or through the hole in his side, enacting the doubts of Saint Thomas. Sutures and holes, untrimmed edges, darker splotches and, on the flesh side, imprints of veins streaking across the page, recalling the animal that owned the skin, far more supple and nerved then. The sutures and marks seem childlike, innocent, but the regular indentations on the hair side strike me as somehow indecent, as if there were an unforgivable cruelty in removing all that would first come in contact with the hand if the animal were alive. Well-read manuscripts have grimy edges and, sometimes, homemade love poems are handwritten on empty flyleaves. Specks of chewed-up bread or parchment spittle—glued to the margin to mark the spot. Doodles of limp-wristed hands extending the index finger, wider at the fingertip, as if pressing against the page. Crowns, crosses, eyes, "n"s topped with two dots for "*nota bene*," words, authors, references to specific lines of poetry, mostly classical. Erased "cleric" and put in "knight" in a love poem, when the book changed lovers. The indescribable silky softness of very fine vellum, melting between the fingers. Pigments bleeding through too thin a page, especially blues and oranges. A remedy: pictures on little extra rectangles of parchment pasted to the page, so the bleeding would not dissolve the poem lines on the verso. The edges of these pasted pieces poke out here and there from under the crumbling gold and blue framelets that were supposed to keep them in place and mask the joint, like a baseboard or a dado. Much later, in French, *lambris doré*, gilt dado, comes to mean an opulent dwelling that would be in doubtful taste if it weren't so rich. Later still, *poutres apparentes*, exposed beams, signify ancient construction, old money, and style. The repetitive rhythm and the unashamed display of structural elements (beams, joints) are now meant to procure a reassuring pleasure. For me, that pleasure belongs to the same category as the satisfaction of seeing a miniature representing two knights at lance point in all of the thirty battle scenes of all of the seven romances bound in one volume. Or, in early Renaissance guidebooks, the woodcut of one city on a river as the illustration to every city the book describes.[2] In the early printings of medieval texts, the woodcut of a port every time anyone in the romance, good or bad, alone or at the head of an army, takes to sea. These are stock illustrations—an expression from the age of print, first attested in English in 1625: "kept regularly in stock for sale," the books that will find buyers, or so the printer speculates.[3] But the practice is medieval. It applies to illuminations, and it also characterizes late medieval book trade, where frequently sold items (books of hours, but also romances) were kept in stock. The buyer's crest was added at purchase if required, sometimes on an extra leaf of better quality.

The practice of adding elements of the book recalls the way a manuscript page was constructed: in layers of one kind. First all of the ruling, then all of the script, then rubrics and initials; then to the illuminator's. First the drawing, then the gold. Burnishing would rub off the pigment if the sequence were reversed. Then, the flat reds, greens, and blues. Then, all the white highlights and gray or brown shading, the latticework in the backgrounds and crisscrossed stonework on castle walls. At each step, the manuscript looks nothing like the next stage, and nothing even approaching the final product. But it does have a completeness of its own. The gold speckles, on a page left at that, stand perfectly balanced, although they were meant to be only a sprinkling of highlights in a thick carpet of flowery vegetation.

Today, reproductions of unfinished manuscripts come under the heading of useful teaching material, demonstrating technique. They show the process that leads to certain effects such as the balance of color in a decoration, and allow us to understand aesthetics as a direct result of procedures used in manuscript painting. Another reason for our interest, less explicit, is that unfinished manuscripts do not look stereotypically gothic. I would say that in-progress decoration looks modern in a number of ways: sparseness of medium, primacy of function, distance from a figurative or totalizing goal—necessarily, since the design is unfinished. The unfinished pages make visible the segmentation and recombination practices that underlie the manuscript culture, but that may not be an obvious characteristic of the gothic style, for instance, in a complete building that presents the typical verticality or expanse of glass.

But my focus on dissection, recombination, and recycling as principal laws of manuscript objects, makes their relevance to the production of literary texts rather more than less enigmatic. Intellectual objects are free of the material constraints that stimulate recycling and recombination of manuscripts, and yet recycling can be often evoked as the principle of authorship, sometimes heroically, sometimes cynically. Some scholars see compilation as the master pattern of the period from the twelfth to the fifteenth centuries. Alistair J. Minnis's *Medieval Theory of Authorship* narrates the evolution of medieval literary theory as a process of "accumulation and refinement" (pp. 3–4), an image intended to replace one of the epistemic breaks between the humanism of the twelfth century and the scholasticism of the thirteenth and fourteenth.[4] Minnis believes the motor of that evolution was the idea that an *auctor* be at once a source of *auctoritates*, of *sententiae*, and fallible, for instance, biblical David: adulterer and homicide; and that a text presents multiple categories of relevance: literal, allegorical, anagogical. Minnis describes the greater tolerance and inclusion of pagan poets in the fourteenth century as the result of the evolution he traces: "Scriptural *auctores* were being read literally, with close attention being paid to those poetic methods believed to be part of the literal sense; pagan poets were being read allegorically or 'moralized'—and thus the twain could meet" (p. 6). Minnis's examples not infrequently deal with fragmentation and reconstitution— among them, Albert the Great's commentary on Baruch (written between 1270 and 1280), justifying "the collection and compilation (the verbs *colligo* and *compilo* are used) of scraps of truth. . .No scrap of inspired Scripture must be wasted for, as St. Paul says, 'all that is written is written for our doc-trine' " (Minnis, *Medieval Theory of Authorship*, p. 99); or Chaucer's adoption of the persona of the compiler, ethically unengaged with the content of his work, "a very self-conscious author who was concerned to manipulate the conventions of *compilatio* for his own literary ends" (p. 210). If compilation is the principle of authorship that does not participate in the materiality of manuscript production, is there a principle that accounts for both?

The phenomena described above, particularly buying incomplete man-uscripts and dismembering old ones, were not uniformly or even primar-ily a matter of clearly expressed aesthetic preference. Quite the opposite, there must have been practical reasons: payments that did not materialize, partial recovery of assets. Medieval manuscripts form a hierarchy of value that is not unlike a monetary system with currency equivalents: script only; with one color letters; with two colors; with gold and colors. That is how manuscripts were priced—by the number of iterations of a specific kind of decoration. If the simpler ones were cheaper, the symbolic value was not infrequently added. The combinatory capacity of the system was multiplied because a practical element such as rubrication could have a range of values: cheap (paint), expensive (gold and lapis lazuli). An obvious example of intersection between manuscript decoration and a currency system is the equivalence in price between gold and lapis lazuli, based on the limited supply and complex refinement process of the latter. Each of the elements works as a complete entity and as a part of a richer scheme and contributes to a gothic aesthetics of dissection, modularity, and recombination, to which we respond by strong if not always conscious fascination with incomplete or visibly jointed works.

There is a surplus of meaning, especially in the case of dismembered man-uscripts, that is not explained by economy. Let's look at it more closely. Dis-membering old manuscripts and reusing the illuminations in new ones fulfills a particular desire: to possess a book one cannot afford to commission, a book impossible to procure in one's material circumstances. Finding no fulfillment in reality, desire leads to dissection and recombination of elements. The con-cept of desire and custom-made identities and objects tailored to fulfill that desire, constitutes the common ground between dissection and cross-dressing.

Cross-dressing allows us to divide identities into segments—clothes (masculine or feminine), social status (independent or dependent), performance of gender norms (heroic or obedient), behavior (bellicose and adventurous or domestic), emotions (courageous or vulnerable), positioning in love scripts (active or passive), facial features (ruddy or smooth-cheeked), body (handsome or pretty), genital (male or female). Cross-dressing recombines these segments as it formulates a new identity. Whether the other characters in the romance are taken in (women fall in love with the cross-dressed woman, men allow the cross-dressed man into women's chambers) or become suspicious (the cross-dressed woman looks too young, too pretty to be a man, leading another character in the romance to the brink of discovery of her identity), either way the pleasure of the reader consists in the surplus of knowledge: the constantly summoned awareness of the split between the enacted and the original identity of the cross-dressed figure. That pleasure entails dissection, recombination, and visibility of the seams.

It need not be queer. As Lacan notes, quoting an example of female cross-dressing, the awareness summoned by cross-dressing is simply a matter of degree, a "more precise way to evoke the absence" of the penis, the absence that defines women as objects of desire:

> Telle est la femme derrière son voile: c'est l'absence du pénis qui la fait phallus, objet du désir. Evoquez cette absence d'une façon plus précise en lui faisant porter un mignon postiche sous un travesti de bal, et vous, ou plutôt elle, nous en direz des nouvelles: l'effet est garanti à 100%, nous l'entendons auprès d'hommes sans ambages. (Lacan, *Ecrits 2*, p. 188)
>
> [Such is woman concealed behind her veil: it is the absence of the penis that makes her the phallus, the object of desire. Evoke this absence in a more precise way by having her wear a cute fake one under a fancy dress [*travesti de bal*], and you, or rather she, will have plenty to tell us about: the effect is 100 percent guaranteed, for men who don't beat about the bush, that is.] (Lacan, *Ecrits*, trans. Fink, p. 310 [p. 825]).[5]

Similarly, Robert Mills, in "Whatever You Do Is a Delight to Me!" an investigation of homoerotic desires clustered around Saint Sebastian, presents the famously libidinized martyr as the epitome of Christian masculinity.[6] Mills ties the interest in inversion to the origins of Christianity as a persecuted religion, a "queer" ideology (n. 55, p. 18, p. 37). Within the now dominant ideology of Christianity, martyrdom is an obvious metaphor and reminder of that originary "alternative" process of subjectivation: a "(mis)taking" of victimhood for heroism: "Martyrdom is more generally a genre in which un-manning literally makes the man" (p. 37). The paradox of Christianity does not end there. Mills recalls Eve Kosofsky Sedgwick's characterization of Catholicism "as a figure of phobic prohibition," "famous for giving countless gay and proto-gay children the shock of the possibility

of adults who don't marry, of men in dresses, of passionate theatre, of
introspective investment, of lives filled with what could, ideally without
diminution, be called the work of the fetish."[7] Independent of the question
whether vulnerable male martyr saints were associated with women, Mills
points out that they provided an alternative to the phallic orthodoxy in
their attractive and transcendent masochism: "exhibitionism and
masochism have the capacity, in certain contexts, to become strengthening
and even ultra-virile pursuits" (n. 33, p. 13). Mills considers this "confusion"
between pleasure and pain as queer: "the queering of the pain-pleasure
nexus." That queer confusion is not reducible, it is situated at the heart of
transcendence: "unmanning" of martyred male saints, naked and vulnerable, "meat for the male gaze" (p. 13) is "what effects the martyr's eventual
recuperation into the masculine symbolic: his transcendence of the flesh
and his assumption into heaven" (p. 33). Since the viewer more strongly
identifies not with the male, "assaultive" gaze, but with the heroic victim,
both unmanliness and "interpassivity" or pleasure through "masochistic
fantasies of. . .bodily abjection" (p. 36), might be opportunities not only for
the modern, but also for the medieval "decentered" or queer consciousness
to emerge: "[m]y point is that the queerness that such images represent for
the modern spectator might not have been entirely lost upon certain view-
ers in the Middle Ages" (p. 6). Mills does not suggest that the "pictures of
martyrs. . .*necessarily* reflect a peculiarly subversive queer sensibility," but
that "the queer wishes that might be inferred from certain written accounts
of martyrdom—that is to say, their alignment of the martyr with abject
fleshliness and humiliation—*could also* have opened up spaces for an alternative conception of masculinity to the one imparted by hegemonic discourse: a vision of masochistic passivity and objectification that falls outside
of the normative phallic pale" (p. 28, emphasis mine).

If Mills concludes his essay: "As such, there is no guarantee that these
images were either subversive or transgressive; it is only through queering,
that is to say (mis)taking the abject rite of passage itself as the permanent
basis for subjectivity, that they potentially take on this role" (p. 37), he notes
that the libidinization of male martyr saints (sometimes specifically a "het-
ero" libidinization) can be detected, among others, as guilt and shame in
confessions and sermons, and in Counter-Reformation's iconoclastic anxiety, expressed by the Council of Trent (1563): "all lasciviousness [shall be]
avoided, so that images shall not be painted and adorned with a seductive
charm" (n. 79, p. 33). This led, for instance, to a shift in the representation
of Saint Sebastian, from a nude tied to a post and pierced with arrows, to a
scene where the saint is "nursed to health by Saint Irene as he eats a bowl
of hot soup" (in a painting by Francisco Pacheco; Mills, "Whatever You Do
Is A Delight to Me!" pp. 32–33). The transformation of Saint Sebastian into

a *heimlich*, domestic saint betrays the fear produced by the confrontation with a repressed object of desire.

It becomes obvious, as we follow this argument, that the same (mis)taken or queer subjectivation is not only the basic covert structure of martyrdom, and of Christianity as an alternative religion at its inception, but that it also characterizes any fictional hero, if we consider him or her in structural terms. A hero is, by definition, without means, and transcends his or her condition, not without passing through a masochistically satisfying low point. If Mills notes: "[p]erverse optic would certainly be an apt expression in relation to *post*-medieval interpretation of male martyrdom imagery" (p. 4), the same can be said of medieval authorship as heroic or ironic recycling, as defined by Minnis.

But I want to distinguish my approach to the problem of cross-dressing from Mills's. Although Mills quotes Hildegard of Bingen, Aelfric, and medieval French mystery plays, his most direct testimonies of libidinization of images of male martyrs, and institutional reaction to that libidinization, as well as his most striking Italian, German, and Spanish examples, come from the end of the fifteenth century to the end of the sixteenth and later (the Counter-Reformation). I focus on an earlier period. It seems to me that at that time, the emergence of a "queer subject" from fragments available in the hostile matrix of the dominant heteronormative discourse, is at the same time less clear-cut and less dependent on the dominant ideology than in Mills. I find the best metaphor for the formation of *that* subject in Lacan's psychoanalysis, with its emphasis on splits and slits: the split subject, the slits in discourse through which peers the unconscious, the partial objects, the orifices through which they emerge.[8]

The articulation between the two: medieval texts and Lacan, is not defined by the technique of using two items (text and historical event; or, contemporary and medieval text) to produce a jarring effect, in order to precipitate the elements of medieval texts that otherwise would have remained transparent. Rather, I want to create an alternative to the existing models of medieval cross-dressing fictions. The dominant models are related to Simon Gaunt's three articles these many years ago. The first model, "carnivalesque reversal," presupposes two competing outcomes: episodic reversal as a safety valve and/or as a reiteration of an alternative, bound to function as a model for the permanent change of paradigm. Another model, of polar opposites, explains that the orthodoxy must constitute an "other" in order to repudiate it and define itself; the necessary representation of the "other" is an unalienable part of the orthodoxy, and the secret of this necessity mines the orthodoxy from the inside. In addition, the polar opposite becomes the site around which unaccounted-for desires agglomerate. One of the problems with these models, from the point of view of queer studies, lies in the indeterminate "and/or" conjunction (Mills's "could also"). In addition, the dichotomy or dialectic models are of limited use at the present, since the stability or even the existence of certain polarized oppositions that formerly may have been taken for granted has been profoundly questioned (what was the status of heterosexuality before the Revolution? One paradigm among many?).

Starting from the same premise: that the fictions of female cross-dressing represent erotic and social fantasies that are not satisfied by culturally available models of heterosexual couples or female friendships—I propose a different framework, assimilating these newly tailored identities to the recycling of manuscripts for their illuminations, a medieval practice specifically associated with women's convents. The violence of cutting up an existing manuscript betrays the desire for an object that is not within reach; but the object thus produced does not represent the exemplars available elsewhere, either. Rather, in the visible marks of cutting and pasting, it bears the traces of its obscene elaboration: it is a partial object. This leads to a connected issue, the visibility of seams as the mark of the partial object (the functioning of a female cross-dressed figure in the narrative depends, among others, on the transparency of her disguise). Lacan's definition of slits and orifices as sites of emergence, not representation, fits my model. I realize that, in the end, in this supposedly new model, I extend a metaphor that Simon Gaunt used over a decade ago: in the title to one of his articles, he spoke of medieval French texts as products of "straight minds, queer wishes," implying an "ego vs. id" relationship.

Lacan asks: given that the unconscious is structured like the language, and given the structure of language as defined by Saussure and Jakobson, how can we define the subject? "Once the structure of language is recognized in the unconscious, what sort of subject can we conceive of for it?" [La structure du langage une fois reconnue dans l'inconscient, quelle sorte de sujet pouvons-nous lui concevoir?] The answer begins with "the right way to answer the question 'Who is speaking?' when the subject of the unconscious is at stake. For the answer cannot come from him if he doesn't know what he is saying, or even that he is speaking, as all of analytic experience teaches us." In other words, the Lacanian subject is not a classical, Carthesian subject that, from a landscape of uncertainty, derives the ultimate certainty "that he is thinking": the certainty of *sum* from the *cogito*. Since the unconscious is that which is prohibited from speaking, it is only in-between, in the slits and cuts of discourse, that it appears:

L'inconscient, à partir de Freud, est une chaîne de signifiants qui quelque part (sur une autre scène, écrit-il) se répète et insiste pour interférer dans les coupures que lui offre le discours effectif et la cogitation qu'il informe. (Lacan, *Ecrits 2*, p. 158)

[Starting with Freud, the unconscious becomes a chain of signifiers that repeats and insists somewhere (on another stage or in a different scene, as he wrote), interfering in the cuts offered it by actual discourse and the cogitation it forms.] (Lacan, *Ecrits*, trans. Fink, p. 286 [p. 799])

The analytical situation is bracketed out from the "actual discourse." Therefore, not only its stumbles and interruptions, but the analytic situation itself is "a break in false discourse":

Pour que ne soit pas vaine notre chasse, à nous analystes, il nous faut tout ramener à la fonction de coupure dans le discours, la plus forte étant celle qui fait barre entre le signifiant et le signifié. Là se surprend le sujet qui nous intéresse puisque à se nouer dans la signification, le voilà logé à l'enseigne du pré-conscient. Par quoi l'on arriverait au paradoxe de concevoir que le discours dans la séance analytique ne vaut que de ce qu'il trébuche ou même s'interrompt: si la séance elle-même ne s'instituait comme rupture dans un faux discours, disons dans ce que le discours réalise à se vider comme parole, à n'être plus que la monnaie à la frappe usée dont parle Mallarmé, qu'on se passe de main à main "en silence." (Lacan, *Ecrits* 2, p. 160)

[Lest our hunt be in vain, we analysts must bring everything back to the cut qua function in discourse, the most significant being the cut that constitutes the bar between the signifier and the signified. Here we come upon the subject who interests us because, being bound up in signification, he seems to be lodging in the preconscious. This would lead to the paradox of conceiving that discourse in analytic session is worthwhile only insofar as it stumbles or even interrupts itself—were not the session itself instituted as a break in a false discourse, that is, in what discourse realizes when it becomes empty as speech, when it is no more than the worn coinage Mallarmé speaks of that is passed from hand to hand "in silence."] (Lacan, *Ecrits*, trans. Fink, p. 288 [p. 801])

The analytical situation, by bracketing out the production of meaning, allows it to arise from within the prohibition, and from within the breaking up of language. In the analytical situation, it is an emergence "between," where "*interdiction*" (prohibition, speechlessness) is opened up by the analytical situation, creating productive splits: "*inter-diction*" (saying between) and "*intra-diction*"(saying within). Instead of a transparent or in(di)visible classical subject, there arises a series of opaque Freudian signifiers that are in an asymptotic relationship to the signified (whence the importance of puns and slips, phenomena that consist in confusing the signifier with the signified, and therefore cannot be considered as part of language, but play on language), a series that Lacan describes as *fading*:

Par quoi la place de l'inter-dit, qu'est l'intra-dit d'un entre-deux-sujets, est celle même où se divise la transparence du sujet classique pour passer aux effets de *fading* qui spécifient le sujet freudien de son occultation par un

signifiant toujours plus pur: que ces effets nous mènent sur les confins où
lapsus et mot d'esprit en leur collusion se confondent, ou même là où l'éli-
sion est tellement la plus allusive à rabattre en son gîte la présence, qu'on
s'étonne que la chasse au Dasein n'en ait pas plus fait son profit. (Lacan, *Ecrits
2*, pp. 159–60)

[Hence the place of the "inter-said" [*inter-dit*], constituted by the "intra-said"
[*intra-dit*] of a between-two-subjects, is the very place at which the transparency of the classical subject divides, undergoing, as it does, the effects of
fading* that specify the Freudian subject due to its occultation by an even
purer signifier; may these effects lead us to the frontiers where slips of the
tongue and jokes become indistinguishable in their collusion, or even where
elision is so much more allusive in driving presence back to its lair, that we
are astonished that the hunt for Dasein hasn't made any more of it.] (Lacan,
Ecrits, trans. Fink, pp. 287–88 [p. 801]; star marks an English word used by
Lacan in the original.)

What is the relationship between the definition of the unconscious as
that which is unspeakable, the observation that the "actual discourse" only
allows the unconscious to emerge in its breaks, the split model of a linguistic sign (signifier/signified), and the observation that the unconscious is
structured like a language? This relationship pivots on breaking up the
"actual discourse" to allow the emergence of the unconscious. Since language preexists and determines the subject of "actual discourse," the breaks
in meaning that affect the "actual discourse" are a proof that there exists
something else that the "actual discourse" does not account for. That
"something else" is the unconscious:

Cette coupure de la chaîne signifiante est seule à vérifier la structure du sujet
comme discontinuité dans le réel. Si la linguistique nous promeut le signifiant
à y voir le déterminant du signifié, l'analyse révèle la vérité de ce rapport à faire
des trous du sens les déterminants de son discours. (Lacan, *Ecrits* 2, p. 160).

[The cut made by the signifying chain is the only cut that verifies the structure of the subject as a discontinuity in the real. If linguistics enables us to
see the signifier as the determinant of the signified, analysis reveals the truth
of this relationship by making holes in meaning the determinants of its
discourse.] (Lacan, *Ecrits*, trans. Fink, p. 288 [p. 801])

It is the structure of language, the cut between the two constitutive categories of meaning: signifier and signified that confirms for Lacan the
importance of cuts, margins, and borders, as "erogenous zones." Language
predetermines the representation of desire ("language speaks us," "*la langue
nous parle*," as Saussure said), but there is also a possibility, immanent
in "anatomical characteristics of a margin or a border," and "no less
obviously prevalent characteristics of the object," of an emergence outside

representation, an emergence that is not a reproduction of an already
available meaning:

> La délimitation même de la "zone érogène" que la pulsion isole du métabo-
> lisme de la fonction (l'acte de la dévoration intéresse d'autres organes que la
> bouche, demandez-le au chien de Pavlov) est le fait d'une coupure qui
> trouve faveur du trait anatomique d'une marge ou d'un bord: lèvres, "enclos
> des dents," marge de l'anus, sillon pénien, vagin, fente palpébrale, voire cor-
> net de l'oreille (nous évitons ici les précisions embryologiques). L'érogénéité
> respiratoire est mal étudiée, mais c'est évidemment par le spasme qu'elle
> entre en jeu. [graphe #3]
>   Observons que ce trait de la coupure n'est pas moins évidemment préva-
> lent dans l'objet que décrit la théorie analytique: mamelon, scybale, phallus
> (comme objet imaginaire), flot urinaire. (Liste impensable, si l'on n'y ajoute
> avec nous le phonème, le regard, la voix,—le rien.) Car ne voit-on pas que le
> trait: partiel, à juste titre souligné dans les objets, ne s'applique pas à ce qu'ils
> soient partie d'un objet total qui serait le corps, mais à ce qu'ils ne représen-
> tent que partiellement la fonction qui les produit. (Lacan, *Ecrits* 2,
> pp. 178–79)
>
> [The very delimitation of the "erogenous zone" that the drive isolates from
> the function's metabolism (the act of devouring involves organs other than the
> mouth—just ask Pavlov's dog) is the result of a cut that takes advantage of
> the anatomical characteristic of a margin or border: the lips, "the enclosure
> of the teeth," the rim of the anus, the penile groove, the vagina, and the slit
> formed by the eyelids, not to mention the hollow of the ear (I am avoiding
> going into embryological detail here). Respiratory erogeneity has been little
> studied, but it is obviously through spasm that it comes into play.
>   Let us note that this characteristic of the cut is no less obviously prevalent
> in the object described by analytic theory: the mamilla, the feces, the phal-
> lus (as an imaginary object), and the urinary flow. (An unthinkable list, unless
> we add, as I do, the phoneme, the gaze, the voice. . .and the nothing.) For
> isn't it plain to see that the characteristic of being partial, rightly emphasized
> in objects, is applicable not because these objects are part of a total object,
> which the body is assumed to be, but because they only partially represent
> the function that produces them?] (Lacan, *Ecrits*, trans. Fink, p. 303 [p. 817])

When the nuns cut up and reconstitute a book they do so in the face
of an absence. That absence is the lack of another suitable solution to procure an object that answers their ambitions and desires. Such an object
exists, but not as part of their library. We could say that it exists in other
libraries, and there ends the parallel between dismembering manuscripts
and emergence outside representation. But the object, when it is realized,
is unlike the others (it does not have an Other): unlike a newly commissioned illuminated manuscript, it is scarred. Like the partial object, the

pasted-in manuscript "partially represents the function that produces it": the marks of cutting and pasting are poignantly visible. In other words, it represents the sisters' limited means, which it was not intended to do, and therefore it is only partially the object that was desired: it is a partial object. A parallel can be made between that paradox and cross-dressing fictions, where objects that the "effective discourse" of romance was intended to conceal emerge in the cuts. That emergence is "the only one that verifies" what the discourse of the romance generally conceals: same-sex desire. This parallel conveys new importance onto the visibility of seams, an effect on which cross-dressing fictions rely.

Dismembering books, for instance, as it was practiced in women's convents, is an apt parallel to the articulation of same-sex desire in a discourse that does not make a dignified, legitimate place for it: an actual or effective place. Dismembering books is a gesture marked by aggression and conflict. Violence is proportionate to the force of desire for that which the community cannot obtain by any other means. That is another significant parallel to cross-dressing. In allowing female characters autonomy, in disconnecting sartorial and other technologies of gender from the anchoring matrix of genital sex, in unsettling gender roles and expectations, in creating circumstances where two women marry, go to bed together, and promise lifelong protection to each other, cross-dressing fictions resonate with erotic and social fantasies that are not satisfied by other romances, by heterosexual marriages, by a single life, or even by female friendships and pious communities. These new identities appear "lesbian-like," to use Judith Bennett's term. Bennett writes:

> As I understand David Halperin's essay in *Representations*, we need no longer flounder on the shoals of the distinction between sex and sexual identities. Even Halperin—perhaps the most fervent of social constructionists—now agrees that there were, indeed, sexual *identities* before the nineteenth century; our job is to try to understand the very different constituents of these past sexual identities. [. . .] This project has perhaps been best illustrated, to date, by Anna Clark's essay on Anne Lister which shows how, long before sexologists like Havelock Ellis or Richard von Kraft-Ebing could have provided her with a ready-made identity, Anne Lister fashioned one for herself, from her "inherent desires," from her "material circumstances," and from the "cultural representations" available to her.[9]

The fictions of cross-dressing allow the formation of custom-made identities through dissection and recombination of the components structuring medieval masculinity and femininity. In my opinion, these fictions fulfill erotic needs and social fantasies, rather than being mere accidents of narrative. I focus my discussion on *Yde et Olive*, an early-fourteenth-century romance, which represents two women publicly getting married and privately conversing in bed.[10] The two episodes are also depicted in the miniature accompanying the text. Just as sensual pleasure is an unalienable part of reading and understanding a medieval text and its aesthetics, the image in *Yde et Olive* presides over the work of this chapter. In reading current studies of cross-dressing in romance, I kept asking myself how they relate to that image. I came to see the miniature not as a simple representation of a series of fictional episodes, but as a complex testimony, both storytelling and a trace of how the story was told, how it was meant to be heard, what pleasures it afforded to those who heard it. As Sylvia Huot observes,

> As the visual representation of an essentially oral text, the medieval illuminated manuscript has a certain theatrical—at the risk of anachronism, one may even say cinematic—quality; it does not merely describe events, but, rather, stages them. The performative quality of the medieval book is of profound importance. . . Writing in the second quarter of the thirteenth century, Richard de Fournival testifies to the theatricality of the illustrated book in the prologue of his *Bestiaire d'amours*. Commenting on the fact that the *Bestiaire* is constructed of speech and illustrations—*parole* and *painture*—Richard explains that the combination of the two allows for a vivid auditory and visual experience of that which is depicted. . .
>
> In *Claris et Laris*, which postdates the *Bestiaire d'amours* by about thirty years, Claris is described as witnessing the events that he reads of in a book of love stories: "*En .I. petit livre veoit / La mort Tibé et Piramus*" (In a little book he saw the death of Thisbe and Pyramus [Alton ed., vv. 162–63]). And the analogy between theater and the illuminated book is still apparent in fifteenth-century English defenses of the mystery plays, in which the dramatic performance is referred to as a "living book."[11]

The image portraying Yde and Olive exchanging wedding vows and in bed had a similar effect on me. It was a point of reference, a resistant, if diminutive, representation against which modern interpretations were measured. This role is entirely out of proportion to its dimensions and its general characteristics—it is not a stylistically outstanding piece of work. But the important role it plays in my thinking is perfectly in keeping with its unique status as a friendly representation of a same-sex union between two women at the start of the fourteenth century. Measured by any standards, that picture is a rare find, because it gives visibility to same-sex fantasies of the manuscript's makers and readers.

The rubric accompanying the miniature on folio 394 verso, column b, resembles a wedding invitation: "Ensi que Ydes, fille Flourent d'Arragon, espousa Olive, le fille Otheviien, l'empereur de Rome" (How Yde, daughter of Florent of Aragon, married Olive, daughter of Otto, emperor of Rome).

Unlike the *Yde et Olive* miniature, some of the illuminations in the volume do not exactly match their rubrics (e.g., on fol. 372r col. b)—a sign that our miniature was prepared with care. As one of eight illuminations (illustrating six Huon de Bordeaux sequels, of unequal length), and the only one in *Yde et Olive*, this image has relative importance. It is also quite distinctive in design compared to other illuminations in the volume (Turin MS. L. II. 14). It presents a domestic scene, part of a love story, unlike most miniatures, which represent battle scenes with the pageantry of caparisoned horses mounted by knights carrying crested shields clad in finely depicted armor. The vignettes in the margins show satirical versions of the battles and encounters represented in the main space of the page. While the vignette accompanying the *Yde et Olive* miniature portrays men at a bird hunt, some of the humorous jousts in the same volume also include women. For instance, there is a repeated image of a mounted woman with a distaff on the left, facing a bishop equipped with a frame (for winding wool?) on the right.

The *Yde et Olive* illumination is slightly damaged and wrinkled from the 1904 fire of the library, when burning manuscripts were thrown out of the windows and doused with water, making the parchment shrink. It is a tribute to the permanence of the medium that the text and illuminations are legible even in heavily shrunk manuscripts. Like other damaged volumes, the one containing *Yde et Olive* was wetted, re-stretched, rebound, and treated with gelatin wash to stabilize pigments, a practice now discontinued. The first ten or so folios, now a quarter of their original size, were not re-stretched, having been burned so badly that they lost plasticity. They are legible, but considering the quality and beauty of the manuscript, they look heartbreaking. Compared to them, the part of the volume containing the text of *Yde et Olive* fared very well. But our illumination is located in the right column of the text on the verso, the vulnerable position closest to the inner margin. The fire not only damaged the first and last folios, but also radiated from the spine, since spines and covers caught fire first. In the process, Turin MS. L. II. 14 lost its original binding; it is now rebound in three volumes. In our miniature, the closeness to the affected inner margin results in significantly more damage to its right side.

The illumination is split in two. The left side represents the marriage, with two identical figures of the lovers. A mitered bishop joins their hands, and some nine attendants look on. A person on the left is holding a long candle—echoing line 7,157, "Tante candaille I avoit alumee" [there were so many candles lit]. Someone on the right is playing a *vielle*. The right portion of the image shows a bed with a white canopy and a gray cover, lined in deep red, strewn with gold *fleurs de lys*. This side, being on the inside of the folio, is less legible due to the fire damage. The two figures lying in bed are still discernible, and there is another figure behind the bed, dressed in blue—perhaps the tattletale page that overhears Yde and Olive's private oath of loyalty and protection. If the split frame and doubling may be seen as a metaphor for the split identity of the cross-dresser Yde, the beauty and harmony of the four figures on both sides of the image translate the narrator's sympathies. The four identical main figures also emphasize the same-sex theme, making it an insistent, inescapable part of the representation.

The split frame, pairing the representation of the couple in a crowd with the couple in their bed, evokes for me a recent shift in our interests. If the social aspects (the heroine's autonomy, her actions in the public sphere, the play of feminine characteristics in the male cross-dressing hero) used to dominate feminist discussions of cross-dressing fictions, erotic archaeology symbolized by the bed, seems to predominate now. The question of the relevance of labels such as *lesbian* and *queer* to premodern texts is essential to that discussion. Some medievalists flatly refuse to admit that medieval texts, including fiction, portray homoerotic themes or same-sex love, despite the fact that there exist, in legal texts, cases of prosecution as well as definitions and descriptions of same-sex acts. It is undeniable that women account for a very minor fraction of sodomy cases. Judith Bennett notes that, for the entire medieval period, we have a record of only four cases involving less than a dozen women, all of them in the fifteenth century.[12]

Following Karma Lochrie, many agree that this is due not to lower frequency of sex between women, but primarily to the fact that laws regulating the life of medieval institutions and communities were written and applied in male-dominated juridical culture, mostly concerned with dealings between men. A similar attitude is reflected by confession manuals, which list the "talking points" and details in their treatment of male penitents, and assume symmetrical treatment of women; or by compilations of customs, which describe and prohibit same-sex acts between men, adding "women likewise." This could be attributed to a greater reluctance to imagine or accept female homosexual acts, but is more likely due to the fact that the practice of confession pertained to clergymen more than to any other category, either male or female. Finally, the "silences of the Middle Ages" in the matter of sex between women may also be a testament to these women's success in maintaining necessary secrecy. As with any study of female homoeroticism, my reading is also "an attempt to make visible those who had every reason to ensure their survival by making themselves invisible" (Sautman, "Invisible Women," p. 177).[13]

A different category of objections to reading cross-dressing characters as representations of queer anxieties and desires is raised by literature scholars who argue that instances of queer and transvestite behavior can be explained in terms of plot requirements. With that interpretation comes the reading of emotions represented in these texts as intense friendship and female solidarity, feelings that can be explained in the heteronormative framework. This reading effectively excludes lesbianism, on Ockham's principle.[14] While these interpretations have unquestionable merit, they are not exclusive. Some medieval texts, including *Yde et Olive*, lend themselves to a lesbian reading of the interactions between women, whom they portray *in extenso* in bed, making a lifelong pact to protect each other, in full knowledge of their vulnerability and because of it. The love and loyalty that brought them together is strangely rewarded: one of them is given "all that a man has of human nature" (l. 7269: "Tout chou c'uns hom a de s'umanité"). It is thanks to that gift, we assume, that in the next lines, the couple produces a legitimate male heir—but this last-ditch dynastic conclusion does not, in my view, erase the unusual proposition of the romance. After what can be described as an accidental marriage, the two women recognize each other as women, and as women promise to give all of themselves and risk all for each other.

The third objection, after the refusal to see homoerotic themes in medieval texts and the reduction of such themes to plot requirements, derives from an approach to sex and gender studies that emphasizes the discontinuity between periods and maintains that past phenomena cannot be read in the light of our experience, particularly for the premodern period. This does not mean, in my view, that we cannot know the Middle Ages. Dinshaw, Bennett, Burger, and others want to resist "the stabilizing push of an absolutely other and distinct Middle Ages against which modernity can define itself and against which medievalists can isolate themselves,"[15] and argue that medieval texts provide "an exceptionally promising location to bring together the canonical and the marginal, the modern and the medieval, the historical and the theoretical, imagined not as a stabilizing difference but as productive continuity and rhizomatic connect" (Burger, *Chaucer's Queer Nation*, p. x). Texts such as *Yde et Olive* reveal themselves more fully in a queer perspective that tests the possibility of the "rootedness" (to appropriate Burger's term) of modern lesbian affect in medieval fictions. These texts show love and eroticism between women in a positive light, and invite great latitude in the interpretation of the events they portray. *Yde et Olive* shows the beginning of Olive's love for Yde, Olive's heroic decision to protect Yde, and the unexpected resolution of the conflict that threatens to destroy them both. In spite of their essentialist, heteronormative conclusions, such texts call out for lesbian readings.

Two erudite articles in the collection *Gender Transgressions* compile lists of cross-dressing episodes in medieval French texts.[16] Keith Busby discusses primarily male cross-dressing, and Michelle Szkilnik discusses female cross-dressing.[17] Male cross-dressing episodes appear in such romances as

Raoul de Houdenc's *Meraugis de Portlesguez* (ca. 1220), *Floire et Blancheflor* (early thirteenth century), *Claris et Laris* (1268), Robert de Blois's *Floris et Lyriopé* (thirteenth century), Douin de Lavesne's fabliau *Trubert*, *Wistasse le moine* (both mid-thirteenth century), the interpolation (ca. 1400) in version IV of *Tristan en prose*, and in *Valentin et Orson* (a prose romance from the fifteenth century). Cross-dressing females appear in the fabliaux *Berengier au lonc cul* and *De la dame excoilliée*, in the legend of Pope Joan, in the chante-fable *Aucassin et Nicolete* (Nicolete disguised as a minstrel; late twelfth or early thirteenth century), and in a number of romances: *Roman de Silence* (Silence; end of the thirteenth century), a brief, earlier analogue of *Silence* that constitutes an episode of *Estoire de Merlin* featuring Julius Caesar as the cuckolded king (chapters 35 and 36), part of the prose *Lancelot* (Grisandoles/Avenable; 1230–35), *Roman d'Ysaïe* (Ysaïe's lover Marte), *Roman de Cassidorus* (empress Helcana/hermit Helcanor; end of the thirteenth century). In these last three romances, there are also secondary plots with males disguised as females: queen Eufeme's lover disguised as a nun in *Silence*, and the twelve young lovers of Julius Caesar's wife disguised as ladies-in-waiting in the earlier *Silence* analogue that forms part of the *Estoire de Merlin*; the dwarf Tronc in *Ysaïe*, and Licorus in *Cassidorus*. Other romances with women dressed as men include *Clarisse et Florent* (Clarisse), *Yde et Olive* (Clarisse's daughter Yde; the two texts are sequels to *Huon de Bordeaux*, contained in the same 1311 manuscript), *Roman de Perceforest* (Roman noblewoman Cerse as the knight Malaquin and Nestor's *amie* Néronès as the squire Cuer d'Acier; beginning of the fourteenth century), *Tristan de Nanteuil* (Blanchandine; first half of the fourteenth century), *Buevfes de Hantone* (Josianne; fifteenth century), and the *Roman du comte d'Artois* (the countess; fifteenth century). Other notable examples of sex change include Christine de Pizan's early-fifteenth-century *Livre de la mutacion de Fortune*, which recounts a dream of becoming a man—a metaphor for Christine's active role as a writer and the head of her family.

Busby links male cross-dressing episodes to Thetis disguising Achilles to keep him from going to war, and he attributes the interest in cross-dressing to the general tendency of later romances to play with the conventions of "classic" twelfth-century texts. For Busby,

> cross-dressing. . .is part of a broader implementation of comic devices which borders on the farcical and which entertains while adding perspective to the depiction of. . .the hero. . .and exploiting another direction in the development of Arthurian romance. In *Meraugis de Portlesguez* and other comparable texts, romance, its ideals, and protagonists, are being deflated and demystified; its sharp edges, which hitherto defined and delineated roles and issues, are gradually becoming blurred. (Busby, " 'Plus acesmez,' "p. 48)

He adds: "[a]s a type of disguise, [cross-dressing] often articulates questions of appearance and reality as well as providing narrative impetus" (Busby, "Plus acesmez,'" p. 57). In *Floris et Lyriopé*, Floris exchanges clothes with his twin sister to approach her girlfriend Lyriopé. She feels attracted to Floris without seeing through his disguise. Similarly, in *Floire et Blancheflor*, Floire dresses up as a woman to penetrate the harem where his beloved Blancheflor is imprisoned, and they make love among the houris. In *Meraugis de Portlesguez*, the disguise serves a different function, allowing Meraugis and Gauvain to escape the island where they are trapped. Meraugis poses as the mistress of the island and convinces the real lady's own servants to ferry him and Gauvain out. In *Claris et Laris*, Calogrenant is changed into a woman, a mirror image of the first person he sees upon entering a magical castle. His clothes are initially unchanged, emphasizing the poor fit with his new, diminutive body. He then dresses the part, changing both clothes and horse to gender-appropriate equivalents, and pursues his search for Laris, Claris, and Gauvain with additional motivation, since his original sex is supposed to be restored at the conclusion of the quest. In the interpolation IV to *Tristan en prose*, other knights play a rough joke on Dinadon, who is ambushed, stripped, and forced to appear in public in feminine attire. He astutely manages to avoid some of the ridicule and is restored to dignity and men's clothes. In *Valentin et Orson*, the dwarf Pacolet reminds Szkilnik of the cross-dressing dwarf Tronc in *Ysaïe*: "both dress as women to seduce and trick their enemies" (Szkilnik, "The Grammar of the Sexes," p. 63).[18]

Busby treats separately the cruder texts, *Trubert* and *Wistasse le moine*, pointing out that their "kind of callous vulgarity is very rare, even in a genre such as the *fabliau*, where the sexual act is openly described and often the source of robust humor" (Busby, "'Plus acesmez,'" p. 56). If the editor of *Wistasse* calls this text a *roman d'aventures*, Raynaud de Lage classifies *Trubert* as a *fabliau*.[19] Trubert assumes a series of disguises that help him to commit acts of gross genital and sexual aggression. These include torture of the duke of Burgundy that focuses on his buttocks and anus, a "cure" that involves covering the duke with excrement, and cutting off a woman's genitals and anus to present them to the duke as war trophies. Finally, Trubert impersonates his own sister, and impregnates Roseite, the duke's daughter. In an extended passage, he persuades childish Roseite that his member is a little bunny, *connetiaus*, who loves to play in vaginas, *cons. Conin*, vagina/bunny in medieval French, stands for Trubert's male member that he passes off as both an animal and a vagina.[20] In a concluding episode, Trubert is married to king Golias and "deflowered." For Golias, Trubert fakes a vagina by means of a purse. In *Wistasse le moine*, Wistasse in drag climbs on a horse, prompting verbal play with the male servant in charge of the mount, exploiting the slippery connection between scatology, bestiality, same-sex and heterosexual acts. While feminine drag either allows a character to sneak into the gynaeceum or makes him ridiculous, masculine drag conveys power. Feminine drag is antiheroic; masculine, heroic. The hierarchy is borne out by the numbers and the narrative length of the episodes. According to Szkilnik, not only are there more fictional episodes of females dressing as males, but also, in comparison to female cross-dressing, "male cross-dressing does not generate abundant writing" (Szkilnik, "The Grammar of the Sexes," p. 63). Is the cross-dressed woman best considered as a female character, does she constitute a category on her own, or is she a variation on the masculine ideal? Is she representative or exemplary? Szkilnik notes that it would be obvious for medieval writers that women cross-dressed as men were superior to others. She quotes Ambroise Paré's observation that "true stories" of sex change ("histoire véritable") always tend toward greater perfection: from female to male (Szkilnik, "The Grammar of the Sexes," p. 62).[21] In *Clothes Make the Man: Female Cross Dressing in Medieval Europe,* Valerie R. Hotchkiss argues that, unlike real and fictional "ordinary women," cross-dressing female characters are active, noteworthy, outstanding. They are celebrated, they offer a challenge to the norm, but their status, according to Hotchkiss, is not representative of women, whether real or fictional.[22] Szkilnik and Hotchkiss seem to agree that cross-dressed women are exceptional. Marjorie Garber's groundbreaking discussion of cross-dressing in *Vested Interests,* focused on film, but whose theoretical impact on the discussion of cross-dressing goes far beyond that context, also emphasizes that a cross-dresser is in a separate category.[23] On the other hand, in examining medieval French romance, Francesca Canadé Sautman notes an interesting correlation between cross-dressed women and women heroes in the romance *corpus.* The two texts Sautman studies, *Tristan de Nanteuil* and *Yde et Olive,* "belong to mini-cycles in which women play important roles; in fact, these are some of the only French epic cycles identified with women's names" (Sautman, "What Can They Possibly Do Together?" p. 202).[24] This would suggest that cross-dressed women and other female protagonists were not dissimilar, but rather constituted variations of the female hero.

Assessing the queering potential of cross-dressing fictions, Szkilnik notes that even the more extensive episodes of female cross-dressing, by superposing sex and gender, "divert us from fully assessing the situation. It is as if the writers were toying with the idea of homosexuality but could not bring themselves to name it, even less to describe the consummation of the act" (Szkilnik, "The Grammar of the Sexes," p. 68). Szkilnik agrees with Michèle Perret that "cross-dressing is an opportunity to hint at homosexuality—a taboo so powerful that we find very few examples of

texts dealing frankly with it." The only exception noted by Szkilnik is the
episode of Agriano in *Bérinus*, a fourteenth-century prose romance that has
previously been discussed by Christiane Marchello-Nizia, among others.[25]
The description of homosexuality in *Bérinus* is quite direct. The handsome
young king Agriano banishes all women and presents his men with a hundred good-looking boys enclosed in a tower. The characterization of
Agriano as manly and beautiful, and at the same time evil, does not square
with the portrayal of same-sex-oriented males as effeminate. Rather, it
recalls the contrast between the aggressively masculine Sodomites and
courtly, friendly "good heterosexual males" that, according to Elizabeth
Keiser, structures the opposition homo/hetero in the fourteenth-century
English poem *Cleanness*:

> The [*Cleanness*] poet's reversal of the gender symbolics of conventional
> homophobic discourse conveys his denial that the feminized attributes of
> courtliness the positive exemplars of *cleannesse* all display could logically be
> predicated of men who make love to each other as the Sodomites did.
> Instead, men thus drawn to sexual acts with each other must exhibit the very
> opposite trait, crude masculine aggressiveness. . .He cannot mean that both
> partners in his Sodomitic pair are "passive" and hence effeminate, since he
> stresses the fact that all Sodomite males, not just half of them, are distortedly
> macho and aggressive. Thus, despite the reference to these men as being tan-
> gled together confusingly in a womanly way, male homosexual relations are
> not being constructed here as emasculating in the traditional sense of that
> term. They are not, that is, being condemned because they involve active
> males betraying their sex by becoming passive partners in intercourse as was
> so offensive to polemicists like Alain de Lille.[26]

In the heterosexual polity of *Cleanness*, men have some "feminine" characteristics such as courtliness and the ability to fall in love with females. The
negative excess of this trait would be "effeminacy" in the classical Latin
sense of "uxoriousness." It is logical that romance as a genre would maintain a distinction between aggressive manliness of same-sex-oriented men
and "properly feminized" heterosexual men, and it is also logical that in that
context, "in women's fashion" would mean "male-oriented desire," just as
Keiser argues (p. 159), and conversely "manly" would mean "woman-
oriented." But romance representations are not characterized by impecca-
ble logic. They are more often conglomerates of mutually exclusive
ideologies, complex testimonies of the passage from one system of thought
to another, whether in time (from classic to medieval) or in genre (combining piety and some theological and philosophical elements with the
often conflicting values of a love plot). For instance, in medieval prose
Alexander discussed by Katherine Coyne Kelly, Alexander was "rewritten"

from same-sex oriented to womanizer. The taste he and his army developed for woman-like soft, silk garments of the conquered peoples, is given as the reason of the army's downfall (balooning baggage train), and may hint at his classical persona, or at his medieval womanizer persona.

Agriano's utopian kingdom survives some fourteen years, but succumbs to its heterosexual, fast-reproducing enemies:

> prirent cuer et vigueur en ce qu'il estoient moult creü de bonne gent pour la grant plenté des femmes qu'il avoient eües, et la gent Agriano estoit malement decreüz et affebliez, car mauvaisement peüssent multiplier selon le pechié [variant: la mauvaise acoustumance] qu'il maintenoient contre Dieu et contre nature. (*Bérinus* par. 142, vol. 1, p. 125)

> [they grew in courage and vigor because their population has grown by many good people thanks to the great abundance of women that they possessed, and Agriano's people were severely diminished and weakened, because their numbers could poorly multiply considering the sin [the bad habits] they maintained against God and nature.][27]

If the direct description of a same-sex polity in that episode is atypical, the sympathies of the reader are mobilized in a typical, homophobic manner. In that respect, the episode of Agriano falls into the same category as the "Potiphar's wife" episodes, frequently associated with the motif of same-sex preference. The story line involves a predatory female character that falls in love with the hero or with the cross-dressed heroine; rebuked, she accuses him of same-sex preference (as in Marie de France's *Lanval*, or Conon de Bethune's poem "L'autrier avint en cel autre pays"), and sometimes also accuses him/her of rape (*Lanval*, *Roman de Silence*). In another case, to extricate himself, the beleaguered young man feigns "effeminacy," an elastic category that combines same-sex preference and eunuchism (Walter Map, *De nugis curialium*). There is usually a heterosexual love plot in the offing for the hero/heroine. Sometimes, the woman cross-dresser not only feigns being male, but continues the "male-type" plot (*Lanval*, *De nugis*) by also feigning s/he is an effeminate male. That is the case of *Ysaïe*'s main character, Marte. Disguised as a minstrel, Marte gives in to a noble lady's desire and exchanges caresses for fear of angering her by rejection, although she does not take pleasure in it. In the end, Marte/the minstrel extricates herself by pretending to be impotent (Szkilnik, "The Grammar of the Sexes," p. 77). Although Marte adopts a minstrel disguise to chase after Ysaïe, and the reader's feelings are with the heterosexual couple, Marte's feint is still an opportunity for a "homosexual interlude" with "much kissing and hugging." All these cases differ significantly from *Yde et Olive*, where the heterosexual alternative is incest. In *Yde et Olive*, the same-sex episode claims our sympathy.

If the cross-dressing episodes are "also an opportunity to reflect on what is innate or acquired in sexual identity" (Szkilnik, "The Grammar of the Sexes," p. 61), Szkilnik detects a chronological progression, from the early thirteenth century on, toward

> less ambiguous, more assertive (if less sympathetic) ways of defining femininity. By the fifteenth century, the topos of cross-dessing is either a commodity. . .or an opportunity for the heroine fully to accomplish her female destiny. . . . It is as if medieval writers, at first interested in trying out different combinations, had later become scared by the consequences of their boldness, scared by the ease with which their heroines were undertaking male tasks and being too good at them, scared by the troubled waters they had stirred by touching on the sensitive topic of homosexuality. It was much more comfortable to fall back on old prejudices and to treat cross-dressing as yet another female trick, though a purely practical one that would not jeopardize the fundamental distinction between the sexes. The later texts imply that gender identities are the products of biological difference. This evolution of the topos may be indicative of a general trend towards a more rigid differentiation between men and women. (Szkilnik, "The Grammar of the Sexes," p. 82)

We could say that this narrative of tightening barriers and definitions in the period from the thirteenth to the fifteenth centuries is consonant with the historical development of legal instruments and law enforcement. It also accords with totalizing tendencies of preaching and reform movements, the cultural context in which Szkilnik interprets her reading of cross-dressing fictions: "[b]y the end of the fifteenth century and in the sixteenth century, female transvestitism was strongly condemned by reforming preachers, linked to sodomy and interpreted as a sign that the coming of Antichrist was near."[28] In a Foucauldian optic, these are the two ways in which the discourse of power shapes the social consciousness of individuals: first, through preaching and a progressively more generalized practice of confession; and second, through the development of legal institutions, which bear upon a widening cross-section of the population. The reminder of that regime—the gallows—is always physically present, even shockingly prominent in the medieval urban landscape.

Two models emerge from these recent articles on cross-dressing in romance. Busby notes that cross-dressing episodes generate humor, help develop the plot, and thematize the problematic of fiction and reality, appearance and identity. In Busby's view, cross-dressing episodes participate in the evolution of the romance as a genre: the later romances play on the conventions of twelfth-century "classical" fictions. According to Szkilnik, the first bold and somewhat tentative "homosexual interludes" give way already in the early thirteenth century to more cautious treatment. In early romances, cross-dressing episodes call into question the connection between sex and gender, and lead us to see "nature" as a modern theorist would (be it Judith Butler or, as quoted by Szkilnik, Roberta Krueger): as a device used to account for and justify asymmetries resulting from socially constructed gender differences. Later treatment resorts to essentialist solutions that tend to unquestioningly rely on "nature" as an essential category.

These two narratives of evolution explain plausibly how cross-dressing episodes were adapted and how they remained relevant to changing audiences of romance fictions throughout the medieval period. Yet, different narratives can be constructed as well. First, cross-dressing and gender bending could have appealed to an aesthetic preference. Second, Busby's and Szkilnik's analyses suggest that cross-dressing was particularly adapted to articulate or reaffirm the dominant ideology through a fictional play with a dialectic "other." Third, same-sex encounters facilitated by cross-dressing may have been the expression of same-sex fantasies. *Yde et Olive* is a particularly likely example. The narrator and the persons involved in the production of the manuscript, the intended reader and later readers whom the text could not anticipate but whom it does concern, collaborated in that project. By their participation, they show knowledge of same-sex desire, a tangible reality to which the fiction calls out in its own desire to please the reader. Pleasure in reading what the narrative offers presupposes knowledge on the part of the subject who reads, no matter what the authors' intentions were. The fit between the desire of a queer subject to read and the book's desire to be read is possible because of the gothic project of cross-dressing and gender bending. That aesthetics is *haute couture*. By definition, it is suited to accommodate desires that cannot be fulfilled by the *prêt-à-porter*, the already existing, ready-made objects or identities. The elements of an available whole (identity, manuscript, etc.) are cut up, reshuffled, and recombined; and discrete entities (masculine, feminine) are merged to fashion a lesbian-like identity where there is no "ready-made identity." A custom-made identity is pulled together from "inherent desires," "material circumstances," and available "cultural representations" (Bennett, " 'Lesbian- Like,' " n. 27, p. 11; quoting Clark on Lister).

Busby insists on the cathartic and obscene quality of cross-dressing episodes, noting some scatological, "sinister and diabolic overtones" (Busby, " 'Plus acesmez,' " p. 57). Szkilnik, after Perret, notes the breach of taboo, although she is careful to "nuance" its portent, and emphasizes "a progressive reconsideration of the practice: suggesting at first the fluidity of gender boundaries, the topos later serves to reinforce their rigidity" (Szkilnik, "The Grammar of the Sexes," p. 62). It is understood that the narrative use of cross-dressing and the pleasure it affords the readers lies precisely in the exploration of the prohibited possibilities opened by the representation of alternative genders, with their richly inventive sartorial and genital combinations. But both Busby and Szkilnik base their narratives of dialectic and evolution on the perception that cross-dressing characters are "always already," that is ontologically, doomed to fall short of the goal they articulate: for Busby, chivalric hero status; for Szkilnik, homosexual potential on one hand, and exposing constructedness of gender on the other hand. In response to their framing of cross-dressing, I would like to adopt a stylistic optic and suggest that cross-dressing characters were attractive to changing medieval audiences because they are essentially ambiguous. While medieval narratives are never fully and unquestioningly sympathetic to homo-eroticism, they are not clearly heteronormative either. I would suggest that these episodes should not be seen as aborted experiments in tolerance and relativism. If we assume a taste for exposed seams, cross-dressing episodes will no longer strike us as oddities, accidents of narrative, marking the decline of romance conventions, as if the romance narrators had nothing more to give in terms of wholesome poetry, and succumbed by default to these odd gender combinations in their characters, even in their protagonists. Instead, composite gender identities of fictional characters would participate in an aesthetics of segmentation and reuse.

In an article criticizing the structuralist reflex, Félix Guattari describes it as a mechanical reading of everything "as a language," a practice he calls "the interpretative illusion:" "any fact, whether social, behavioral, mythical, imaginary, etc., can be expressed by language; it will be therefore considered 'structured like a language.' "[29] In opposing that reductionism, he points out that the relationships that can be described as "language" may be more effectively and fully defined. He proposes a list of four types of "encoding" that include, but are not limited to language: "natural" (general preexisting conditions, e.g., time, distance, population); "symbolic" (gesture, ritual, mythography, with no particular emphasis on language; these symbolic relationships bind an individual into a social matrix, and are both enabling and restrictive, since they define the modalities of an individual's participation in the social); "signifying" (articulation between discourse and writing, and "subordination of all other semiotic systems to linear chains of signifiers"); and "a—signifying"—mathematics, music, etc.,—what he calls the "writing machines" ("*machines à écriture*").

This taxonomy was conceived to address particular questions: the relationship of money to fulfillment, and the modalities of assignation of value. Guattari sketches out a chronological succession of power formations defined by these four subsequent encodings. He notes that the effects of historical subservience to different modes of encoding are cumulative, resulting in the crisscrossing (*quadrillage*) or rootedness (the image is that of a tentacular root, *rhizome tentaculaire*) of multiple strata of power, which infiltrate all "individual value systems," defining individual "micro-politics of desire" (Guattari, "La valeur," pp. 296–97). That argument is not transferable here. Rather, Guattari's distinctions help me justify my hypothesis of aesthetic preference for gender bending and cross-dressing. Guattari says that desire is the key to these rhizomic systems, and this helps me link sexual and aesthetic desire in representations of cross-dressing. Aesthetic preference would cut through the categories proposed by Guattari like a tentacular root.

If we were to hypothesize that gender-bending fictions fulfilled an aesthetic desire, it would not be difficult, in my view, to summon a disciplinary consensus that a fundamental characteristic of medieval fictions and artifacts was a tendency for dissection and fragmentation grounded in basic circumstances of production (Guattari's "natural encoding"). An economy of dearth breeds an "aesthetics" of dissection and recombination, for instance, when women's religious communities recycle old manuscripts and buildings because they have no other means to fulfill their needs. But the stylistic preference for heterogeneity, everywhere present, is not always traceable to limited funds. Classical myths recast as contemporary dynastic propaganda and Carolingian manuscripts cut up to save historiated initials participate in a shared experience of fragmentation, recombination, and ambiguity (Guattari's "symbolic encoding"). I think that this experience is widely shared across geographical and time lines, and that it can be detected in multiple relationships that medieval authors establish with classical works: creation of dynastic legend in the *matière de Rome* romances such as *Enéas*, or accumulation of intellectual capital through the use of mythology in *Roman de la Rose*.

Medieval artifacts show both the awareness of and the willingness to manipulate the conflicting values that are attached to heterogeneous parts of their composite wholes. Copying and binding texts in a codex also entails segmentation, alteration, reconstitution of segments into a syntagmatic whole that can be very unlike the original. For instance, a romance can be bound with other fictions or with chronicles, implying very different interpretive values.[30] A section of a book can be copied as a stand-alone work; for instance, section fifteen, on geography, of Bartholomaeus Anglicus's *De proprietatibus rerum*, missing from some manuscripts of *De proprietatibus*, but on the other hand present in other manuscripts as an independent text.[31] The evolution of anthologies of poets and poems (compilational patterns, auctorial design of books of songs, etc.) is another example.[32] Segmentation affected the entire spectrum of the book market. On the low end, the system of *pecia* developed for high-volume copying of "everyday" books in university centers: one scribe produced multiple copies of one section of a work, allowing other sections to be copied in multiples simultaneously by someone else. On the high end of the market, we observe the rise of specialized workshops participating in production of luxury books, protracting the phase during which quires or other workable portions of the text were separated. Semantic systems participating in the creation of meaning on the manuscript page—rubrics, initials, paragraph marks, illuminations, borders, arms—were produced in isolation from one another in space (different sites or workshops) as well as in time. Some manuscripts were sold or circulated even though their illumination cycles were never finished. These systems, produced separately, gave birth to sec- ondary structures of meaning—stylistic coherence, patterns, workshop style, genesis and influence of representative "hands." These secondary structures of meaning are so well articulated and interesting that they, not the individual manuscripts, are the traditional subject of art history. In Guattari's terms, this would correspond to the transformation of an "a- signifying system" ("machine à écriture": *pecia* and high-end specialization) to one more meaningfully invested: the hermeneutics of the selection and arrangement of texts in a given manuscript, workshop stylistics. We observe that the postulate underlying Guattari's approach, the tendency of a-signifying systems to adapt to producing meaning, is confirmed. It can be docu- mented by the inevitable transformation of "writing machines" into signi- fying systems, as if attribution of meaning was desirable and necessary.

This gives me the impetus to argue that even the phenomena that can be explained in terms of economy (manuscripts a community could not afford) are overdetermined by desire. Dismembered old books are often associated with women's convents (including Syon Abbey and the royal French foundation at Poissy).[33] This leads us to believe that cutting out illu- minations made sense in less well-endowed women's convents, while wealthier men's communities would prefer to sacrifice part of their income to have new books illuminated without dismembering old ones. The taste for manuscripts beyond a community's collective means indicates a split between what is available and what is desirable, a split bridged by the highly emotive gesture of dismembering a complete but no longer used book. The resistance of books to dismembering gives a measure of its necessity where it was performed.

The comparison with composite manuscripts helps explain the func- tioning of cross-dressing fictions. The act of dismembering a manuscript is aggressive, emotionally charged. That act is physical and therefore, in my opinion, more violent than creating a fictional character in a romance or, *a fortiori*, in a *fabliau*, a genre where violence has less consequence, much like children's cartoons today.[34] Just as the split between desire and availability is bridged by creating composite, pasted-in manuscripts, the split between what is desirable and what is possible in terms of erotic investments or social roles may be expressed by the fantasy of a woman dressing up as a man, a *chevalier fendu* or split knight, but also a knight with a split, a problematic but somehow necessary figure.[35]

Used as the epithet of a cross-dressing woman knight in *Roman de Perceforest*, this term—*chevalier fendu*—is doubly a *blason*. First, it reflects her/his split identity in a concentrated, heraldic, symbolic fashion, like a *blason*, a device or coat of arms, similar for instance, to another cross-dressing woman in *Perceforest* renamed Cuer d'Acier (Iron Heart). Second, *chevalier fendu* (split knight? crotch knight? dyke knight?) isolates and reveals a body part, as in the poetic genre of *blason*. If the vogue of *blason*/small poetic form, which defines the word in modern French, postdates *Perceforest* by two centuries, *blason*/defamatory statement is attested since the end of the fourteenth century (*Cent nouvelles nouvelles*). This particular *blason* highlights an obscene, unnamable body part; the nickname associates public/heraldic and obscene/bodily meaning. If Szkilnik notes that *fendace* "refers to female sex" ("The Grammar of the Sexes," pp. 71–72), it also specifically refers to male sex, for instance, in *Enéas*, where Lavinia says Aeneas would have liked her better if she wore pants, "se j'aüsse fandus les dras," l. 9,156 [if I had split cloths/clothes], and that the boys he uses always have their shirt open for him: "fandue trove lor chemise," l. 9161 [he finds their shirt split]; and in *Trubert*, where "li fenduz" is revealed between the duke of Burgundy's exposed, naked buttocks (*nache*, *Trubert*, l. 279), which Trubert penetrates (Li dus li a le cul tourné, / apareillé et descouvert, / si que toz li fenduz apert. *Trubert,* ll. 272–74 [The duke turned his ass toward him, prepared and uncovered, so that the whole crack opens up/shows]). In the *blason* "*chevalier fendu*," the text exacts violence on the character in a manner similar to dismembering a book for its initials. It bespeaks a fulfillment (of the desire to possess and to preserve) that resolves its initial fascination (lack) by reducing the desired object to one particular part. It is a "split" part, either the female genitalia or the anus, that appears (*apert*). Because they open themselves, these split body parts are perceived as more intimate than the penis; they are associated by Lacan with the slit of the penis. The gesture that reveals them can be seen as more aggressive, because it can penetrate as well. Fragmentation gives permission to open up, expose, penetrate ("vos fis un pertuis en la nage," *Trubert* 832 [I made a hole in your buttocks]), while denying its initial object its wholeness, and using it for parts (fragmenting, dismembering). The final result is a composite whole that may strike us as artificially construed. However, that composite entity is exactly what was desired, what was aimed at in the act of dismembering and regrouping. Medieval authors and audiences wanted queer characters; they did not just happen as accidents of narrative.

Another parallel to writing composite genders is *translatio studii et imperii*, a term that embraces the various technologies of loose translation and recycling of classical material by vernacular authors. *Translatio studii et imperii* bespeaks an appreciation for prestige similar to that which led the nuns to reuse old illuminations. Vehicles of symbolic value, Latin sources are often mobilized in dynastic projects, or in projects expressing somewhat inflated cultural aspirations. At the roots of recycling classical myths is a rupture, a separation from initial purpose similar to that which allows the nuns to dismember a codex. In her recent work on mythology, Renate Blumenfeld-Kosinski quotes an earlier critic, Stierle, who compared this rupture to the "separation between *signifiant* [signifier] and *signifié* [signified]"—a comparison testifying to the theoretical preoccupations of the moment, but that may perhaps usefully be developed in the context of Lacan.[36] Blumenfeld-Kosinski extends Stierle's metaphor by comparing the medieval survival of classical myths to segmentation and recombination in new syntactic strains. These strains are imbedded in new material, culminating in the interweaving of biblical and Latin narratives, in such compilations as the *Histoire ancienne jusqu'à César*, or the *Mer des histoires*. The redeployment of myth in the vernacular can sustain many uses: political legitimating, moral authorization, erotic fantasy, and biographical fiction. In the later period (fourteenth and fifteenth centuries), the use of myth can be an index to an interpretive stance rather than to a specific moral or other univocal interpretation. Following Jauss, Blumenfeld-Kosinski also reminds us that the new grammar of myth (new syntagms composed of old segments) accompanies developments in myth "semantics." Some figures (Venus, Cupid, Genius, Nature) acquire in the Middle Ages a density and complexity to which they do not seem predestined in the classical sources. As Blumenfeld-Kosinski points out, these phenomena show that each iteration of the myth is both utterance and *parole*, an event that not only reiterates, but also contributes meaning.

This property of segmentation and recombination is also at work in cross-dressing characters. The elements that constitute a gender syntagm—physiology, clothes, language, emotions—are cut up and pasted together in a new phrase, corresponding to a composite gender, inscribed somewhere on a continuum whose extremes—masculine and feminine—are perhaps only theoretical. The appearance of cross-dressing in fiction queers the gender norm: no longer a polarized dichotomy, it must rather be described as a continuum from masculine through queer to feminine. Queer episodes produced in the framework of heterosexual ideology are ambiguous both in terms of exclusively queer and exclusively heteronormative. Queer representations are both liberating and frustrating as antecedents of homosexual identity, but their heterosexual effects are ambiguous as well.

Through castration, transvestitism, androgyny, or sex change, a "straight" male or female character turns queer—for instance, becomes a passing transvestite (*Yde et Olive, Silence, Roman d'Ysaïe*). By transvestite I mean more than a cross-dresser—someone (like Yde, Silence, or Marte) capable of arousing feelings of pleasurable amorous suffering in women who declare themselves heterosexual. Some manuscripts dwell with obvious relish on these sexually ambiguous protagonists and their genital and emotional tribulations, focusing on queer scenes both in the text and in the illuminations (*Yde et Olive*). What work are these episodes doing? There are many possibilities here. For instance, one can suppose that the economy of heterosexual pleasure is secretly served by transvestite plots and resulting female homoeroticism, similar to voyeuristic pleasure that fuelled the production of nineteenth-century lesbian novels, or to cinematographic tradition dating back to the "celluloid closet" of the 1920s and 1930s. In that sense, bed scenes with Yde and Olive or Floire and Blancheflor (Floire disguised as a woman and hiding in the harem, pretending to be Blancheflor's girlfriend) are similar—they may appeal to a male audience imagining two, or two hundred, women in bed.

Another interpretation would explain sustained representation of queer love in heteronormative romance tradition, in spite of the taboo on homoeroticism, in terms of construction of communal identity. In their transgressive presence, enacting the taboo, queer episodes in romance resemble a ritual reenactment at allowed periods or places, a liminal experience, in the sense theorized by Victor Turner: bordering the social fabric and therefore constitutive of it. This corresponds to the dialectic noted by Szkilnik and Busby: quoting a composite or ambiguous gender and sexual identity can have the effect of firming up the central ideology of the narrative. This is the role that borders and margins often play in a manuscript, allowing an explicit, obscene, or scatological expression of concerns that are entertained with more decorum in the main body of the text. An alternative gender and sexual configuration can play a similar role. We may suppose that some texts lend themselves to this interpretation better than others; those, in particular, where the emotive gesture that segments, then recomposes a gender identity plays a greater role. Instead of the ambiguity (resulting from segmentation and recombination), the emphasis is on cutting up, for instance, on castration. Instead of dwelling pleasurably on two women in bed (*Yde et Olive*), the text anxiously focuses on torture and suffering (*Parzival*).

When a queer episode is used to reaffirm essential dichotomies, it often undergoes a kind of "repair," or exorcism, which erases to some extent the previous functioning of the queer character as an alternative model of sexual and gender identity. The "repair" consists in reinserting the queer character into the social fabric *via* the patriarchal heterosexual family, by reinstating the previously collapsed dichotomies (male versus female, hetero-versus same-sex preference). This can occur within the text (in *Yde et Olive*, Yde is miraculously given male genitals; in *Silence* and *Estoire de Merlin*, the protagonist is undressed; revealed as female, she marries the king). The examples discussed in chapter 1 focus on other types of "repair": in the gloss accompanying the text (Bersuire's commentary to Ovid, Raoul de Presles's commentary to Saint Augustine), or in the continuations that postdate the text proper (*Graal*). As I have shown, later interpretations sometimes erase the queer potential of the original. In most continuations of *Graal*, the ambiguous gender identity of the Fisher King is veiled or dropped. In Chrétien's original, brief account, there is a queer potential but nothing explicit. This, as I have shown, allows two developments. One— the Fisher King's genital wound is a punishment for philandering; and two—Fisher King as a castrate is a queer figure. I have noted that Wolfram von Eschenbach's *Parzival* develops both potentialities by doubling the figure of the castrate. The magician Clinschor is punished for philandering, and the Fisher King is a sexually ambiguous figure. I also pointed out that some later French versions (e.g., Manessier) preserve the ambiguity of Chrétien's original. On the other hand, the majority of continuations, as well as the manuscript tradition of Chrétien's *Graal* (particularly the iconography of the Fisher King episode) tend to reduce this ambiguity. Even as the Grail romances become part of French dynastic legend, the ambiguity is resolved.[37]

The case of Christine de Pizan, analyzed by Jane Chance, illustrates well the procedure of "repair" of gender idiosyncrasies.[38] In the *Livre de la muta-cion de Fortune*, in a dream vision, Christine, widowed and destitute, realizes a solution to her problems—she becomes a man. Here, sex change is the metaphor for authority. Chance comments that sex change is also, ironi-cally, the condition of transmission and procurement under which Chris-tine de Pizan's works are translated into English, copied, and printed. The "repair" of a split identity (woman author) proceeds in the predictable fash-ion. Christine's texts are attributed to male tutors or students, and presented under the sole name of the translator, scribe, or printer. The printing of Christine's texts is also accompanied by "immasculation" (a term Chance borrows from Judith Fetterly) of female mythological figures, both classical and invented by Christine (her "gynography").[39] The illustrations undergo "repairs" similar to the text. Compared to manuscript illuminations prob-ably supervised by Christine, in later, independently printed woodcuts, women are made smaller, disappear, or are boxed in or cornered, while men become more prominent, bigger, or appear in scenes where they were pre-viously absent. There also exist examples of a symmetrical reversal, for instance, feminization of male lovers from the classical tradition such as Alcibiades. It is as a famous woman that the Athenian general and politician appears in commentaries to Boethius's *De consolatione Philosophiae*, and most famously in French in François Villon's "Ballade des dames du temps jadis," recounting women worthies, and preceding the ballad on famous men (part of Villon's *Testament* written in 1461–62; "Ballade des dames," l. 3).[40]

The presence of cross-dressed characters, however episodic, produces a permanent queering effect in medieval culture. This is by no means an isolated reading, but rather a well-known strategy exploiting the structural fallacy of polarized systems of oppositions that cannot be constructed without articulating their Other, double, or obverse. A deconstructive reading allows us to recover the marginalized entity and unsettle the norm. In a structuralist framework, that type of reading is also possible, and it can be associated with Bakhtin's interpretation of carnivalesque reversals as safety valves that enable the continuance of a repressive regime.[41] An aesthetic and philosophical appreciation for the role of incongruous, displaced elements as a means to transcendence was an integral part of medieval thought. That appreciation is expressed in the dirt and scatology of fabliaux, in the ascetic tradition, in alchemy and medicine (homeopathy), among others. By focusing on these aspects, structuralist and deconstructive approaches were "writing theory from the Middle Ages." Although they may seem un-Foucauldian in their periodization, structuralist and poststructuralist readings of the functioning of queer episodes in medieval romance can be related to Foucault's statement that the homophobic discourse of sexual hygiene is the site of emergence of homosexual identity. That is, I believe, the ideal relationship of queer studies to Foucault's work, a stance that Francesca Canadé Sautman and Pamela Sheingorn advocate when, following Karma Lochrie, they criticize "pure Foucauldians" for using the medieval period as the background against which modern sexuality is defined: "Foucault's revolutionary thinking on the production of knowledge within society and on the mechanisms by which discourses constitute power, and his attack on the social undergirdings of intellectual authority have paradoxically been subsumed at times into a hasty reading of the history of sexuality, then made into canon and dogma," a gesture of which Foucault would most certainly disapprove. As Lochrie notes, such dogmatic Foucauldianism cannot "aid in the kind of cultural genealogies that Foucault's work so admirably fostered" (Sautman and Sheingorn, *Same Sex Love and Desire*, pp. 5–6, quoting Lochrie).[42]

One of the formative references in queer studies, John Boswell's *Same-Sex Unions in Pre-Modern Europe*, presents an interesting variant of the history of homosexual subjectivity.[43] Boswell's and Foucault's positions on the formation of homosexual subjectivity are mutually dependent: Boswell's early work apparently influenced Foucault's later work.[44] It can be summarized as follows: where the straight will see an exemplary exception—a limit to the norm that defines self—the queer will see a mirror self. In essence, in *Same-Sex Unions*, Boswell proposed a reader-bound interpretation of queer practices and texts. He pointed to multiple examples of doubly polarized models used in same-sex marriage or adoption rites. For instance, he showed that same-sex couples of saints, frequent in Christian traditions influenced by Byzantium (including Russia, Central Europe, and Italy), were recognized by the official orthodoxy, and yet simultaneously, within the same chronological and geographical space, served as patron saints of same-sex unions.

While Boswell's understanding of queer texts' double polarity rests on a historical and cultural analysis, queer readings that are not chronologically or spatially anchored, and can treat a text as disconnected from its context, also abound. For instance, in his article on the French *Life of St. Euphrosine* (a cross-dressed woman who achieves sainthood as a monk), Simon Gaunt highlights the classic paradox: if queer is the polar opposite of heterosexual, the representation of queerness is necessary in order to define the heterosexual norm.[45] The gesture that defines the norm carries the means of its own undoing, or deconstruction. In order to "prove a heterosexual," we have to "assume a queer," but once we assume a queer, we create a locus around which feelings, models, and rituals of queerness coalesce.

Boswell's and Gaunt's conclusions, although concerning widely dissimilar bodies of evidence, are concordant: the presence of queer protagonists queers the text, in spite of the heteronormative framing. Queering can be an explicit function of the text, or arise in the use of the text. However, for Gaunt, texts with queer women figures follow patterns that are not the same as, or symmetrical to, those he defined in his discussion of Eneas, Lanval, and other male figures he analyzed in an earlier article.[46] Gaunt notes that in queer texts with female protagonists, the outcome is different from the one observed previously for male heroes. He emphasizes that the cross-dressing female protagonist is always straightened out in the end, either defrocked or endowed with a penis. Both solutions eliminate the earlier disagreement between genital and sartorial indices: a defrocked cross-dressed female is now just female, a be-penised cross-dressed female now has genital equipment to match her masculine drag. According to Gaunt, the reasons for this final folding into the bipolar, heterosexual mold are on the order of the text's audience, reception, and functioning. Gaunt's remarks allow us to distinguish two kinds of this "higher order of narrative necessity" that justify both the queer device (cross-dressing) and its straight resolution (*post mortem* defrocking, post-marriage sex change). As Gaunt points out, the narrative's explicit meaning lies not in erotic adventures but in exemplary sainthood (in the case of saints' lives, e.g., *Euphrosine*). In the case of romance fictions, heterosexual orthodoxy and biological means of reproduction matter more than queer desires (*Yde et Olive, Silence, Estoire de Merlin*). On that count, Gaunt's reading is in agreement with the widely shared view that romance as a genre is essentially motivated by dynastic concerns.

In that reading, the episodic nature of women's cross-dressing is made to play a negative role in the constitution of their identity. In the process of heterosexual self-elaboration that, as Gaunt shows, depends on the production of queer behaviors and desires, the texts with female protagonists present an outcome different from that of male cross-dressing episodes. In *Eneas* and *Lanval*, sexual orientation is separate from, and may exist in the absence of, acts: "it is implicit in these diatribes (and in others from vernacular texts) that some men are represented as having an irrevocable and immanent sexual orientation toward other men that transcends their acts, thus belying the 'constructionist' argument that object choice is a more recent defining category of sexual identity" (Gaunt, "Straight Minds/Queer Wishes," p. 441). Are we to understand that medieval fictions represent male homosexuality differently from female, and specifically that the cultural paradigm comprehends male homosexuality but not female? Do texts on women reveal a premodern fictional construct of female desire, showing sexual orientation as immanent in acts, whereas male homosexuality is represented in the modern fashion, through desire and object choice? Are the Middle Ages on both sides of the "essentialist/constructionist" argument: premodern in their treatment of women, early modern in that of men? Perhaps premodern in some texts about women or men, modern in others?

In the romance that bears their names, Yde and Olive are the third generation of lovers in a cycle that forms a sequel to *Huon de Bordeaux* and consists of a series of *romans d'aventure* connected by the genealogy of their protagonists, as well as by the repetition of plot devices. *Yde et Olive* is represented by one manuscript only, Turin MS. L. II. 14, although a summary of its plot appears in BN f. fr. 1451 on fol. 225r, lines 19–29, another manuscript of *Huon* followed by sequels (an alexandrine version of *Esclarmonde*) (Barbara Brewka, *Esclarmonde. . .*, vol. 1, pp. 3 and 5). There also exist Middle English versions of *Huon* and adaptations of *Yde et Olive*.[47] The Turin manuscript, unique witness of *Yde et Olive*, dates to 1311, while the Huon de Bordeaux cycle was copied from the mid–thirteenth century through the fifteenth (the most recent manuscript is BN f. fr. 22,555). In addition to interesting marginalia, initials, and poles dividing the two columns of text in the Turin manuscript, the sequels are decorated with eight illuminations. One of the eight depicts the marriage and bed scene from *Yde et Olive*, giving this episode a remarkable visibility in the context of the entire volume.

Yde et Olive opens as a "Constance/Manekine" story, with Yde fleeing her incestuous father. In the course of her adventures, she dresses as a man and fights valiantly, as her mother Clarisse did in *Clarisse et Florent*. When Yde heroically serves the Roman emperor, his daughter, Olive, falls in love with Yde. The emperor, in order to reward Yde, gives her Olive in marriage. Yde marries Olive reluctantly and, after feigning illness to avoid intimacy, she reveals to Olive that she is a woman. Olive, who loves Yde, accepts this news with equanimity, and even praises Yde's virtue. The two women decide to live together as a married couple, and keep Yde's identity a secret. However, the emperor is informed of their pact, and somewhat unenthusiastically decides to expose the couple and burn them at the stake. To gather evidence, he orders Yde to bathe with him. An angel intervenes, announcing that God has altered Yde: "Dix li envoie et donne par bonté / Tout chou c'uns hom a de s'umanité," ll. 7,268–69 [God sends her/him and gives from his goodness / All that a man has of human nature]. In the context, human nature ("umanité") can be interpreted as male genital organs, because after this intervention the marriage can reproduce. In the closing words of the poem, the angel foretells that the emperor will die soon, and that Yde and Olive will have a son to succeed him. The emphasis, as modern readers agree, is not on purging the couple of homoerotic desire, but rather on enabling the two women to procreate. There is another dimension to the gift of "umanité": theological. God is not human, and therefore lacks "umanité," human nature: for where there is death, there is also copulation (John Chrysostom, *On Virginity*: "There where there is death, there is also sexual copulation; and there where there is not death, there is not sexual copulation either)."[48] The wording of the angel's announcement represents Yde and Olive's marriage as nonhuman, and in one sense, prelapsarian. The woman–woman couple, like Adam and Eve before the fall, is exempt from the curse announced as the first human couple is being thrown out of the Garden of Eden: that Eve shall give birth in pain. It is only when Yde is given "all that man has of human nature" that Olive will give birth. I would also emphasize that the lack of punishment and the bestowing of "human nature" on Yde do not prove that there is no awareness of lesbian subjectivity in the text. Rather, this lack of punishment and this gift of "humanity" can be interpreted as corollaries of a different order of narrative economy, where romance functions primarily as a dynastic fiction, a narrative of filiation set in the heroic mode. The dynastic dimension need not erase the erotic. Even when incompatible, these two dimensions can coexist. Here as in many other genres, the apparently subordinate erotic stratum can be viewed as far more meaningful than the didactic.

What interests me, therefore, is the bed scene. Not only is that scene lengthy, but it is also given extraordinary relative emphasis as the subject of the one and only illumination to *Yde et Olive*. The same-sex configuration ostensibly heightens the attraction of the bed episode, compared to heterosexual bed scenes, usually dispatched with a couplet. The length of Yde's and Olive's bed negotiations (7,156–95) is comparable to that of Yde's heroic exploits during the recent campaign (6,975–7,035), proving that two women almost having sex are as attractive a romance subject as a host engaged in battle—a parallel that the bellicose metaphor underscores: "During this night there were no cries or battle" [En cele nuit n'i [ot] cri ne mellee, l. 7,191].

When Yde forewarns Olive that she may not rise to the occasion, she says: " 'Car jou l'arai mout griés si com jou bee: Jou ai .j. mal dont j'ai ciere tourblee.' / A ices mos fu Olive accollee" (7,169–71). "Car jou l'arai mout griés si com jou bee," a difficult line, could be translated as "It will be difficult, I think," or, "although I would love to," but Guiraud's research on the "b-vowel-b" group, showing semantic equivalence between the mouth and the vagina in the word *bee*, suggests another reading. In the verbal or adjectival form, *bee* would signify round, open; in the substantive, oral, vaginal, or anal aperture. This equivalence is borne out by the examples of the use of *bee* in medieval texts.[49] Along with many examples of *bouche bée* or *gueule baee* (mouth agape), there is this attestation from *Renard*: "Lieve sa queue, le cul bee" (l. 715) [lifts his tail, the asshole staring out], showing the equivalence between the body's various orifices in the use of *bee*. Since medieval *bee* signifies to be open, to desire, to dream, to yearn for, to covet, to gape, to be confounded, to await, anticipate, as well as to wait in vain (*paier la bee*), the line could be read as a pun on waiting, perhaps waiting in vain for the consummation of marriage, specifically because an orifice opens (*bee*, from verb *beer*, *baer*, to open) where a penis was expected. Thus, "*Si com jou bee*" could mean both "I think" and "I have a vagina (instead of a penis)": " 'It will be difficult, because I am female: I have a weakness which troubles my body.' With these words Olive was embraced."

Olive herself forestalls the sexual act with a stock romance request: that consummation of marriage be delayed a fortnight, until the departure of guests. This request is to remain a secret ("*ci sommes a celee*," l. 7,173: we are here in private), just as Yde's half-confession was made "*coiement a celee*" (l. 7,166: softly in private). "*A celee*"—the words that punctuate the bed scenes in *Yde et Olive* (ll. 7,166, 7,173)—can be read as an adverb of place as well as of manner, and can be translated as "in hiding," "in the closet," as well as "in private." The deferral recalls Christine de Pizan's ballad *Douce chose est que mariage*:

La premiere nuit de ménage
Tres lors poz-je bien éprouver
Son grand bien, car onques outrage
Ne me fit dont me dus grever

Mais, ains qu'il fut temps de lever
Cent fois baisa, si comm' je tien,
Sans vilenie autre rouver:
Et certes le Doux m'aime bien (ll. 9–16)

[The first night of marriage I could sense his kindness very soon because
he never harmed me in a way that I could deplore. But, before it was time
to rise, he kissed me a hundred times, as it pleases me, without seeking
other villainy, and the Sweet surely loves me well.]

Olive gives a different context to this request: she wishes to delay the
consummation of marriage because of the presence of wedding guests who
would laugh at her ("Que jou n'en soie escarnie et gabee," l. 7,181 [So I
shall not be mocked and ridiculed because of it]). The request is formal and
formally granted. However, the many forms in which intercourse is
described in this passage, in negative terms—"I want not this. . .but
that"—purposefully make us imagine what two women do in a marriage
bed. Olive says she does not want to "jouer. . .a la pate levee," l. 7,177 [play
at the paw in the air], and protests she never desired it ("Onques de chou
ne fu entalentee," l. 7,178 [I was never keen on that]). Concerning
"jouer. . .a la pate levee," Brewka notes: "This is perhaps the most colorful
phrase in the sequels. I have been unable to find instances of its use in other
texts; however, the meaning seems to be clear; that is, to have sexual intercourse" (Brewka, *Esclarmonde*, vol. 2, p. 542). Tobler and Lommatzsch give
two phrases, from *Some de Nausay* and *De Constant du Hamel*: "Amours li a
le piet levé / L'oreille li a escaufé / Et le cuer ou ventre engrossié" (*Some de
Nausay*, ll. 1,439–1,410 [love has lifted her foot, heated her ear, and swollen
her belly]. As for the ear, it sometimes stands in for the vagina in the erotic
geography of the body, for instance, in the Virgin Birth or in Rabelais's
Gargamelle who, like the Virgin Mary, conceives through her ear; and the
"swelling in the belly" is a pregnancy, as the choice of "engroissir" also
implies. The lexicographers modestly propose "Hat ihn in Begewung
gesetzt" [has set her foot in motion] for "li a le piet levé," but I believe we
can propose a fairly specific coital posture, since all three lines are clearly
metaphors for arousal, intercourse, or its effects. That posture is described
directly in the second example quoted by Tobler and Lommatzsch, a rape
scene from the *fabliau De Constant du Hamel*. Constant rapes the provost's
wife in his presence, to take revenge on him, and the expression is part of
a detailed description, not a hint: "la dame fu toute esperdue. . ., / Et cil la
vait aus jambes prendre; / Se li a levees amont, / Les genouz li huerta au
front. / Por ce qu'ele se defendoit / C'on l peust jouer aus dez" (IV, ll.
192–98) [the lady was terrified. . ./and he went and took her by the legs,
and lifted them up, knocking her knees against her forehead, because she

was fighting him off, so that one could play dice there]. Seen in the light of these examples, the text of *Yde et Olive* graphically represents what the two women did not do in bed.

Olive refers to intercourse in the "pate levee" metaphor as well as in a euphemism she attributes to others: "Mais de l'amour c'on dist qui est privee / Vous requier jou que je soie deportee" (l. 7,186–87) [But I request of you to be excused from the love which one describes as intimate]. This evokes the stock *fabliau* motif of the aloof maiden. As it does in the *fabliau*, here also the rhetoric of aloofness functions as the anticipation of seduction. Olive proposes that their pleasure be consummated at leisure ("A no deduit arons bien recouvree," 7,182) [We will make up for that at our leisure] after the wedding guests depart. Meanwhile, she repeatedly wishes to be excused ("Que, s'il vous plaist, je serai deportee," 7,184; "Vous requier jou que je soie deportee," 7,187). In the meantime, Olive likes to be embraced ("Fors du baisier bien voel estre accolee," 7,185), and they seal the pact with kisses and hugs ("Dont l'ont l'un l'autre baisie et accolee," 7,190 [On account of this then they kissed and embraced each other]).

But perhaps the most interesting reading of Yde and Olive's bed negotiations would be to take Olive's words at their face value. She says she never wanted to have sex, "onques de chou ne fui entalentée" (l. 7,178) [I was never keen on that], and refuses "l'amour c'on dist est privee" (l. 7,186) [love which is called private]. On the morning after the wedding night, asked: "comment iés mariee?" (l. 7,198) [how were you married?], Olive responds: "ensi com moi agree" (l. 7,199) [as I like it], provoking laughter. That laughter, "grant risée" of the palace crowd ("u palais," l. 7,201) is a very nice touch. It echoes "escarnie et gabee" of line 7,181, the jokes that meet the deflowered virgin on the first morning of her marriage, as the knowledge of her sex becomes public. The audience, though, appreciates her enigmatic reply: the courtiers are the butt of the joke. Refusing to "play at the paw in the air" is to refuse the threatening aspects of sex with men: rape, violence, private and public humiliation.

What are we to make of Olive's pleasure in her marriage, in view of her attraction to Yde? That attraction is described emphatically, and Olive is presented as an active, desiring subject: "Her whole body shakes with joy and she says softly, so that no one hears her: 'He will be my lover. I will tell him before the day is out. I have never been so taken with a man. It is well and right that I should tell him' " (ll. 7,026–7,030); "The king's daughter has fallen so deeply in love with her/him/ That she told him/her—she could no longer hide it" (ll. 7,046–7,047); " 'Now I have what I want / I haven't wasted my time on this earth / Since I will get what I so much desired' She fell on her knees at her father's feet; / As she stood up, she loudly exclaimed: / 'Father,' said she, 'now please make haste/ It always seems to me as if he were to disappear' " (ll. 7,087–7,093).[50] Linking incest and same—sex marriage episodes, the verb *fourmir* is used twice, in both instances to describe the erotic urge provoked by the sight of Yde. *Fourmir* is an interesting word. If its modern French translation, *frémir* (to tremble, shiver, quiver, simmer) is close in spelling to Latin *fremere* (to roar, growl, howl, din, grumble, complain, demand, murmur, resound), one can imagine only with difficulty the passage from grumbling and howling to being thrilled; perhaps the etymon of *frémir* is not what lexicographers think. Rather, the Old French form puts one in mind of Latin *formicare*, derived from *formica*, ant, describing a bodily sensation that seems an apt metaphor for the quiver of pleasure or the trembling of fear. *Fourmir* is glossed by Brewka as "to stir," "to move." "To electrify," anachronistic, could also be a translation. The examples recorded by Tobler and Lommatzsch show that *fourmir* can be used to describe both positive and negative reactions (joy, fear, worry are among the most common). There are also uses connected to desirable properties of objects. It is said of liquids (wine, milk) and of shimmering light. We note two examples of use identical to *Yde et Olive* in Gautier de Coincy's *Miracles de la Sainte Vierge*: "Par le palais s'esmaient, tout en vont fourmïant / De çou k'elle a le ciere si clere et si riant" ("Christ," l. 1,387) [throughout the palace they are astounded and start to stir because she has such a clear and smiling face]; and a lovely proverb, "Cuers qui bien ainme, adès fremie" (ll. 640, 721) [the heart that loves well, trembles at once]. In the incest episode, the noblemen of the court are stirred by Yde's beauty. That reaction introduces the detailed description of Yde, including her breasts, hips, and feet: "Encontre li est li barnés drecïés; / De sa biauté est cascuns formïés" (ll. 6,502–6,503) [The noblemen have risen in greeting, everyone is stirred by her beauty]. Gentlemen rise regularly at the sight of female beauty in French romance, leading us to wonder what was conveyed beyond the gesture of greeting, notably in Lanval (ll. 621–24). Sometimes, the near-homonym body (*corps*, *cors*) is used as well as heart (*coeur*, *cuer*) in expressions with *fourmir*. In the part leading to the same-sex marriage, Olive's body is stirred by the sight of Yde: "Car des crestiax l'avoit veüe Olive. / Trestous li cors de joie li fourmie" (ll. 7,025–7,026) [For Olive saw her [Yde] from the ramparts. Her whole body stirs with joy]. This repetition erases the distinction between men and women's reactions to Yde. Although it is the cross-dressed Yde that moves Olive, the simple repetition of *fourmir* reinforces the resistance to heteronormative distinctions, a resistance that transvestite episodes make possible.

Similarly to *fourmir*, the words *ciere* and *carnés* (face or flesh, body, oneself, and bodily) appear in the incest and same-sex marriage episodes with an insistence that becomes especially apparent when we notice their near-absence from battle episodes. It is the eroticized body that the text narrates.

The frequency of the use of *body* to signify "self" is especially striking (ll. 7,107, 7,115, 7,116–17, 7,119, 7,183–84). It forces us to focus on the body as the foundation of identity even as we are led through the cross-dressing fantasy. In that fantasy, elements of heterosexual love stories are cut from their discursive, heteronormative matrix and refashioned into a same-sex marriage plot. At the same time, the elements of male and female behavior, public and private roles (warrior and beauty, lover and beloved), bodily and sartorial indices of masculinity and femininity, are disconnected from their organic, genital matrix and recombined into a composite "lesbian-like" identity. In my opinion, the insistence on the body is a way to authenticate or to assert the reality of that newly fashioned identity. It is in her body that Olive feels the tremor of her desire for Yde (l. 7,026); it is her body, says Yde, that Olive wants ("La fille au roi a mon corps enamé," l. 7,119 [the king's daughter fell in love with my body/me]). It is as a "body" that Yde remembers her flight from incest ("En maint peril a puis mon cors esté," l. 7,115 [my body/I was in many a peril since]) and feels the danger of her forced marriage to another woman ("Or me cuidai dedens Rome garder, / Mais jou voi bien mes cors ert encusés," ll. 7,116–17 [I already thought I was safe in Rome, but now I see my body/I myself will be in danger]). That doubling of body/self is augmented by a third, unrelated term, the near-homonym *cor*; a conjunction, "thus," "because," or an adverb that functions somewhat like "already" does in colloquial English:"do it already!", *cor* is usually spelled *car* (Modern French *car, donc*), and it translates as "would that. . ." *Car* is frequently used in romance verse for added emphasis as well as to pad the meter. When Yde asks for mercy, she cries out:"take pity on this poor woman" (l. 7,107:"De ceste lasse cor vous prengne pitiés" [would it that you took pity / please feel pity for this poor woman]).[51] Echoed in this homonymous, adverbial *cor*, the linking of body/self through the word *cor* is so tight that sometimes it is not possible to distinguish between them. For instance, the common denominator body/self reappears during the wedding night conversation when Yde avoids Olive, Olive agrees to that, and even asks Yde to delay the consummation of the marriage. To preface her request, Olive summons the goodness that permeates Yde's being, her *cors*:"Tant sench bonté en vo cors arrestee" (l. 7,183) [I feel so much goodness present in your body/in you].

Queer lexicography is also informed by the final episode of the romance, the bath with the emperor that is supposed to seal Yde's fate by uncovering her for the impostor she is. The narrative does not offer us a simple condemnation, nor does it describe Yde as a woman. Instead, she is described by a curious epithet applied to her body, *cors*: "Yde of the *mollé* body" (l. 7,248) [Yde au cors mollé]. *Mollé* (which can be loosely translated as gorgeous) can be used to describe either a masculine or a feminine beauty; Tobler and Lommatzsch give an equal share of examples. Yet, interestingly, *Huon de Bordeaux*, to which *Yde et Olive* is a sequel, only uses *mollé* in association with male beauty: "Amaouris fu parcreüs et maullés" (l. 56) [Amauris was tall and *maullés*]; "Hües au cors mollé" (l. 108) [Huon of the *mollé* body]; "Gros fu et cras [Hües], parcreüs et mollés" (l. 191) [[Huon] was big and well built, tall and *mollés*].

It can be said that the insistence on the body in *Yde et Olive* oscillates between these two poles: on one hand the complex linking of body/self and the ambiguity surrounding the use of *mollé*; and, on the other hand, the reduction of all the possibilities articulated in the narrative to genital masculinity, especially in the last scene of the romance. The problematic nature of Yde's marriage is at one point described as a lack of penis: "N'a membre nul qu'a li puist abiter" (l. 7,104) [she [Yde] has no member with which to cohabit with her [Olive]]. When an angel intervenes, conveying the order to Otto from the Almighty himself to go take a bath and leave Yde alone, and describing the miracle that alters the same-sex marriage, the social dimension of the sex change is followed by the bodily, which receives greater emphasis: "For I am telling you, forsooth, you have a good knight in your vassal Yde. God, in his goodness, sends and gives Yde all that a man has of his humanity [umanité] . . . This morning s/he was a woman, now s/he is a bodily man" (ll. 7,266–72) [Car jou te di en bonne verité, / Bon chevalier a u vassal Ydé: / Dix li envoie et donne par bonté / Tout chou c'uns hom a de s'umanité /. . . Hui main iert feme, or est uns hom carnés]. This emphasis on the bodily, *carnés,* is necessary since, as we know from the story, Yde is a good vassal and knight, "a man" in every other sense, political, military, or sartorial, and when she unwillingly becomes a husband, she is a careful and gentle one. Now, with "all that a man has of his human nature" (l. 7,269), Yde is a *bona fide* knight, "bon chevalier" (l. 7,267). For us, the alteration that makes Yde "human" may be disconcerting or frightening, like the New York Times ads enjoining gays to "convert" to heterosexuality. But it is quite necessary considering that *Yde et Olive* is one in a series of sequels. There must be an heir whose deeds can be narrated in the next episode. The last word of the text is *engenrés* (l. 7,283), when Yde fathers a son: a new fictional body from a long string of body talk that, for a considerable and memorable time, allowed us to venture beyond the reproductive imperative.

Reproductive concerns are not part of the love plot in the romance, but they are assumed to be its corollary. They are never articulated as part of the lovers' dialogue in romance as a genre. Yde and Olive follow the standard pattern of romance lovers in that they give not a single thought to posterity as they contemplate marriage and then lie in bed together. Sex, not reproduction, is the only dimension of their intimacy. Concerning the marriage, Olive's enthusiasm is in contrast with Yde's reluctance. Yde first refuses the emperor's offer of Olive's hand, then reconciles herself to it. When the marriage becomes final, she is still anxious: "[Yde] does not know how she will acquit herself: she has no member with which to cohabit with her" (ll. 7,103–104) [Ne set comment se porra demener; N'a membre nul qu'a li puist habiter]. If Olive is happy with Yde, as time goes on, she also begins to worry: "Olive s'est durement mespensee" (l. 7,208) [Olive became seriously worried]. The insistence on the characters' fluctuating emotions is very important in the economy of the romance, where lovers' emotions create an ethical imperative that captures the sympathy of the reader and overrides a universal morality. We could say that this is another instance of the fashioning of lesbian identity: the reader is made to sympathize not with the concerns of heterodoxy (same-sex marriage is prohibited), but rather with the concerns of the characters in the story (how does a same-sex marriage work). The solution is highly interesting, and also concerns the process of the tailoring and representation of queer love. Yde and Olive do not have "sex" at all, as far as the heterosexual, penetrative norm is concerned. But there is a lot of kissing and hugging, recalling the "homoerotic interlude" in the *Roman d'Ysaïe*. Except that in *Ysaïe*, the hugging and kissing is scripted as a comedy of errors. Marte pretends to be a man, and her seducer, the noblewoman, believes her. Marte also only pretends to give in to the seduction, the better to extricate herself and follow her heterosexual love interest (Ysaïe). The plot of *Yde et Olive* differs drastically. The "accidental" same-sex marriage and two women lying in bed as a result of it are an alternative to the heterosexual love plot. Although Yde pretends to be a man and Olive believes her, there is no man in the offing for the heroine. In fact, the heterosexual plot is fatally vitiated because it is incestuous. Its revelation mobilizes Olive's sympathy for Yde. The hierarchy established in the narrative privileges same-sex marriage over incest, a heterosexual transgression. After Yde reveals her sex to Olive, they stay in bed. The fashioning of a lesbian love plot proceeds by a detailed description of bodily intimacy, and an insistence on the freedom of choice and lifelong commitment at all cost.

After the wedding night, we are given a short respite to acknowledge the two-week feasting, and return to bed with Yde who "lay beside her spouse, and did not talk to her more than before, nor prod about the kidneys, or clasp from the back" [Et Yde jut avoecques s'espousee, / Ne l'a nient plus que soloit aparlee, / Devers les rains pointe ne adesee] (ll. 5,205–208). As earlier, the specificity of that which Yde did not do allows the description of the erotic body in a variety of non-missionary acts. As Olive approaches Yde, the double meaning of French "*bee*" is again exploited: "Et Yde set mout bien u elle bee" (l. 7,210) [and Yde knows very well what Olive intends, where she is headed, what she is waiting, yearning for, or: where her orifices are]. Yde then reveals the secret "from head to head," thoroughly [De cief en cief li a l'uevre contee] (l. 7,212)—again, the locution puts the body first (Brewka's edition misspells one letter in this line, substituting *cier* for the second *cief*). She reveals everything, and Olive comforts her [Ydain a mout doucement confortee] (l. 7,217); [Mais or soiés toute rasseüree] (l. 7,221) and decides to cast her lot with Yde because of the honorable motivation of Yde's cross-dressing adventure: "Puis que vous estes pour loiauté gardée, Ensamble o vou[s] prendrai ma destinee" (ll. 7,222–23) [Since you have kept yourself honorable (kept a secret for an honest reason?), I will take the fate that befalls me with you]. The verb *"prendrai"* (I will take) emphasizes that, in view of the new developments, Olive has a choice in the matter. Her continuing commitment is emphasized in the first word of the line: *ensemble*, together. When Yde finally reveals her secret identity, Olive renews her vows instead of breaking them. The exchange of marriage vows is also represented in the miniature, where two identical figures, Yde and Olive, are first joined before an assembly of courtiers (on the left), and then lying in bed (on the right). The private exchange is the only one quoted in the text. The public one receives no symmetrical treatment—it is simply reported to have taken place. The private exchange of vows, given this interesting prominence in the text, both overshadows and confirms the public ceremony, echoing its probable formulation—"I will share whatever befalls you." In my view, the text oscillates between these two poles: a fiction that portrays two women in love against all odds; and a fiction that offers two women in bed to titillate a male heterosexual audience. The first allows Yde to escape the horror of incest into a safe haven of union with another woman, with all the privileges that manhood bestows (power and land), but none of the suffering that "humanity" entails for women (reproductive sex, birth, and death). Not only does this scenario eliminate the fear of rape, but it also creates a deeply meaningful bond of loyalty and protection between two women, and an option for women's participation in power (however fantastic, since it is dependent on maintaining the cross-dressing illusion). The second creates a possibility that would be best interpreted in the framework of Lacanian desire for the phallus: a cross-dressed woman, or two women in bed, by providing an occasion to speak in detail about the lack of a penis, constitute the ideal instance of the phallus, object of desire.

I would like to acknowledge my debt to Claire Goldstein for the idea that same-sex utopia is a remedy for heterosexual marriage, which entails thinking of incest, "heterosexual marriage's gross extreme," as the opposite of same-sex marriage; and to Robert L.A. Clark, who elaborates an opposite reading where same-sex marriage is an equivalent of incest in the

narrative economy. Clark's "A Heroine's Sexual Itinerary" explores the relationship between incest and same-sex marriage, noting that incest is
described in *Yde et Olive* as *bougrenie* (heresy), a term usually reserved for
same-sex acts (sodomy, "buggery"), "a fascinating and revelatory slippage"
(p. 102). Clark emphasizes the indeterminacy of that category, possibly a
carryover from the classical usage of *incestus* as unspecified impurity. The
point that Clark articulates is not only the twinning of incest and sodomy
in terms of "horror," but also in terms of the role they played in "medieval
culture's tremendous effort to define and delimit sexual transgressions."
While that process was under way in the writings of Thomas Aquinas,
Peter Damian, or Alain de Lille, the categories "incest" and "sodomy" were
characterized by "conceptual vagueness, a certain fluctuation between general and more specific meanings," allowing for slippage between incest and
other sexual transgressions, including same-sex acts (Clark, "A Heroine's
Sexual Itinerary," p. 101). That vagueness is a symptom of "deep and multiple category crises," which call out for the intervention of a "third term,"
in this case a cross-dressing character that

> not only blurs the boundaries between male and female but also undermines
> the whole attempt to construct stable binary categories of oppositional dif-
> ference. It is a figure onto which irresolvable crises of boundary definition
> can, at specific historical and cultural junctures, be displaced. (Clark, "A
> Heroine's Sexual Itinerary," p. 98)

In the specific context of *Yde et Olive*, "*Yde. . .*participate[s]. . .in the elaboration of regimes of sexual and other forms of repression." Her character
"lifts the veil on a range of anxieties and ambiguities surrounding the regulation of the socio-sexual domain and of female sexuality especially," creating "discursive spaces around the linked motifs of incest and sodomy. It is
the cross-dressed heroine who is called upon to negotiate, for herself and
her audience, the twin horrors of sodomy and incest, and her cross-dressing
is the device which makes this possible" (Clark, "A Heroine's Sexual
Itinerary," p. 102).

Following Marjorie Garber, Clark calls attention to the visibility of
joints that characterizes cross-dressing.[52] Because it is born of dissection
and composition, cross-dressing not only queers desire, but also problematizes representation. What Garber calls "the transvestite effect" (Garber,
Vested Interests, pp. 9–17), Clark sums up as follows:

> it is precisely because cross-dressing is characterized by a complex inter-play
> between "reality" and representation that the cross-dresser is inherently a pol-
> ysemous figure which allows for the problematization of the dynamics of
> desire and of representation itself. (Clark, "A Heroine's Sexual Itinerary," p. 98)

In reflecting on the function of cross-dressing in romance as a genre, Busby notes the same effect:

> [cross-dressing] often articulates questions of appearance and reality as well as providing narrative impetus. . .it causes the audience to reflect on the Arthurian intertext generally. . .[it] points to the rigidity of the Arthurian world and its inability to cope with the customs its own tradition has generated. (Busby, " 'Plus acesmez,' " p. 57)

The connection between Busby, Clark, and Garber derives in part from their shared interest in metonymic relations between representation and its objects, and between fiction and its social context. That similarity reveals as much about our interests (in *mise en abyme*, in cultural studies) as about the texts it interprets. If Busby relates cross-dressing to the questioning of the chivalric ideal of "classical" (twelfth-century) romance, Clark proposes a cultural interpretation of cross-dressing steeped in anthropological approaches, relating cross-dressing fictions to Promethean myths. Clark notes that in the "overcoming of seemingly irreconcilable cultural contradictions," the role of the cross-dresser is similar to the "mediating function" assumed by "the trickster, the bisexual, the phallic woman"—a model developed by Claude Lévi-Strauss in structural analysis of myths (Clark, "A Heroine's Sexual Itinerary," pp. 102–103). Cross-dressing fictions resemble the functioning of mythical trickster narratives described by Lévi-Strauss both in terms of an "opening up of the socio-cultural field for the main character" and the "deep ambivalence about this opening, most particularly through the machinery of recuperation which they ultimately deploy in the service of social order and heteronormativity," where heteronormativity is an instance of the coercive, disciplinary social regime (Clark, "A Heroine's Sexual Itinerary," p. 103). Clark notes that cultural (Marjorie Garber) and anthropological, structuralist projects (Lévi-Strauss) shed more light on medieval fictions of cross-dressing than does a Freudian approach that may result in "forcing of these narratives into predictable paradigms of interpretation which potentially mask as much as they illumine" (p. 103). The optic that allows us to grasp these texts more fully is for Clark "one that makes use of the notion of category as a construct constantly under the threat of indeterminacy and collapse" (p. 103)—in a word, a deconstructive reading.

Clark, Garber, Lévi-Strauss, Gaunt, Busby: five readings of cross-dressing that originate in different disciplines but produce similar conclusions. It may be that cross-dressing is a special case, one that our interpretive tools are particularly apt to illumine. But it is also clear that we are interested in cross-dressing because it lends itself to deconstructive criticism and, more generally, to a reflection on representation. We must be cautious if we are to interpret cross-dressing fictions rather than use them as pretexts. I respond to this imperative by focusing on the body, as does Clark when he touches on the reality of incest, not only its fictional representation. In *Yde et Olive*, the category crisis is not abstract. It is not even an allegory. Instead, it is a series of erotically charged *tableaux*. Clark notes: "[i]n what is itself a highly ambiguous move, the poet seeks to implicate the reader in the king's [incestuous] desire," and then, we may add, seeks to implicate the reader in same-sex desire, "to make the text's audience feel at once the erotic pull and the revulsion of the incestuous dynamic" and of the same-sex dynamic (Clark, "A Heroine's Sexual Itinerary," pp. 99–100). Is it only today that the twinning of incest and sodomy as "horrors" appears lop-sided? Our laws prosecute the everyday horror of adults using children for sexual gratification. However, we are beginning to end the too-long episode in Western history when consensual relations between same-sex adults, for reasons we are trying to understand through our work in queer studies, were prohibited, feared, burdened with shame, and violently punished. For us, the two are only "twinned" in one sense: they provoke the same intense sadness and outrage against a society that does not keep either its children or its gay adults safe.

Clark points out the greater horror of father–daughter incest, and the complexity of its representation in the romance and in medieval discourse on sex:

> It has already been remarked that nuclear family incest was not the object of the same obsessive attention which consanguineous marriage elicited in normative texts. Kathryn Gravdal has suggested that this repression of nuclear family incest may have resulted in a return of the cultural repressed in the form of a proliferation in the medieval imaginary of texts like the *Manekine* that have as their theme nuclear family incest.[53] *Yde et Olive* bears the mark of this symptomatic masking and unmasking of incest, for when the king makes his stunning announcement to his barons that he will marry his own daughter, they exclaim, with a properly judicial horror: [. . .] "you can't have her within the fourth [degree] or else it will be heresy!" (ll. 6,450–51; Clark, "A Heroine's Sexual Itinerary," pp. 101–102)

As Clark shows, the scandal of *Yde et Olive* is not only the reduction of father–daughter incest to arithmetic of consanguinity. It is also child pornography and the unspoken social contract that, now just as then, humanizes child molesters. The text is putting us in a series of corrupt positions, from incest carried out to its reprehensible limits, a father's sexual use of a daughter who is still a child—in order to mark that, the narrator invites us to look at Yde's breasts, which are undeveloped (l. 6,483)—to sympathy with the father, who faces the impossible choice: incest or madness ("Du sense istra, se ne l'a espouzee," l. 6,417: he will lose his mind if he does not marry her).

Instead of incest and sodomy as "twin horrors," two categories "in and of crisis," I note the lopsidedness of the twinning that would not be apparent without Clark's careful analysis. I see same-sex marriage as a utopian solution both for Yde (an alternative to the horror of incest) and for Olive (an alternative to an oppressive, violent, heterosexual marriage). If incest is the gross extreme of the dynastic prerogative, any heterosexual marriage contract is tainted by patriarchal hegemony, and perpetuates "*umanité*," the "human condition," linking sex, death, and Eve's suffering in childbearing. The same-sex marriage in *Yde et Olive* is a happy fantasy that allows the woman to choose her partner, to dictate terms, to be vulnerable but not end up hurt, to consent and love as an equal, whether she wants to avoid marrying her father (Yde) or for her father (Olive).[54]

The father's desire and Olive's desire for Yde are linked through the use of the same terms, and both episodes "seek to implicate the reader" by representing Yde's charms. Although the terms are identical, the positioning of the characters is different. That difference can be used in support of the idea that same-sex marriage represents a positive escape from both incest and heterosexual marriage. For instance, Florent's courtiers realize that, left alone with her, he will use her sexually: "S'il le tenoit en sa cambre a celee, / Ja ne seroit de Florent deportee / Qu'il nel eüst tantost despucelee" (ll. 6,429–31: if he kept her privately in his room, she would never be excused by Florent unless he would have deflowered her first). The same expressions—*a celee*, *deportee*—are used in the episode with Yde and Olive, but the lexical identity only emphasizes the complete reversal of the situation. It is now the lover (Olive) who, upon learning that Yde is ill (Yde's ruse to avoid more intimate physical contact), first allows, and then requests the beloved (Yde) to "let her [Olive] be" (*deportee*, ll. 7,184, 7,187). They both use the term "in private" (*a celee*, ll. 7,166, 7,173) to say, in effect: "we're in private, so—just between you and me—let's take advantage of it and only hug and kiss instead." Yde later uses *deportee* to avoid taking a bath with the emperor, the trial he devised to verify the rumor that she is not a man (ll. 7,248–49). The emperor's bath mirrors the one Yde's father makes her take in preparation for the incestuous wedding (l. 6,556). The bath motif in both episodes evokes the figurative use of "hot bath," which covers the spectrum from the erotic to the sadistic. The bath can be a metaphor for a vengeful trap: "Je vous cuit tel baing caufer / Dont vous avrés chaut as costés" (Barbazan and Méon, *Fabliaux et contes,* Paris, 1808, vol. 4, p. 40, ll. 632–33: I think of making such a bath for you as will make your sides burn). Prepared by Love himself, the bath stands in for the slow burn of amorous suffering in Chrétien de Troyes's *Cligès* and the anonymous *Roman de Poire* (Chrétien de Troyes,

Cligès, ll. 470–71: "Amors li a chaufé un baing / Qui moult l'eschaufe et moult la cuit" [Love has prepared a bath for her that greatly heats her up and sears her]); *Roman de Poire*, ll. 2,836–37: "Amors li ot un doleros / Baing chaufé et mal atempré" [Love has heated her a painful and intemperate bath]). The vulnerability of the heroine is emphasized by this repeated threat of the bath, directly linking incest and the inexorable application of the heterosexual prerogative. Another example twinning incest and heteronormative prerogative is the repeated metaphor for meting out death, "l'ame du corps sevrer" [to part the soul from the body]. Like *deportee* and *celee*, it is highlighted by its place in the rhyme (l. 6,405, l. 7,226). Yde's father Florent uses this expression to threaten his vassals and coerce them into accepting his incestuous marriage. The spy who overhears Yde and Olive uses it when he anticipates denouncing the same-sex couple. If there is a narrative design in these repetitions, where the spy denouncing the same-sex couple echoes the incestuous father, it implies the narrator's equal resistance to heterodoxy and incest.

The accidental witness to Yde and Olive's private vows, the young servant who overhears the women and denounces them to the emperor, is a paradoxical figure. He both confirms and undoes the union. He incorporates the public dimension and, by his mere presence, transforms the closet vows into a public contract. He also starts the chain of disclosures that threaten to reveal Yde and Olive's secret bond and destroy them. The narrator curses the boy: "mal de l'ame son pere!" (l. 7,229) [his father's soul be damned!], with a contempt that contributes to the assimilation of this character to the despicable informer of courtly love narratives, the *losengier*. The two love scripts, *fin' amor* and *Yde et Olive's* same-sex narrative, share *dramatis personae* (the *losengier*), fear of disclosure, and the closet space of vows and embraces. The ease of translation from courtly love to homoerotic desire seems independent from the undeniably homoerotic origins of *fin' amor* in Arabic love poetry, which could have warranted that courtly love was primarily considered as a cipher for same-sex love, but did not, as far as we know.[55] Most scholars assume at present that courtly love was disconnected from its homoerotic roots when it passed to the East (langue d'oc) and even more so when it reached the North (langue d'oïl). That disconnection is so strongly felt by contemporary critics that even a *canso* addressed to a lady by one of the few trobairitz, Bietris de Roman, is not always highlighted as an expression of queer love.[56] The poem uses the traditional forms of love address to a lady, and is attributed to a woman by the manuscript. I think that *Yde et Olive* and Bietris's *canso* are both examples of a conscious reinvention of homoeroticism in courtly love that participates in the fashioning of a lesbian literary voice in the Middle Ages. The *fin' amor* script is tailored to represent a same-sex couple.

Would a heterosexual marriage be followed by a bed scene, or is it only *fin' amor* (*Chevalier de la charrette*) or same-sex love (*Yde et Olive*) that affords us the intimate representation of *surplus*? An accepted interpretation assumes that "the happily ever after" of the heterosexual love plot is not narratable because there is no suspense in perfect happiness. But perhaps the opposite is true. Let us assume, on the contrary, that it is the violent and improbable nature of the heterosexual marriage contract that dooms it to silence. If *fin' amor* and same-sex pairs constitute a subject, it is not because they are transgressive, but rather because they are the only ones worth narrating. Both represent utopian exceptions from the impossible and oppressive heteronormative rule. Elisabeth Keiser in *Courtly Desire and Medieval Homophobia* analyzes a different instance of such utopia, the ideal heterosexual contract narrated in *Cleanness*. Many contexts analyzed by Keiser, including Alain de Lille and the *Roman de la Rose*, intersect with the texts cited in this book. One might say that *Yde et Olive* proposes a same-sex alternative to the perfect love described in *Cleanness*. The emphasis on consent and the continuation of the marriage in spite of the revelation of Yde's genital sex; the form of the vows; and the fact that they are spoken in bed and followed by physical contact are striking. They fulfill three of the requirements of legal marriage: exchange of vows, knowing consent, consummation. The medieval narrator and the illuminator of *Yde et Olive* represent same-sex marriage as they would a heterosexual one, the only difference being its aesthetic perfection, as the newlyweds are symmetrical reflections of each other.

Given the condemnation of heterosexual incest inscribed in *Yde et Olive*, the tolerance of same-sex desire, the erasure of difference between same-sex and heterosexual affect in the representation of Olive's desire for the transvestite Yde, the closeness to the script of *fin' amor*, and the blurring of distinctions between same-sex and heterosexual marriage, we may contrast this text with those described by Gaunt, the texts that "occlude but do not erase" their homoerotic potential. The text of *Yde et Olive* ostensibly dwells on the fantasy of two women in bed, wedded spouses and lovers, not just friends. The emphasis on the erotic as well as the legal aspects of the same-sex union is strong, detailed, and amplified by the resonance between text and image. In articulating this contrast, however, we still follow Gaunt who, over a decade ago, spoke of medieval French texts as products of "straight minds, queer wishes."

CHAPTER 3

THE PLACE OF HOMOEROTIC MOTIFS IN THE
MEDIEVAL FRENCH CANON: DISCONTINUITIES
AND DISPLACEMENTS

This chapter analyzes selected fictional representations of same-sex
themes, from the late twelfth to the late thirteenth century. It opens
with false accusations of same-sex preference in two works associated with
the literary patronage of Europe's most powerful couple, Henry II Plantagenet and Eleanor of Aquitaine, in England in the second half of the twelfth
century: *Roman d'Enéas*, a *translatio* of Virgil, and Marie de France's *Lanval*.
Both these texts have been discussed from the point of view of queer
studies, notably by Christopher Baswell, Simon Gaunt, Noah K. Guynn,
and David M. Halperin.[1] Two other texts use a similar motif, false attribution of same-sex preference as an explanation for heterosexual indifference
or a convenient excuse used to shield a man from unwanted attentions of
a powerful woman: Walter Map's *De nugis curialium*, a collection of courtly
anecdotes in Latin also connected to Henry II's court, and a lyric poem
by a northern *trouvère* Conon de Bethune (died 1224).[2] Other texts mentioned in this chapter date approximately from the time of the likely composition of *Enéas, Lanval*, and *De nugis*, to the end of Conon's life: *Aucassin
et Nicolete*, a text dated between 1175 and 1250; and the early-thirteenth-
century Lancelot–Grail cycle. The latest text is the *Roman de la Rose*, written by Guillaume de Lorris ca. 1230 and later continued by Jean de Meun
ca. 1275–80.[3]

While Martha Powell Harley, Michael Camille, and Pamela Sheingorn
interpret same-sex couples in *Rose* as narcissistic or homosocial, Ellen
Friedrich proposes a strictly homoerotic reading of such elements as the
description of the rose, the behavior of male allegorical figures (God of
Love and Bel Acueil) toward the male lover, and the abrupt ending of the

first part.[4] Simon Gaunt reads the *Rose* as an allegory that creates and sustains tension between a homoerotic meaning on a literal level, and a heteroerotic reading on the allegorical level.[5]

In a thorough review of over half a century of scholarly controversy concerning the allegorical same-sex couple formed by Amant and Bel Acueil in the *Rose*, an allegory sometimes called "absurd" or "improper" (from a twentieth-century heteronormative point of view), Gaunt succinctly describes the positions occupied by C.S. Lewis, who considered the tension between homoerotic literal level and heteroerotic allegory level a "failure" of Jean de Meun. In turn, John V. Fleming, Alan M.F. Gunn, Douglas Kelly, and Heather M. Arden discounted that tension. The hypothesis they shared was that grammatical or allegorical gender is wholly or predominantly abstract, not "sexual" (in my experience as a native speaker of a language with three grammatical genders, this hypothesis is theoretically possible but, empirically, erroneous). Next, Gaunt mentions scholars such as Daniel Poirion, Michel Zink, Jean-Charles Payen, and Peter Allen, David F. Hult, and Sarah Kay, who favor a homosocial rather than homoerotic explanation of the same-sex couple, but who (in contrast with the previous group) strongly emphasize the homoerotic, narcissistic, or "ho(m)mosexual" dimensions of same-sex allegorical couple ("ho(m)mosexual" is Luce Irigaray's term that refers to "the refusal of men to recognize sexual difference"; Gaunt, "Bel Acueil," p. 67).[6] At the opposite end of the interpretive spectrum to both C.S. Lewis (with his hypothesis of Jean de Meun's "failure") and the "grammatical accident" school of interpretation (Fleming, Arden, Gunn, Kelly), Gaunt notes the intervention of a historian, Jo Ann Hoeppner Moran, who assumes that the *Rose* intentionally evokes homosexuality to engage with the contemporary debate on clerical homosexuality.[7]

Following this assessment of the field, Gaunt examines the shifting representation of couples in *Rose* as either homo- or heteroerotic, the play of the illuminations that portray Bel Acueil as female or male, and the vacillation introduced by different versions of the text and interpolations that either erase or alter Bel Acueil's gender ("Bel Acueil," pp. 74–84). Gaunt concludes:

> [t]he *Rose*'s ability to sustain multiple readings makes it a perilous expositor of morality. Moreover, because of the way sex and writing become reciprocal metaphors for each other and because of the play that I have described in the allegorical representation of sex, the *Rose* does not simply tell a story of deviant sexual acts; it also. . .evinces an interest in sexual deviance on the more profound level of allegorical discourse itself. (Gaunt, "Bel Acueil," p. 85)

For Gaunt, *Rose* is a successful allegory precisely because of the play between the two meanings.[8]

Gaunt's argument strongly resonates with my interest in supersaturation of the signifying system in *Perceval* as a tag for same-sex desires and anxieties (chapter 1), as well as with Barthes's statement that homosexuality is the "invokable goddess" of ultimate *jouissance* in reading (conclusion, below):

> [*Rose*] seems wantonly amenable to appropriation by readers for their own interpretive agendas. I have suggested that this multivalency is deliberate and that it is enabled by the allegorical play that ultimately prohibits the determination of a fixed meaning. I would submit that the *Rose* was popular not despite this apparent incoherence, but because of it, and that the pleasure afforded by allegories like this derived not from the convergence of the literal and allegorical in one inevitable and morally uplifting truth, but from the possibilities that allegory offers for the exuberant exploratory play and indeterminacy that seem to pervade the *Rose*. The pleasure taken in indeterminacy—both linguistic and sexual—subverts a series of apparently neat and irrefutable oppositions that Jean [de Meun] seems deliberately to invoke, only to deconstruct through play: the allegorical and the literal, the proper and the improper, the "straight" and the "perverted" in writing and in sex. (Gaunt, "Bel Acueil," p. 91)

The *Rose*, in Gaunt's interpretation, becomes a model of the formation of a queer medieval subject. This is particularly interesting since *Rose* is a medieval vernacular bestseller.[9] The play and indeterminacy of *Rose* that concern both sexuality and writing, the allegorical figure of Bel Acueil that constantly evokes homoeroticism in this ostensibly heteronormative text, result in the production of subjectivity and sexuality that is neither heteronormative, nor polarized between heteroeroticism and homoeroticism, with heteroeroticism as the privileged term:

> The text promotes, yet simultaneously subverts a model of sexuality (and subjectivity) that functions through the opposition of heterosexual to homosexual desire: it promotes this model by making the repudiation of homosexual activities foundational in the definition and production of the sexual orientation (reproductive heterosexuality) that is ostensibly sanctioned by the text (19,513–656); it subverts it by collapsing the distinction between the homoerotic and the heterosexual since the theoretically excluded deviant impulse turns out to be part of that which is defined against it. The *Rose* may condemn homosexual activity, but its allegorical love plot is articulated through the love story of two masculine figures while its erotic metaphors are susceptible to a reading that renders them potentially homoerotic rather than heteronormative. The boundaries between the homoerotic and heteronormative are thus consistently blurred and this would suggest therefore that there are queer impulses at work in the *Rose*, not so much because of its

homoerotic seam (though this can of course be construed as queer), but rather because it challenges the repressive binary structure that subordinates non-heteronormative sexualities to a heterosexual matrix. If. . .illuminators sought to reassure readers looking for a heteronormative love story in the *Rose* by feminizing Bel Acueil and thereby "normalizing" the allegory, the text ultimately resists their efforts, leaving such readers with a vision of the sexual acts that is neither reassuring (for them) nor heteronormative. (Gaunt, "Bel Acueil," pp. 91–92)

All these studies have shown that the *Rose*, traditionally seen as a canonical example of the dominant, heteronormative discourse of the romance, can accommodate homosocial or homoerotic interpretations. In this chapter, I want to demonstrate that *Rose* is not alone in hinting at homoeroticism, but rather it participates in a tradition of texts about love and seduction that openly mention same-sex preference. It is not a function of medieval fiction, but rather of nineteenth- and twentieth-century medievalism, that the presence of homoerotic themes in these works is an obscure footnote.

The fact that prominent homoerotic motifs in these works are little known is, no doubt, the corollary of the nineteenth-century invention of heteronormative "courtly love" as an operative concept in medieval studies. We recognize and warn against the constricting influence of the method on the object of study, or the encroachment of anachronistic categories that stand in the way of our full understanding of the evidence offered by distant historical periods. An awareness of the differences between the twelfth- and twentieth-century categories of sexual normalcy was also expressed by the editor of the *Roman d'Eneas*, J.-J. Salvedra de Grave (author of the 1891 and the 1925–29 editions). Expressed in a slip (rare in his text), Salvedra de Grave's awareness may well be taken as a symptom of a deeper-reaching issue. Speaking of the "crudity" of *Eneas*, and evoking specifically the accusation of same-sex preference in *Eneas* and *Lanval*, Salvedra de Grave notes: "[t]hese are certainly not [*sic*] passages that seem to us, indeed, inappropriate for women's ears; in the 12th century, they did not shock as much. . ." (Introduction, p. xxii).[10]

I follow, but *à rebours*, Stephen Jaeger's call to restore the lost twelfth-century sensibilities, by saying that it is time to reinstate the homoerotic references to a visible place in medieval texts of which they are a part. Brought together in this chapter, the late twelfth- to mid-thirteenth-century texts show that the prestige of classical and Occitan tradition enabled the representation of same-sex desires and anxieties. It provided an opportunity not only to translate, but also to add references to same-sex preference. Taken separately, these examples present different modalities of representation of same-sex preference. It can be framed as false accusation or a convenient excuse, worded identically to opposite-sex preference, or distinguished by labels specific to the medieval period, such as *heresy*. I begin by the examination of fictional stereotypes and vocabulary of same-sex preference. Not surprisingly, we observe some continuations from Latin, but also, perhaps mostly, discontinuities and displacements. The complexity of this situation is compounded by the fact that in major genres, references to sex acts are veiled. It would be a mistake to attach the discussion of Latin vocabulary of penetrative acts to the study of romance. However, some Latin stereotypes concerning receptive males that are more removed from sexual acts can be compared to French. One stereotype that medieval French texts such as *Enéas* inherit from Latin is the assimilation of receptive men to specific "cultures": Trojans, Carthaginians, actors. Ganymede, Zeus's cupbearer, was a Trojan prince. In Virgil, Eneas's alleged same-sex preference is identified as a Trojan trait. But that similarity between French and Latin stereotypes is overshadowed by major differences. Latin labels focus on the body. Words describing appearance, especially hair (*calamistratus, depilator*), neighbor words that refer to specific sexual acts (*fellator, irrumator, pedicator*), orifices (*scultimidonus*), or roles (*pathicus*). They represent same-sex availability through reference to a profession or station in life (*cinaedus*, dancer; *puer delicatus*, young male fit for sexual gratification), gestures or general appearance (*mollies*, soft), or grooming (*depilator*). Few of these terms have an equivalent in medieval French (*molz, fout-en-cul*). As Halperin and Williams have shown, a major difference is the categorization of specific acts, some of which we distinguish today as "same-sex," some of which we combine as "oral," but that would be distinguished in Rome with the reference to the orifice, and to the role (insertive or receptive), independent of genital sex.[11] This produces the following list: *irrumare* (oral, insertive)/*fellare* (oral, receptive), *futuere* (vaginal, i.)/*crisare* (vaginal, r.), and *pedicare* (anal, i.)/*cevere* (anal, r.). While some terms appear more frequently than others, the list is striking by its completeness: "a specificity not seen in other languages' sexual vocabularies" (Williams, pp. 161–62). Males were assumed to be insertive (rare literary references to insertive females confirm the rule). Persons of all ages and either sex, and all orifices, were available to insertive males. The language as presented above did not distinguish between receptive partners, whether they were male or female, young or old, free or slave, although a verb like *crisare* would be only applicable to females. According to Williams, *pathica* and *cinaedior* mark a woman's particular lasciviousness, although he mentions Seneca's remark that women are " 'born' to that role" [pati nate, Seneca's *Epistles* 95.21] (Williams, *Roman Homosexuality*, p. 178).

Like Latin, French uses specific words referring to body parts and their actions, but these expressions are not necessarily Latin derivatives. For example, *fout-en-cul,* a term used by the narrator of *Wistasse le Moine* when Wistasse, dressed up as a woman, is propositioned by a man: "n'est pas herites / Ne fout-en-cul ne sodomites" [he is not a heretic, or a fuck-in-ass or a sodomite] may be considered as a semantic near-equivalent of either *pathicus* or *pedicator,* or of the rare Latin word *scultimidonus* ("those who bestow for free their *scultima,* that is, their anal orifice," Williams, *Roman Homosexuality,* p. 174), but it is not etymologically related to them. Rather, it derives from Latin *futuere,* here clearly expanded to cover the meaning of Latin *pedicare.*[12] Only the context can establish whether the French label is receptive or insertive, an indeterminacy unlikely in Latin. Other French verbs, like *croistre* (used in *Trubert*) need further study. Medieval French, like English and Latin, has two nouns, *erites* (heretic) and *sodomites* (sodomite), that it uses in the extended sense of "same-sex oriented" (as opposed to orthodox, heterosexual). Their emergence, evolution, and use have been described by Dinshaw (heresy in English) and Jordan (sodomy in Latin).[13] Some classical Latin stereotypes appear in medieval Latin texts composed within the zone of influence of French (*facie dealbata* may be connected to the palor evoked as a tell-tale sign of effeminacy in Walter Map's *De nugis curialium*). Dinshaw notes that the description of Chaucer's Pardoner—pale, effete—must be understood in the context of that stereotype. I have not yet found an occurrence of "pallor" as a sign of same-sex preference in French that would be independent from a Latin source (the example from Raoul de Presles, *Cité de Dieu,* cited in chapter 1, is a translation).

Hair and depilation constitute another Latin stereotype that maps covert sexual preference onto overt bodily characteristics. It is a particularly interesting case because it cuts across several categories: sex, age, gender, status, and profession. Lilja and Williams discuss texts from the Augustan period that describe how hair as a marker of virility or effeminacy can be used either to reveal the secret of a man's preference for receptive sex, or to mask that preference.[14] The absence of facial hair is the attribute of the beardless youth, *puer delicatus,* usually the receptive partner, sometimes encoded as the virginal object of the adult male's desire. If being hairless, and being a sexually receptive male, is a generational episode in classical Rome and Greece, depilation proclaims a chosen identity. By artificially removing bodily hair, the male passes from an undifferentiated to a marked position. But depilatories, tweezers, and pitch are not univocal signs of male receptiveness. Curled hair and beard denote effeminacy as effectively as the use of depilatories. The gesture of curling one's hair with one finger is also a marker of receptiveness, Lilja notes. Conversely, the defining characteristic of the portraits of Augustus, his tousled, unkempt hair, is understood as a reference to his manliness. The indices may be compatible in designating a receptive male when the depilated lower body accompanies a curled and perfumed beard, but they may also be contradictory when the perfumed beard and shaved legs are combined with overdeveloped muscles.

Although Williams and Lilja document the prevalent association between depilation and male receptiveness, Williams highlights the complexities of this issue. Roman masculine norm may have included depilated underarms and nostrils, but not legs or anus, trimmed beard and hair, but not genitalia, and the absence of body odor or bad breath, but also of perfume. However, this norm designated by Ovid and other writers

> seems to come as a reaction against relatively widespread practices, and if we add that consideration to the evidence provided by Martial's epigram on Labienus,[15] it seems clear that in the urban landscape of first-century A.D. Rome there were men who, in hopes of attracting women (among other possible reasons), went to the extremes of beautification—for example, by depilating their arms, legs, and chest—even if doing so laid them open to charges of effeminacy. (Williams, *Roman Homosexuality*, p. 132)

Medieval French texts must be contrasted with Lilja's and Williams's examples in that references to men's hair have become so rare. The casual appearance of a recipe for depilatories in Villard de Honnecourt's notebook of architectural patterns may indicate that the practice was mainstream. In romance, the one use of depilatories I encountered is connected to a sex scandal: disguising men as ladies-in-waiting. As in most cases of male cross-dressing in medieval romance, the disguise facilitates an illicit heteroerotic liaison. It occurs in the *History of Merlin* (cited in chapter 2). Julius Caesar's wife has her young partners disguised as ladies-in-waiting ("damoisiaus atornes a guise de damoiseles," p. 281, l. 38 [young lords dressed up as young ladies]), their faces depilated to avoid detection: "And because she was afraid that beards would grow on her twelve boys [*serieans*, servants or hirelings, p. 282, l. 1], she had their chins smothered with lime and yellow arsenic [*orpiement*, tri-sulfide of arsenic, a pigment] steeped and boiled in stale urine, and they were dressed in big, flowing gowns and wrapped in wimples, and their hair was long and grown out, and cut in the manner of maidens, so that they looked very much like girls" (*puceles*, p. 282, l. 3) (*Lancelot-Grail*, ed. Lacy, p. 323).[16]

The examination of the few medieval French texts that do mention men's hair confirms that hair and its appearance remained an important marker of gender, and excessive preoccupation with hair continued to connote excessive eroticism, two functions shared with Latin. Unlike in Latin, hair no longer functioned as one of the primary characteristics of sexual preference in males (receptive or insertive). If *cinaedus* (literally, dancer, actor) is the most common Latin designator of the receptive male, Lilja emphasizes the frequency of the collocation *cinaedus calamistratus*, curly-haired (from *calamus*, reed, or curler that serves to shape the hair).[17] A synonym for *calamistratus* is *cincinnatus*, from Greek *kinkinnos*. Webster and OED only give the Middle High German *kinken* as the root of Modern English *kinky*, and the early uses are apparently limited to nautical terminology (a kink in the rope is the earliest quote). The adjectival use only appears in the mid-nineteenth century, interestingly contemporary with the elaboration of the category "homosexual." It seems possible that Latin *cincinnatus* as a synonym of *calamistratus* may have been present at the lexical horizon of educated English-speakers when the adjective kinky was applied to sexual practices. No such connivance can be suggested for French—the closest and irrelevant lexical item is *cincinerium*, umbrella, from the fifteenth century on—but in French during the Middle Ages, curly hair continues to imply excessive preoccupation with sex.

Old French *dorenlot* is a rare word whose semantic field resembles Latin *cincinnus, cincinnatus*. *Cincinnus* has the following uses: (1) ringlets of hair; (2) luxurious effeminacy; (3) frayed (*cincinnosus*), referring for example to the tails of comets; (4) curled hair, lock; and (5) a (sometimes excessively) artificial, elaborate poetic ornament. *Dorenlot* has a similar range of meanings: (1) a lock of hair on the forehead; (2) flourish, excessive ornament, embellishment, be it in clothing, hairstyles, music, poetry, or rhetoric; (3) melody, refrain; (4) care or caress (of a child, or an erotic partner). It is exclusively in the last sense that *dorenlot* persists in modern French: *dorloter*, to caress, pamper, or spoil, can be said of a beloved or a child.[18] *Dorenlot* taps into a system of related words and homonyms describing sexual play and caress, along with braids and fringes.[19] It is associated with sartorial excesses that hint at moral opprobrium. For the meaning "grosse boucle de cheveux relevée sur le front des hommes" (Godefroi) [a large wave or curl on a man's forehead], Tobler-Lommatzsch quotes: "in capite, ut patet per oculum, plura sunt signa superbiae quam in aliis membris; ut patet in multis clericis qui faciunt 'le dorenlot' " [in the head, as it is easy to see, there are more signs of vainglory than in other parts of the body; this is obvious in many clerics who wear "the *dorenlot*"]. *Dorenlot* preserves the connection between luxurious hairstyles and sexual excess, one aspect of *cinaedus calamistratus*. And the meaning "fringe, ornament" of the Old French *fraise* might have been the metaphor for penis in Lavinia's mother's monologue where she accuses Eneas of preferring "young men's *fraise*" (penis?): "Molt aime fraise de vallet" [He really likes a young man's *fraise*] (l. 8,576).

Virgil's *Aeneiad* exploits the Latin stereotype linking hairstyles, effeminacy, homoeroticism, and womanizing. Aeneas's foes impute to him male receptiveness as a Trojan characteristic. Numanus refers to the Trojans not as *Phryges*, but *Phrygiae* (she-Phrygians), while Turnus calls Aeneas *semivir*

Phryx (half-male Phrygian). The reference to the Phrygian cult of Cybele and her castrated priests ("half-male") is obliquely present. Turnus comments on Aeneas's appearance: "crinis vibratos callido ferro murraque madentis" [hair curled with hot iron and smothered in myrrh].

Confirming medieval relative disinterest in men's hair, the French poem omits references to it, but maintains and expands the motif of Eneas's sexual preference in two monologues.[20] The two fragments amount to 124 octosyllabic lines. Lavinia's mother attributes same-sex preference to Eneas to promote Lavinia's match with Turnus, ll. 8,565–621, and Lavinia suspects Eneas's same-sex preference because she feels she has been rejected by him, ll. 9,130–9,188. Other French texts of that period (*Lanval*, Conon de Bethune's poem) echo the general situation of *Enéas* (false accusation or false attribution of same-sex preference), as well as certain terms (wretch, coward, heretic, sodomite). However, *Enéas* passages occupy a unique place in French because they are so long; we can't compare them with any other text. They constitute the richest resource on the articulation of same-sex preference in any early medieval French text.

Enéas passages show the maintenance of one stereotype, male same-sex preference as Trojan usage, but at the same time they demonstrate a discontinuity in the specific sexual acts and roles that are attached to that stereotype, of which one minor instance is the disappearance, from the stereotypical image of *cinaedus* in medieval French, of *calamistratus* (curly-haired) and other references to hair (use of pomade and perfume). More significantly, explicit formulations in *Enéas* allow us to determine that there had been a shift between the classical and the medieval understanding of what the Trojan custom specifically designates. In spite of great specificity of the description, we cannot determine whether Eneas is imagined as receptive or insertive. Representation of same-sex couples in *Enéas* (Eneas with his servants, with his *godel* or mignon, and with his Ganymede) imply a shift in the understanding of the "Trojan custom" from receptive, to either receptive or insertive, now undifferentiated and subsumed under a new category: same-sex.

Eneas is portrayed as the employer of youths whose trousers he often pulls down, and as a prospective husband who would likely offer his wife to a man be likes (*un godel*, a mignon) so that he can "trot on him" in exchange. "Sor lui troter" (l. 8,594) [trot on him] suggests insertive sex, but the pronouns don't allow us to distinguish who is on top:

se il avoit alcun godel,
ce li seroit et bon et bel
quel laissasses a ses druz faire;
nel troveroit ja si estrange

qu'il ne feïst asez tel change,
que il feïst son bon de toi
por ce qu'il lo sofrist de soi;
bien lo lairoit sor toi monter,
s'il repueit sor lui troter; (ll. 8,585–94)

[If he had a mignon (*godel*), it would please him and agree with him that you
would let his lover do it (*quel laissasses a ses druz faire*). He would not think
it's wrong (*estrange*), [and as a consequence nothing would prevent him
from] frequently making this exchange: he [the *godel* or mignon] would do
as he pleases with you, so that he would suffer him with him. He would well
let him mount on you, if he would climb to trot on him.]

Although the pronouns are identical, the verb *repueit*, from *repuier*, to climb,
may indicate that it is the boyfriend who trots on Eneas after he has
mounted Eneas's wife. A confirmation would come from Lavinia's speech
where Eneas is described as a female animal: "he is in rut for a long time"
(l. 9,137) [il est molt longuement an ruit]. In that case, the references to
young boys and Ganymede would indicate either that the medieval discourse imagined Ganymede and young boys as insertive partners, which is
contrary to the classical tradition in the case of Ganymede; or, that the
French text did not distinguish between insertive and receptive partners as
long as they were same-sex. I suggest the latter. The discourse of Lavinia
and her mother erases the difference between insertive and receptive sex.
The fact that Enéas has sex with boys or men defines him, to a far greater
extent than it would have defined a character in classical discourse
described by Williams and Lilja. That would explain why it is so difficult to
us to translate the passages from *Enéas* with certainty about who is on top
of whom: the text does not care. It anticipates the modern categorization
of same-sex acts as the principal category of sexual preference, as opposed
to the principal classical distinction between insertive and receptive acts.
This is not to say that, for centuries after Eneas and in the present, there is
no distinction between insertive and receptive sex; quite the contrary. But
even that difference is co-opted to maintain the polarization between same
and opposite as categories of sexual difference. For example, in patriarchal
societies like ours, men define themselves as "straight" (i.e., masculine, heterosexual) no matter what their casual or habitual partners' sex. Perhaps
they identify as "straight" because they are insertive, perhaps because they
"renew" their straight credentials by occasionally having sex with females,
or perhaps they identify as straight simply because they are men. What we
witness in the case of *Enéas* and in the present is the actual coexistence of
two theoretically discrete and incompatible discourses. This coexistence
must be the defining characteristic of the medieval period, since Williams

and Halperin show that Roman and Greek discourse is far more definite about the roles (insertive or receptive) and far less invested in the sex of the partner (same or opposite).

The most frequently used paraphrases for male same-sex preference in *Enéas* are either negative: avoiding women (or their metonymical and metaphorical substitutes: hen, bunny fur [pubic hair]), or positive: liking men (or corresponding metaphors and metonymies: cock, pants). The negative phrases are about as frequent as the positive. Negative paraphrases occur eight times in 124 lines. They have a few variations: not caring for, or little caring for, women, a specific woman, or "that" pleasure. *Avoir cure* is the most frequent (ll. 8,568, 8,605, 9,166). Its synonyms, occurring only once, are *avoir soing*, l. 9,147, and *chaloir*, l. 9,140. *Etre po de* [to be of little [importance]] occurs twice (ll. 9,131, 9,136), "not to need"—once (l. 9,148). When Lavinia imagines that Eneas prefers men, she thinks that Eneas avoids her because he knows she loves him (ll. 9,149–9,153). She imagines that Eneas is sickened at the sight of her ("de moi veor ot mal al cuer," l. 9,154).

The other most frequent paraphrase is positive: taking pleasure in, only loving, preferring, or having around oneself, a boy, a young man, a boyfriend or mignon [*godel*], Ganymede, boys, young men, male servants, "them." In my view, taking pleasure in a "bad" [*male*] or "male" (a homonym usually spelled differently, *masle*) whore, belongs here ("n'aime se males putains non," Lavinia, l. 9,134 [he only likes bad/male whores]). Boy [*garçon*] occurs three times (ll. 8,572, 9,133, 9,138). Designations of male partner(s) that occur only once are: young man or servant (*valet*, l. 8,576), mignon or boyfriend (*godel*, l. 8,585), they (l. 9,139), Ganymede (l. 9,135), bad/male whore (l. 9,134), enough boys [*assez garçons*] (l. 9,159), many of them (l. 9,161), a man (l. 9,170).

Words for pleasure are, in the order of frequency, *avoir/prendre deduit* [to have/take pleasure] (used for same-sex male couples, ll. 9,133, 9,138, and opposite sex, l. 9,148), and occurring once: to carry one's *galt* ("quant a mené o als son galt," l. 9,139), to be in rut for a long time ("il est molt longuement an ruit," l. 9,137). The different words for preference are: to prefer or hold dear, *priser* (l. 9,155), to have (young men etc.) ("il a. . .o soi," l. 9,159). Unlike *galt* and *rut*, the terms *avoir/prendre deduit*, *priser*, *avoir o soi* are frequently encountered in romance to describe opposite-sex couples.

The paraphrases used to describe the male same-sex acts or pleasures are also, in most cases, the same as the ones used for opposite sex. Only the context indicates the same-sex preference. Among them are references to taking pleasure (*deduit*), doing or needing "it" or "that trade" (*mestier*), mentioned above, and more explicit "por ce qu'il lo sofrist de soi" (l. 8,592) [so that he [the boyfriend] would suffer him [Eneas] with him [the boyfriend]]; "sor lui troter" (l. 8,594) [to trot on him]. There are four paraphrases that are not transitive: "the Trojan custom" ("An ce sont Troïen norri," l. 8,577 [the Trojans are brought up like that]), "doing that/acting thus against nature" [qui si fet contre nature](l. 8,606), and a man that "leaves women, takes men" (ll. 8,607, 9,170). The enigmatic "lo ploin mestier" may perhaps mean "to intertwine" (l. 8,569; *ploier* is to flex, twine, or interlace, and *ploin mestier* may refer to sex as an activity where two bodies intertwine). However, since it is intended to connote Eneas's preference in particular, it may signify "to bend over," or "to hoe." There are other, more colorful images. The mother refers to a preference for eating males, "char de maslon" (l. 8,571) [the flesh of a cock]. "Molt aime fraise de vallet" (l. 8,576) may mean "he likes young men's penis/pants/fringe/berry a lot." Lavinia offers an extended metaphor concerning preference for men's garments, and describes boys being paid for having their pants frequently pulled off:

Molt me prisast mialz Eneas,
se j'aüsse fandus les dras
et qu'eüsse braies chalcies
et lasnieres estroit lïees.
Il a asez garçons o soi,
lo peor aime mialz de moi,
fandue trove lor chemise;
maint an i a an son servise,
lor braies sovant avalees:
issi deservent lor soldees. (ll. 9,155–64)

[Eneas would like me much better if I had split clothes [*fanduz les dras*], and were wearing pants, and tightly tied laces [going up the leg]. He has enough boys with him, he likes the puniest one better than me. He finds their shirt split [*fandue trove lor chemise*]; he has many a of them at his service, their pans often pulled down: that's how they earn their pay.]

Another fragment of Lavinia's monologue anticipates the bed episode from *Yde et Olive*, where Olive is "spared" (*desportee*) by Yde (cited in chapter 2):

Buer sera or la dame nee,
qui a tel home est mariee,
molt avra de lui bon confort,
et bele amor et bel deport,
il l'esparnerat longuement,
ne l'en prendra longues talant, (ll. 9,141–46)

[The woman who is married to such a man will, truly, be born under a lucky star / born a lord [*buer. . .nee*]; she will find much good comfort in him and pretty love and pretty amusement [*deport*]. He will spare her [*esparnerat*] for a long time, he will not delight in her for long.]

A pun is possible in l. 9,141: "*buer*". . .*nee*" would usually mean "born under a lucky star," as in *Enéas* l. 211: ". . .buer furent né / cil qui a Troie la cité / furent detranchié et ocis" (ll. 211–13) [they were born under a lucky star, those who were cut down and killed in the city of Troy], but it can also be taken to mean "born a husband" or "born a lord." The passage can translate, ironically: "the lady married to such a man will, indeed, be born under a lucky star. . .he will spare her and not use her much," or "the lady married to such a man will in fact be born a lord" (i.e., only men are eligible). I suggest that the pun was intended, as in l. 9,134 (n'aime se males putains non" [he only likes bad/male whores]).

The paraphrases used to describe acts involving women in *Enéas* are negative. Eneas does not like to "eat hen" [Il ne velt pas biset mangier] (l. 8,570) but much prefers the flesh of a cock [Molt par ainme char de maslon] (l. 8,571). He would prefer a boy [Il priseroit mialz un garçon] (l. 8,572) rather than embracing you [Lavinia] or another woman [Que toi ne altre acoler] (l. 8,573). He will not parlay at the wicket gate [Ne parlerast pas a guichet] (l. 8,575). He does not like "bunny fur" [poil de conin] (l. 8,595) (*con* in French means female genitalia, and *conin, connetiaus* means bunny, and is used as a pun or interchangeably with *con*). The nouns used to describe Eneas are: wretch (*cuiverz*, l. 8,567), traitor (l. 8,583), sodomite (l. 8,611), coward (*coart*, l. 8,611).

When Lavinia's mother imagines Eneas trading the sexual use of Lavinia for the services of his male lover (ll. 8,585–95, cited above), she reiterates a classical commonplace that can be linked to Catullus (two siblings of Verona) and Ovid (a man punishing his rival by raping him). Lavinia's mother's next argument can be connected to another classical cliché: excessive preoccupation with same-sex partners, especially receptivity, considered as an impediment to reproduction. For instance, in Juvenal's ninth satire, the receptive client also pays his hired insertive male partner, Naevolus, to impregnate his wife in order to produce heirs (70–90; discussed in Williams, Halperin, and Lilja). We have seen (in chapter 1) how Augustine's text on the rites of Cybele ties together castration, same-sex promiscuity, and the sterility of paganism, a bundle whose iconographic symbol is the castrated Attis. For Augustine, Cybele is a paradox: a fertility goddess who requires infertility from her castrated priests. Augustine's description of male promiscuity connected with castration rites was expanded by his French translator and commentator, Raoul de Presles. Medieval French romances also link infertility and castration, including the allusions to sterility in Chrétien's *Perceval*, and the articulation between genital wound of the king and the wasting macrocosm of the realm in the Fisher King episode in Wolfram von Eschenbach's *Parzival*. In my view, these romance texts, dating to late twelfth and early thirteenth century, anticipate the articulation between same-sex preference and castration present in the French *City of God* (1375). Two other fourteenth-century texts, discussed in chapter 2, present a direct causal link between same-sex couples and infertility: the narrative of the fall of Agriano in *Bérinus* (fourteenth century) and the genealogical crisis in *Yde et Olive* (1311) resolved by God's gift of full "humanity" to Yde, and immediately followed by Yde engendering an heir (both cited in chapter 2).

Enéas shares with *Yde et Olive* the concern with "humanity," and it imagines a worldwide extension of the tragic scenario of Agriano. In *Enéas*, it would be the end of the human world, *cest sigle* (l. 8,596: *sigle* connotes the secular world, as opposed to the City of God, the eternal, metaphysical world), if everywhere in the world [par tot lo mont] (l. 8,598) all the humans/men that are in it [tuit li home qui i sont] (l. 8,697) were that way (*autel*, l. 8,598; "that way," that is exclusively interested in same-sex partners, like Eneas). No women would ever conceive [ja mes feme ne concevroit] (l. 8,699), there would be great shortage of people [grant sofraite de gent seroit] (l. 8,600), no children would be made [l'an ne feroit ja mes anfanz] (l. 8,601), and the human world would end before a century was over [li siegles faudroit ainz cent anz] (l. 8,602). The concern with "humanity" and with a worldwide crisis of reproduction is followed by concerns over "nature." By taking men and leaving women [les homes prent, les fames let] (l. 8,607), a male-oriented male "undoes the natural couple/coupling" [la natural cople desfait] (l. 8,608).

Lavinia's mother's exhortation dissolves in epithets: "*sodomite,. . .coart*" (l. 8,611: sodomite. . .coward), "*traïtor*" (l. 8,618: traitor), ending with "cil te seroit toz tens estrange" (l. 8,621) [he would always be a stranger to you]. This is the same Eneas whom the vernacular French text now enshrines as the *pater familias* of French royal dynasty. The conflicted relationship between the nascent French national identity and legendary Trojan origins resembles the proto-humanist attitude of Raoul de Presles in his commentary on Augustine, made up of equal parts vanity, fascination, and anxiety.

Given the role of *Enéas* in the formation of French national legend, Noah D. Guynn is interested in the functioning of same-sex preference in the foundation of a heteronormative regime, especially the repudiation of the "deviant characters" (Pallas and Camille), simultaneously displayed and contained in elaborate tombs. For Guynn, these mausoleums constitute an architectural allegory where the "monumentality of same-sex eroticism" plays a fundamental but also a destabilizing role in state formation:

> *Eneas* uses rhetorical, narrative and allegorical strategies to consolidate power in an incorporated, patriarchal and dynastic model of the state and, as its corollary, a procreative, phallocentric, and heteronormative sexual regime. The allegorical production of the polity suggests, on the one hand, a coherent

system of rigidly constructed, multiply articulated levels of meaning in which timeless truths of political order are predicated through hypostatized metaphors. But on the other hand, the polysemic configuration of allegorical meaning might be understood to repudiate absolute structure and point instead to a multiplicity of possible semantic and phantasmic investments and to the potential disruption of metaphors of power through an anarchic or disordered production of political and sexual meaning. (Guynn, "Eternal Flame," 287)

Guynn's argument resonates with Gaunt's analysis of episodes that transgress bipolar sexual roles in *Enéas* and other French texts, including *Lanval*, *Vie de Ste Euphrosine*, and *Roman de Silence*.[21] Gaunt asks how "transgressive sexualities define and produce the limits of heterosexual norms" (Gaunt, "Straight Minds/Queer Wishes," p. 441). He notes a structural fallacy in the functioning of these episodes, a fallacy that deconstructive criticism is quick to identify: while these episodes always serve to reaffirm the heteronormative, patriarchal orthodoxy, their very presence unsettles that orthodoxy. Even though the ostensible reason for their inclusion is to repudiate the possibility of sexual pluralism, "the mechanisms by which homosexuality is repudiated guarantee and produce a heterosexual matrix but they also fail to occlude what they seek to repress" (Gaunt, "Straight Minds/Queer Wishes," p. 453). To the extent that both Gaunt and Guynn focus on the tension between an element's role in the system and its intrinsic, inalienable value, Gaunt's summary reflection on the constitution of sexual binaries and the paradoxal relationship between the limits and the norm, is like Guynn's analytical reading, exploring the "polysemic configuration of allegorical meaning."

I do not want to reach a premature simplification, but I would like to provisionally contrast Gaunt and Guynn's conclusions with James A. Schultz's observations, based on slightly later German texts. Schultz focuses on specific ways in which these texts represent desire that is not like the modern, polarized homo/hetero opposition. Gaunt and Guynn see same-sex preference in French texts as constructing something else—either the homo/hetero binary or the national self/other binary. Schultz says that the homo/hetero binary was less relevant in somewhat later German texts. When men and women alike admire Tristan's shapely legs, they do not fantasize about same-sex preference. Desire is awakened by Tristan's *noble* legs, not by his *masculine* legs. Men gazing at Tristan's legs unsettle modern heteronormativity, but medieval readers were not unsettled by it, because homoerotic orientation was not as clearly differentiated from heteroerotic. They were not opposites, but two ways to inflect a single, mostly status-oriented desire: "aristophilia inflected by gender" (Schultz).

I now turn to two lesser examples of same-sex preference motif in vernacular French, relatively close in time to *Enéas*: Marie de France's *Lanval* and Conon de Bethune's lyric poem. The twinning of eroticism and wealth (and very good clothes) that defines the German *Tristan* also anchors the plot of *Lanval*, but here the similarity ends. Unlike in the German *Tristan*, the sexual desire in the French poem is structured by the opposition between same-sex and opposite-sex preference, presented as mutually exclusive. The *lai* opens with the crisis of the feudal system of *don*, the form of transaction between the vassals and the king that resembles a courtship much more than a payroll. Two approaches shed light on the economy of desire described in *Lanval*: Claude Lévi-Strauss's *Elementary Structures of Kinship*, with its fundamental assumption that social rules (such as the pro-hibition of incest) warrant circulation of wealth, and Brigitte Buettner's research on gifts at the court of Valois at the turn of the fourteenth cen-tury.[22] Ideally, the exchange of gifts in the court would ensure the circula-tion of wealth. However, this exchange never consists of immediate reciprocity, unlike an exchange transaction in a currency economy. Several steps separate the donor from the beneficiary. The gift is mediated by a series of equivalent objects, manipulated by a number of people, each of whom may derive wealth from his role in the transaction. The donor could never directly request compensation, or confront the beneficiary the way a creditor confronts a debtor (that is precisely the problem facing Lanval, who expended his entire fortune in the service of the king). Buettner's study shows that mediation remained the central element in the later period that she describes. Although the value of the exchanged objects would be specified with as much certainty as if money was used, not money, but rather luxury goods would be exchanged, and several interme-diary steps and persons would be involved.

Why is mediation necessary? When the vassals expend their resources in *dons* (gifts) and the lord rewards them in *contredon*, both sides have the opportunity to adjust the symbolic hierarchy by choosing the amount of economic value they convert into symbolic value by *don*. The procedure carries obvious risks and rewards: one speculates by increasing one's sym-bolic value, at the risk of losing that investment. A crisis of this type is por-trayed in *Lanval*. Lanval spent all he had, but the king granted him no income from his store of "wives and land" [*Femmes et tere*] (l. 17). No one intervened with Arthur on Lanval's behalf for two reasons: he is a foreigner, and he is envied (ll. 21–22). Lanval rides out to brood in a prairie, where an irresistible fulfilment fantasy unfolds. He is seduced by a fairy, who sends him back to court, enriched by her magical means and assured of her companionship whenever he desires her, as long as he can keep their relationship secret.

The first part ends with the fairy satisfying Lanval's need for wealth and companionship—"Ore est Lanval en dreite veie!" (l. 134), famously exclaims the narrator: now Lanval has it made! The second part resembles the story of Joseph and Potiphar's wife, or Hippolytus and Phaedra. It begins with Guinevere's unrequited desire for Lanval and her false accusation of same-sex preference (in private, to Lanval) and rape (in public, to Arthur and the court). In the second part of the story, status and beauty are still connected, and beauty is presented as a relative value, by the beauty contest between Guinevere and the fairy, and the comparison between the fairy and her servants.

Back at court, Lanval briefly enjoys prosperity and secret happiness, until Guinevere tries to seduce him, and is rejected.[23] The queen "misspeaks" (*mesparla*), accusing Lanval of preferring his male servants:

Lanval, fet ele, bien le quit:
Vus n'aimez gueres cel delit.
Asez me l'ad hum dit sovent
Que des femmes n'avez talent.
Vallez avez bien afeitiez,
Ensemble od eus vus deduiez,
Villeins cuarz! Mauveis failliz!
Mut est mi sires maubailliz,
Que pres de lui vus a suffert,
Mun escïent que Deus en pert. (ll. 277–86)

[Lanval, says she, I am quite aware: you don't care for this sort of pleasure. People told me often enough that you don't go for women. You have well endowed young men/servants, and find your pleasure in them, base villain! Malformed freak! My lord is very ill advised to have suffered you near him, if you ask me, God will punish him(?)]

To me, this is not just a token insult. *Lanval* is a frankly sexual and playful narrative, as in a later scene where the fairy appears before Arthur and removes her cloak, and the king and court rise.[24] It is in this playful, open, and sensual context that we may read the queen's accusation of Lanval. The fairy's riches are described in detail, and Lanval's same-sex acts are mentioned in passing. The fairy is a powerful, distant object of desire, the servants—social subordinates. The fairy is singular, irreplaceable, the servants—plural. Guinevere's phrasing of the accusation is obviously calculated to degrade same-sex desire by making it blind to wealth, anti-aristophiliac, and transferable, that is worthless. But although Guinevere portrays same-sex desire as uncourtly, the equivalence that she implies has one upper-class lady replaced by good-looking young men or servants. Some fantasize about a fairy, others, about good-looking youths.

Guinevere's speech brings God's retribution to bear on same-sex acts, and portrays same-sex desire as uncourtly, just as we would expect. But same-sex preference is also described in identical terms as a preference for the opposite sex. Guinevere speaks of Lanval as a prominent man, well known for his same-sex preference ("assez me l'ad hum dit sovent," l. 279), close to the king ("pres de lui," l. 285). He has no desire for women ("des femmes n'avez talent," l. 280), he has good-looking servants ("Vallez avez bien afeitiez," l. 281; I suppose that the use of *avez*, "you have," in relation to *vallez* implies they are servants, not just young men; *bien afeitiez*, well built, well dressed, or well trained, is not a frequently used expression), and he disports himself with them ("Ensemble od eus vus deduiez," l. 282). There is no condemnation or secrecy specifically in this description. Apart from plurality and lower-class status of love objects, nothing allows us to distinguish this from a description of opposite-sex preference. The words for pleasure (*delit, talent, deduit*: delight, desire, pleasure) and relations ("ensemble od eus," l. 282 [together with them]) are standard. Two conditions of courtly love, singularity and aristophilia, are transgressed, but otherwise, there is no negative charge, or any sort of mark, in any aspect of this description, except for the perfectly neutral presence of *vallez* (young men) where in another context women would appear. Invectives immediately follow: *vileinz cuarz* (base coward), *mauveis failliz* (sinister wretch?), but the queen's description of same-sex preference in a man at court is strikingly similar to opposite-sex preference.

When Lanval responds to the queen's accusation, and refers to same-sex preference, he does not use the word *ierites* (heretic) that Lavinia's mother uses, or *iresie* (heresy) that Conon de Bethune's knight uses (perhaps several decades later), but rather a circumlocution, "n'avoir mestier": "Dame, dist il, de cel mestier / Ne me sai jeo nïent aidier, / Mes jo aim et si sui amis / Cele ki. . ." (ll. 291–294) [Madam, says he, I don't go in for that, but I love, and am the beloved of, her who. . .]. Unlike Conon's interlocutor who ironically imagines uses for the false accusation of same-sex preference between two heterosexual partners, Lanval simply denies it. "*Avoir mestier*" is to need, *avoir besoin* in modern French. *Mestier* is attested early, in the eleventh-century Life of St Léger (*mistier*), and is derived from classical Latin *ministerium* via Vulgar Latin *misterium*. If the original meaning is "need," and then "ceremony, service, function" or, by extension, "trade," another *misterium* (a sacred play, a secret, an initiation) plays up the dimension of ceremony and initiatory rite. These meanings, secrecy and initiation, may account for the frequent use of "*mestier*" in reference to sexual acts. A more common expression is "n'ai cure de cel mestier" [I don't go in for that]. It is usually used in the negative, emphatically, like the similar euphemism "*n'ai talent de*" (*cure*: care, *talent*: desire). The phrase is often used as a euphemism addressed by a female hero to a man who is conniving to rape her. In *Enéas*, Lavinia's mother says: "He prefers the *ploin mestier*" [Il prise plus lo ploin mestier] (l. 8,569), and Lavinia says of same-sex preference: "That *mestier* is very bad" [Molt par est malvés cist mestiers] (l. 9,168). *Mestier,* usually used for opposite-sex acts, is different from *iresie.* Lanval's choice of language in speaking of same-sex preference not only emphasizes his courtliness, but also shows that it is possible in the twelfth century to phrase same-sex preference identically to heterosexual preference.

My last example of false accusation of same-sex preference appears in a poem by Conon de Bethune (d. 1224). The author was a Picard trouvère, a continuator in the north of France of the Provençal troubadour tradition. Like most troubadours but unlike most trouvères, he was a notable. He took part in the crusades and profited from them: the chronicle of Geoffroy de Villehardouin, the early monument of French prose, mentions his part in the Fourth crusade, which captured Constantinople from the Greeks. Conon's poem, "L'autrier avint en cel autre pays," is a dialogue between a lady and her knight. The lady is no longer "en son bon pris" [in her prime], and she chooses that moment to give in to the knight. He decides it is too late: "I am quite unfortunate, he says, that you haven't thought of that earlier. Your radiant face [*clair vis*] that looked like a lily flower is gone, my lady, so much from bad to worse, that it seems to me that you have been stolen from me [*me soies emblee*]" (ll. 11–15) [Dame, fait il, certes sui mal baillis / Ke n'eüstes piech'a ceste pensee. / Vostre clair vis, qui sambloit flors de lis, / Est si alés, dame, de mal em pis / K'il m'est a vis ke me soies emblee]. The lady, deeply offended, retracts her offer, and doubts he could love a worthy woman [*dame de pris*]: "Not at all, by God! But rather the fancy to kiss and embrace a pretty young man would take you" (ll. 23–24) [Nenil, par Dieu! Ians vos prendroit envie / D'un bel vallet baisier et acoler]. They continue the quarrel, she—invoking her connections in high places, he—comparing her to the ruins of Troy, once, too, a great city.

The knight takes up the reference to his preference for a good-looking young man. He suggests that the lady should always blame lack of interest in her on men's *iresie* (heresy), here understood as preference for young men, with the negative charge that the lack of orthodoxy automatically implies (ll. 30–32): "Et si vous lo ensi a excuser / Ke cil soient reté de l'iresie/ Qui des or mais ne vous vauront aimer" [And therefore I commend you [*vous lo*] for providing an excuse / Let them be accused of heresy / Those who henceforth would not love you]. Conon de Bethune's courtly interlocutors are aware that same-sex preference is an option that explains men's lack of interest in women. The setting makes it clear that the man is interested in young women, but he ironically implies that a supposed interest in a young man (the lady's accusation is in the singular) allows this woman's suitors to save face (in fact, it allows the lady to save face). Preferences for same and opposite sex are, like in *Lanval* and *Eneas*, equal, plausible, and mutually exclusive.

The poem shares the reference to Troy with *Eneas*, and the specific framework with *Lanval*: false accusation of same-sex preference as a way for the rejected woman to save face. Like Lanval, it also explores the articulation between money, power, and youthful beauty. The three come under one heading: *pris*. The lady wants to make the translation between them seamless: social status as a substitute for beauty. Her partner replies that youthful beauty is irreplaceable: a ruined Troy is not desirable.

I now turn to some texts that are not directly concerned with same-sex preference, to determine whether certain body parts are particularly masculine or eroticized as masculine. My question is: when *Lanval's* Guinevere imagined good-looking young men [vallez. . .bien afeitiez] that Lanval prefers to her, what did she have in mind? Based on his reading of German texts, Schultz comes to the conclusion that legs were particularly masculine (they were exposed by dress in men but not in women), while breasts were undervalued as a feminine attribute. I wanted to see whether that paradigm also obtained in medieval French texts. What I found were confirmations and counterexamples to any tendency one could identify. If, in German romances, breasts are undervalued as a feminine trait, Peggy McCracken discusses the golden nipple in *Le livre de Caradoc* (a replacement for the one severed in the miraculous cure of Caradoc) and shows how the breast becomes a focus for concerns over femininity, desire, intimacy, and loyalty.[25] Breasts are also eroticized in vernacular literature in corporeal ways, as edible and fertile. Small breasts were usually preferred, like those, the size of walnuts, and just as hard, in *Aucassin et Nicolete* (verse 12, ll. 24–25). Some four centuries after Nicolete (1573), when Tasso speaks of the virginal heroine in his pastoral play, he mentions "the unpicked apples of her breasts" (*Aminta*, 1, 2, 356), and so does Clément Marot in a poem based on a medieval romance, *l'Epître de Maguelonne à son amy Pierre de Provence* (ca. 1519).[26] And in Adam de la Halle's *pastourelle* play, *Le jeu de Robin et Marion* (ca. 1283), Marion pulls out her picnic—bread and fat cheese, "fromage cras"—from her bosom to share with Robin.

German *Tristan's* focus on men's legs can be contrasted with the French *chantefable Aucassin et Nicolete*, which devotes a couple of lyrical scenes to the heroine's legs and feet—but not without some comments on this peculiar work. An anonymous text written between the end of the twelfth and the first half of the thirteenth century (single manuscript, BN f. fr. 2,168), *Aucassin et Nicolete* has all the elements of a cross-dressing fiction that Busby enumerates: parody of genres and of ideology, of the chivalric romance, of the courtly love tradition, of social roles and gender stereotypes, of war, power, and marriage. Nicolete dresses up as a minstrel to search for Aucassin, like Marthe in *Ysaïe*, but the range of subversion in *Aucassin* is wider than in any other cross-dressing romance. In the kingdom of Turelure that the lovers visit, the king is in bed after childbirth, while the queen leads into battle an army armed with cheeses. The tone and the verbal and situational humor of *Aucassin* recall the playful moments in *Lancelot en prose* or *Lanval*, but they are sustained throughout, dictating the tone of the *chantefable*. The two heroes can be compared, love's fools both—Lancelot so preoccupied with Guinevere he walks his horse into the river and very nearly drowns, were it not for Galehot who pulls them both out at the last minute; Aucassin indolent, weeping and thinking of his *amie* until a near loss of a battle spurs him into action of Rolandesque proportions. But *Lancelot* can be melodramatic and serious, while in my view *Aucassin's* only serious moments are the intensely poetic descriptions, alternating verse and prose. I would describe it as camp.

     Imprisoned for the love of Nicolete, Aucassin falls into a reverie on her pretty leg. The leg works miracles, he recalls, having restored one paralyzed pilgrim to health (verse 11, ll. 16–31). With Aucassin, we never get to touch. All we do is look at her as a bedridden invalid would. Our eyes, with those of the pilgrim, slide from the bed up Nicolete's leg following the many-layered hems she is lifting: the train, the furry tunic, and the thin white slip. The hems, the fur, the naked skin, the upward glance suggest, but only suggest, her sex. Unlike in Lavinia's mother's list of metaphors for same-sex acts, including mounting and trotting, the leg reverie in *Aucassin* does not make a spectacle of the obscene, but instead speaks of the bodily sites and objects that maintain a tantalizing distance to the focus of desire. In some romances, the site is a body part (feet, hands) or a birthmark (resembling a rose in *Le Roman de la rose, ou de Guillaume de Dole*, a violet in *Le Roman de la violette*). The work that has been done on that subject by Peggy McCracken, E. Jane Burns, and Nancy Vine Durling, among others, has shown that these exceptional body sites provide a way to talk about intimacy. Because it is missing, the nipple in *Caradoc* can be talked about, gazed at, and even found in the forest in ways that a regular nipple cannot. Because they are so strange, big feet or birthmarks focus the gaze in the romance in a way that genital organs are not allowed to do in this genre's convention.[27] Whether or not genital organs are seen and thematized, seems to determine the genre: romance or fabliau. When we take romance as a genre into consideration, the displaced focus of desire appears ambulatory. Rather than a different erotic map of the body confirmed through a number of texts, romances offer us a map redrawn for each text, based on one rule: that the erotic zones of the romance not coincide with those of the body, but rather displace them. This makes for a poor prognosis in finding, in romance, a specific vocabulary for same-sex or any sex acts that may compare to Latin, but it opens up other possibilities.

Displacement and abstraction characteristic of medieval allegory, assisted by the focus on body parts other than the genitals, and their metaphorization, allow flirting with homoeroticism. This is the case of *fin' amor* poetry, where the lady is addressed as *midons*, my lord, and it may also be the case of an allegorical Occitan poem, *La Cort d'amor*, earlier than the *Romance of the Rose* (and perhaps responding to Andreas Capellanus's *De Amore*), where Amor is a man, although in Occitan *amor* is a feminine noun.[28] As Matthew Bardell, the editor of *Cort d'amor* notes, Amor is a frequent exception to the rule that the grammatical gender determines the gender of the allegory, because of the literary tradition that links the masculine Amor/Cupid and feminine Venus, and because of the grammatically masculine *amor* in Latin and Old French.[29] Other allegorical characters in *La Cort d'amor* whose "grammatical gender is overriden" are Larguesza, Proessa, and Merce (four out of thirty; Bardell, *La Cort d'amor*, p. 25). If Bardell links the masculine Amor in *La Cort d'amor* to its "reactionary masculine" message, and the remaining three cases of gender shift to the poem's tendency to "undermine a realist attitude towards personification" and "question the gender of abstractions" (p. 25), a homoerotic reading need not be excluded. Likewise, gender ambiguities of the *Rose* can be discounted as a carryover of Occitan tradition of courtly lyric, perhaps even a vestigial trait of its origins in openly homoerotic Arabic lyric tradition, but that explanation needs not exclude the possibility of a queer reading.

I now return to the *Rose* and map the recent interventions of American scholars, a summary complementary to that of Gaunt (cited above; only a few references intersect). In the first part of *Rose* written by Guillaume de Lorris (the second, much longer part was added decades later by Jean de Meun), in the first description in the romance, the rose appears as a stem tipped by a bud, and its erectness and uprightness are emphasized: "The stem was straight as a sapling, and the bud sat on the top, neither bent nor inclined" (53). Classical myths (Narcissus, Hermaphroditus, Attis) are combined with allegorical figures (Fair Welcome/Bel Acueil, God of Love/Amors, Lover/Amant), creating a fictional space where men talk about love and engage in physical intimacy.[30] Medievalists have been aware of that (Poirion, Uitti), but the mention was only made in passing until Martha Powell Harley devoted a section of an article to the discussion of "sexual ambiguity and homosexuality" in *Rose* in 1986; she coined the phrase "flirting with homoeroticism." Harley's work was followed a decade later by discussions by Michael Camille, Ellen Friedrich, and Pamela Sheingorn, the latter analyzing a same-sex erotic scene between women, a dance where two maidens exchange a teasing almost-kiss, described in the text (ll. 757–69) and sometimes illuminated. Harley and Camille, following Girard and Sedgwick, read *Rose's* homoeroticism as "homosocial desire between males" (Camille, *Medieval Art of Love,* p. 140).[31] Friedrich, on the other hand, proposes an exclusively homoerotic reading of the first part of *Rose* as a love story between Bel Acueil and Amant.

Harley notes that three figures can be seen as ciphers of same-sex love in *Rose*: the hermaphrodite, the narcissist, and the castrate. Three myths flesh out the landscape inhabited by these figures: Hermaphroditus, Narcissus, and Attis. A crucial moment in the first part of *Rose*, Amant musing at the Fountain of Love, invokes these three myths in their Ovidian version in a number of ways, including the dramatis personae and topography. Oiseuse recalls Salmacis (the nymph from Ovid who captures Hermaphroditus and is fused with him, so that he becomes "semivir"); the eye-like crystal into which the Lover gazes also recalls the fall of Hermaphroditus; the mirror-like fountain connotes Narcissus, the pine tree—the metamorphosis of Attis. Harley observes that the three myths strongly modulate the message of the *Rose*, although she concludes that Rose's "Ovidian lovers" are not homoerotic but rather self-absorbed. That conclusion, however, should not obscure her prior observation in the section on homoeroticism in *Rose*:

> In the Introduction to *Homosexualities and French Literature*, Stambolian and Marx observe that "the works of many writers who never wrote about homo-sexuality nevertheless contain fantasies, patterns of imagery, or structures of lan-guage that some critics have begun tentatively to identify as 'homosexual' " (6). It would be inaccurate to say that Guillaume "never wrote about homosexu-ality" [he did, in fact, warn against it]. . .But neither the [homophobic] allusion nor the announced [heteronormative] intent [of *Rose*] impedes the homo-erotic undercurrent in the poem. The constellation of phenomena surround-ing the myths—autoeroticism, bisexuality, effeminacy, and eunuchry—is of sufficient magnitude to warrant a conjecture that Guillaume is consciously flirting with sexual ambiguity and homosexuality. (Harley, "Narcissus," p. 333)

Harley lists a good number of other passages that invite a queer reading. In addition to the three "Ovidian lovers," she discusses the dance and kiss of the two maidens (ll. 757–69) and Amors cautioning Amant not to use rouge or face paint as do fallen women or men who love "sanz droiture" (literally, "without right" or righteousness, l. 2,161; or in Langlois's edition of the romance, "contre nature," against Nature). Harley points out that Narcissus's sexuality was straightened by medieval tradition: his relationship with feminine Echo is emphasized, his love for young boys is silenced, the homoerotic aspects of his self-love are distorted. Around the time of composition of *Rose*, in the late-twelfth-century French Latin poem *Narcisus*, and the thirteenth-century German translation of *Metamorphoses* by Albrecht von Halberstadt, the reference to young men in love with Narcissus is omitted, and the reflection with which he falls in love is given "neutral designations" and feminized. These deletions and changes "reveal. . .anxiety about [Ovidian] Narcissus's homosexuality." Guillaume de Lorris follows this tradition, but only to a point. He omits the mention of boys in love with Narcissus and he emphasizes the role of Echo. He does not, however, change the gender of Narcissus's reflection, which in French *Narcisus* is a nymph or goddess, and in Albrecht von Halberstadt is neutral and feminized. In *Rose*, Narcissus falls in love with a pretty child, "un esfant bel a demesure" (1486). Harley notes: "[t]hat one troubled scribe, in a manuscript of lesser authority, performs sex-change surgery on the phrase, alternating 'esfant bel' to 'fame bielle,' makes Guillaume's preservation of masculine gender appear striking" (Harley, "Narcissus," p. 331). She points out that Guillaume de Lorris's choice of a masculine figure for his allegory was deliberate: he "may have chosen another abstract noun, but instead he seems to have reached for this unusual, grammatically masculine representation" (Harley, "Narcissus," p. 334). Harley also suggests that Lorris was aware of the homoerotic reading of his own work: "Guillaume could not have been insensitive to the uneasiness his selection caused—an uneasiness significant enough to prompt early illuminators to represent Bel Acueil as female or as male and female alternately in a single manuscript" (Harley, "Narcissus," p. 334), a point discussed more fully by Camille.

Harley then focuses on the relationship between Amant and the two other male figures in the romance, Amors and Bel Acueil. Love embraces the Lover (ll. 1,953–56) and locks his heart (ll. 1,997–2,008) with a key that hangs with his jewels ("mi joal," l. 2,002), a key that he pulls out of his *aumouniere*, purse (l. 1,997). Friedrich, based on semantic analysis, interprets that scene as a metaphor or a pun on a same-sex act. Likewise, Harley notes that the lock and key are a pun on intercourse, and that an illumination in one of the manuscripts of the Rose takes this pun literally (Morgan 245, fol. 15v), illustrating "a ritual intercourse." She also mentions that the language of Amors is used elsewhere in the poem to signify male genitalia: "*borses*" (l. 7,113) and "*aumosniere*" (l. 19,637). The last example is particularly significant because it occurs in the context of Genius's attack on homosexuals, in the later, Jean de Meun's portion of the romance:

Ainz qu'il muirent, puissent il perdre
Et laumosniere et les estalles
Don il ont signe d'estre malles! (19,636–38)

[May they. . .suffer, before their death, the loss of their purse and testicles, the sign that they are male!]

Concerning Bel Acueil, Harley notes: "on the literal level of allegory, Amant and Bel Acueil behave like lovers: Amant woos Bel Acueil, Bel Acueil acquiesces, and the two are unhappily separated. To expect an audience to suppress a consciousness of the gender of a character (or a personification) in an allegory of sexual seduction is perhaps to expect too much. Male Bouche [Bad Mouth] certainly does not ignore it. Noticing the '*bel atret*' 'fair reception' that Bel Acueil gives Amant, he slanders the pair's '*mauvés acointement*' 'evil relationship' (3,496, 3,507)" (Harley, "Narcissus," p. 334). She then quotes Daniel Poirion: "the substitution of Bel Acueil for the rose, in the love protests that end the work of Guillaume [de Lorris], leaves us with a troubling ambiguity" (Poirion, "Narcise et Pygmalion," p. 161).[32] This is also Friedrich's reading. As she does with the scene between Amant and Dieu d'Amour, Friedrich discusses the kiss between Amant and Bel Acueil, drawing out its semantic possibilities and making an argument for a homoerotic reading of both the name (Bel Acueil) and the scene. She suggests that *accueil* is a pun that refers to male erogenous organs (*a* translated as "has" and *cueil* as *coilles*, testicles, or *cul*, ass, anus), connoting the character's same-sex preference. On the basis of semantic analysis, leading to a literal, sexual interpretation of *jeux de mots* in the names of allegorical figures, she claims that Guillaume's main (and misunderstood) purpose was to represent the homoerotic relationship between Amant and Bel Acueil, perhaps responding to unusually open homoerotic culture documented at the close of the twelfth century in Orléans (Lorris is in the Orléanais) and other university centers in France.[33] Friedrich also attributes significance to the ending of Guillaume de Lorris's part of *Rose*: the imprisonment of Bel Acueil and the lament of Amant. While most critics see this ending as an outside interruption rather than auctorial choice, Friedrich suggests that Bel Acueil is imprisoned for same-sex acts. According to Friedrich, in the final lament Amant "addresses himself to his one and only beloved Bel Acueil, who. . .granted him access to the Rosebud and especially to the Rose/y anus so desired by the Lover" (Friedrich, "When a Rose," p. 37).

Harley focuses on two descriptions of the Rose and briefly notes their phallic potential:

La tige ere droite con jons,
Et par desus siet li boutons
Si qu'il ne cline ne ne pent. (ll. 1,663–65)

[The stem was straight as a sapling, and the bud sat on the top, neither bent nor inclined.] (p. 53)

 . . .[la graine] estoit encor enclose
entre les fueilles de la rose

qui amont droites se levoient
et la place dedenz emploient,
si ne pooit paroir la graine
por la rose qui estoit pleine. (ll. 3,347–52)

[[The seed] was still enclosed within the rose leaves, which raised it straight up and filled the space within, so that the seed with which the rose was full, could not appear.] (p. 78)

Friedrich, too, unpacks the semantics and cultural connotations of the rose, including the possibility of reading the rosebud on the stem as the penis, and the open rose as the anus. If in the exegesis of the *Roman de la rose* the rose traditionally stands for the female beloved or her *pudenda*, the bud— for her virginity ready to be plucked, some earlier critics including Uitti have noted that the elongated rose, enclosing the seed, appears distinctly phallic.[34] Others, such as *Rose* editor Armand Strubel, have noted that the rose is never identified as a woman (cited by Friedrich, "When a Rose," p. 22, *Roman de la Rose*, ed. Strubel, p. 34). Harley and Friedrich were the first to make more extensive sense of the phallic reading: Harley by putting it in the context of three "homoerotic and autoerotic" myths, and Friedrich by detailed semantic analysis conducted in the context of Arabic love poetry, secrecy (*sub rosa*), and Amant's relationship with Bel Acueil. Rather than see- ing in Rose–Amant–Bel Acueil a triangle allowing the creation of the homosocial bond expressed by rivalry over a woman, as theorized by René Girard; or homosocial desire, as defined by Eve Kosofsky Sedgwick, Friedrich pointed out that the love story of *Rose* may be about the homo- erotic desire between two men. In this and other respects, Friedrich creates a very different model of *Rose* from that to which we are accustomed.

As Camille shows, some illuminations make clear what the text of *Rose* leaves ambiguous: that, in Harley's words, "the game of personifications" leads to the portrayal of Bel Acueil "in very intimate interactions with the lover." In a late-fifteenth-century manuscript illuminated by Robinet Testard, "the handsome young God of Love seems over-eager to grasp the lover" (Camille, *Medieval Art of Love*, p. 139). Camille follows the rebounds of this configuration of same-sex allegorical figures who incorporate the love theme of the poem in their gestures and caresses—yet, like Harley, he stops short of a queer reading. For Camille, male couples demonstrate that courtly love excludes women, but not necessarily that it includes eroti- cism between men. The book's three strata—text, illuminations, material presence—assign to women the role of voyeur, not participant, in the game of love. Women on a pedestal in the text, women glancing from behind a wall in the illuminations, and Louise of Savoy for whom the manuscript was executed, as she considers it from without, are locked out of what Camille, following Girard and Sedgwick, reads as "homosocial desire between males" (p. 140).

My last example of homoerotic potential in romance is the motif of perfect male friendship. I associate representations of perfect same-sex friendships with other forms of diffuseness in representing homoeroticism, characteristic of romance as a genre, as outlined above. Just as birthmarks and mis-shapen or mutilated body parts displace, and thereby allow us to see and to talk about sexual organs, perfect friendship diffuses and, thanks to that displacement, represents same-sex desire. Like allegory and dream vision, the tradition of perfect friendship creates an ambiguous narrative context. In *Rose*, gender indeterminacy of objects used as stand-ins for sexual organs (such as the rose) is mobilized to flirt with homoeroticism. In stories of perfect friendship, the indeterminacy of the relationship between two men also allows such flirting. One example is the friendship between Lancelot and Galehot, the Lord of the Distant Isles, in *Lancelot*; others are *Ami et Amile*, *Athis et Prophilias*, and other narratives of perfect friendship, including the male couples in epic (e.g., the pairs in the *Song of Roland*, Roland and Olivier), *roman d'aventures*, and romance. In describing a perfect friendship, these stories call for ultimate (and therefore similar from one text to the next) sacrifices: wealth, status, life, and sometimes exchange or gift of female lovers or wives. Not only in *Lancelot*, but also throughout Perceval continuations, Galehot, whose usual epithet is "king of the Distant Isles," is sometimes called he who "loved Lancelot."[35] The word "love" is borrowed from the glossary of courtly love, as are other words and actions. Among the startling gestures that mark the exceptional friendship between the two men are Lancelot's dispositions concerning his burial. Interestingly, in view of its decreased interest in Lancelot's love for Guinevere, it is the Post-Vulgate version that adds episodes to the story of Lancelot, connecting the death of the hero to his passionate friendship. Lancelot asks to be buried with Galehot: "He saw clearly that he could not escape death, and he asked the archbishop and Blioberis to take him, as soon as he was dead, to Joyous Guard and put him in the tomb where Galehot, the lord of the Distant Isles, lay" (vol. 5, p. 310). The friends keep the promise. Galehot's tomb is opened, and Lancelot's body is laid next to his friend's. The tombstone also joins them. It names Galehot and Lancelot, "the best knight who ever bore arms in Britain, except only Galahad his son," so that Galahad, his name so close to Galehot, also becomes associated with the couple (vol. 5, p. 310). In the next chapter, when Mark raids Logres, he destroys the tomb and burns Lancelot's uncorrupted body with Galehot's bones. The words and actions that represent the love of Galehot for Lancelot would, in a heterosexual couple, bespeak passionate love. In the case of friendship between two men, they allow the text to flirt with homoeroticism.

In an article on Lancelot and Galehot in *Prose Lancelot*, Gretchen Mieszkowski discusses the parallels between Galehot's passionate friendship and a courtly love scenario.[36] Christiane Marchello-Nizia mentions this text as an example of homosocial triangulation of desire.[37] According to Mieszkowski, same-sex friendship in *Lancelot* invites a homoerotic reading because of the vocabulary, plot, and other characteristics that resemble love stories of heterosexual couples. Jill Gorman has performed a similar reading of same-sex friendship between women in *Acts* of two female saints, *Xantippe and Polyxena*, a text that she compared to late classical novels narrating the adventures of heterosexual lovers.[38] She pointed out that standard episodes in late classical romance plots—separation, chastity preserved among pirates and thugs, kiss on the deathbed—also structure the *Acts* of the female saints. Gorman's reading of the saints' lives in the light of romance fictions enables us to appreciate the homoerotic potential of hagiography.

Medieval writers actively exploit the security that the prestige of the classical and Occitan tradition provides them to explore the themes of same-sex preference and homoeroticism. Whether bundled with moral condemnation (French Augustine) or discredited in relation to narrative truth (false accusations in *Lanval, Enéas,* Conon de Bethune's poem), so vague as to be frequently dismissed or omitted in the interpretation of allegorical love scripts (*Rose, Cort d'amor*), or flirting with homoeroticism by heavily borrowing from the arsenal of heterosexual romance in "perfect friendship" narratives, same-sex preference seems a rather pervasive interest. It is smuggled into canonical works in recognizable ways. Starting from that realization, we can begin the queer re-reading of the medieval French corpus.

CONCLUSION

Throughout the work on this project, Roland Barthes's *Pleasure of the Text* stayed near, like a fellow passenger on a train. I am thinking of the way Barthes justifies reading as pleasure. He is not afraid to say that ultimate pleasure is perversion, and he discreetly lets on, in another text published within a couple of years of *Pleasure*, that homosexuality, specifically, is the way to the ultimate pleasure of the text. These few facts have configured Barthes's intervention in my memory since the very beginning of my work. Over the years, *Pleasure of the Text* would come to mind at crucial moments of our collective work. When we talked about differences between same-sex and opposite-sex relationships in terms of hierarchies and relationships to power, *Pleasure of the Text* appeared as an unexpected precursor, in Barthes's explicit concern that perversion and same-sex relation are at risk of reproducing hierarchies and ideologies, but also in his conviction that they are better suited to abolish them than are the "orthodox" sexual configurations.

The universal quality of Barthes's thoughts on the pleasure of the text accounts for the fact that, in the final form of my work, they are found not at the heart of a discussion, but contained in a separate section of their own. The specific, brief mention of homosexuality and the general trajectory of the theory associating reading with pleasure is an important verification of my own work, but Barthes's thought, even when he particularizes it to the point of making homosexuality intervene as a figure for reading, is still more universal than my approach: grittier, messier, and less abstract. In its level of abstraction, his theory of pleasure has the serenity of descriptions of protagonists in medieval romance. Frequently detailed, they bring us sensual pleasure, but they are curiously void of any distinguishing marks prompting us to imagine the described character as a unique face or even a type. In *Aucassin et Nicolete* or *Lanval*, I see with great precision the detail of a specific kind of cloth against the bare skin, but that detail can be found on any person. When I read Barthes's theory of pleasure, I feel it applies to any text, and does not lead me to think about particular texts in their specificity, the way I feel compelled to read them, as separate, even idiosyncratic, objects.

Especially when texts are found in unique, distinctive manuscripts, they possess an individuality closer to that of a person ("manuscript witnesses"). There, Barthes's *Fragments of a Lover's Discourse* are a better parallel, a model I have attempted to follow in the discussion of body parts in chapter 3.

But a conclusion is also a privileged space where we are expected to say the most important things—and Barthes's idea that texts procure pleasure has just that ultimate importance. His argument reminds us that pleasure is a legitimate way of reading, although a personal and sometimes a frightening one. It seems to me that medieval studies are an intellectual space where, by and large, we have safeguarded the right *not* to seek pleasure in a text. A scholarly reading of a medieval text needs to be accurate, erudite, establish new connections, and bring out aspects that other readers have overlooked: for instance, symbolic capital, political relevance, representation of women, or queerness. Pleasure is associated with pedagogy, where it is defined as other people's pleasure: to entice the students to read medieval texts, we need to think of their pleasure, or pain (that, too, is valued). It may be reassuring to participate in a collective intellectual endeavor where most practitioners' pleasure is furtive or, sometimes, defined as finding an obscure reference. Pleasure is embarrassing and personal. The erudition required by our texts and the field's more than usual respect for tradition, may provide a safe refuge from it. Yet, it seems that at our most assertive, when we publicly embrace our fetish and are able to speak of our pleasure in little known facts, we are less pathetic.

Barthes, on the other hand, reflects on ways of procuring maximum pleasure, *jouissance*, from a text through a reading that is "perverse" or "homosexual" (both terms are his). Such a reading presupposes the reader's, the text's, and the writer's perversion. The goal of a perverted reading is not to document the existence of homosexuality in the Middle Ages, but rather to experience ultimate pleasure in reading the text, while appreciating the Middle Ages in the fullness of their difference. The perverse or homosexual reading, as Barthes describes it, deviates from the trajectory prepared by the ideology of the text and anticipated by the ideology of the reader. It produces an unsuspected pleasure, a surplus of enjoyment that "goes beyond the satisfaction anticipated by desire," says Barthes, quoting Ruysbroeck.[1] For Barthes, a divinity presides over this transcendent pleasure, "goddess Homosexuality." Closely borrowing from Barthes, I want to articulate a conclusion that is not based on superficial resemblance of metaphorical fields between queer readings (concerned with desires and pleasures) and Barthes's "pleasure of the text." When Barthes designates "goddess Homosexuality" as the presiding deity of ultimate pleasure in reading, it is not merely a rhetorical device. Rather, Barthes's practice of reading reminds him of the aspects of his particular, individual, subjective, sexual pleasure, what he calls his "perversion," in opposition to the less sat-isfying "nature" and "doxa." Barthes's same-sex preference and its practice prefigure and define the ideal reading practice. Same-sex preference, whether or not it is thematized in a medieval text, is not only a legitimate contemporary way of reading (medievalist interpretation) but also a legiti-mate reading (medieval text's signification). Barthes struggles with this idea—he replaces "goddess Homosexuality" in the manuscript notes by a cryptonym, "goddess H.," in the printed version. In my view, this encrypt-ing indicates fear or shame, but also the pleasure in encrypting a sexual message and hoping to be found out, and therefore, further, the necessity of an openly homosexual reading. This folding together of fear, pleasure, and desire is best unpacked through psychoanalytic theory. My guide here is Jean Laplanche, a significant voice in French psychoanalysis, contempo-rary of Barthes and Lacan, coauthor of the *Dictionary of Psychoanalysis*. Pub-lished as a series of volumes, Laplanche's advanced university seminar on anxiety digests and problematizes issues in Freud and Lacan.[2] While Barthes scholars find that his use of psychoanalysis was not systematic, his ideas evolved in the context of Lacan's and Laplanche's work, as well as the critique of the Freudian concept of desire by Gilles Deleuze and Félix Guattari in *Anti-Oedipus* and *A Thousand Plateaus*.

A psychoanalytic approach is not the only way to ask questions con-cerning sex and gender in medieval texts. A pragmatic, narrative, or cultural studies approach would also yield interesting answers. For example, "false positionings" in terms of pragmatics (obvious, sometimes willful mistakes concerning a character's gender and sexual preference), and narrative "truth" (false accusation of same-sex preference) could suggest that same-sex preference is only a token narrative *empêchement*, a function with indif-ferent content, an obstacle of indifferent nature that separates the lovers. But the accusation of same-sex preference had to correspond to either real or imagined phenomenon for the device to work. Since the narrative con-structs meaning in a social context, these episodes point to a closeted social phenomenon. That much would be possible to say from a pragmatic, nar-rative theory, or historical standpoint. By opening up a way of speaking about repression and the unconscious, a psychoanalytic approach allows us to say that same-sex preference, even (or especially) framed as an accusation and condemned, may be indicative of desire. We could say that same-sex desire and the anxiety accompanying it are symbolized metonymically by false accusations, and metaphorically by castration. Psychoanalytic theory also shares tools with literary criticism. Such concepts as symbolization are mutually comprehensible, while the methodology of history and literary criticism can be mutually exclusive. Finally, and for me most importantly, a psychoanalytic approach allows us to account with precision for the presence of same-sex desire in the absence of same-sex themes. By work-ing out a model that accounts for the process of symbolization and its increasingly remote reformulations of the original content, psychoanalytic theory provides one of the few successful models of a hint. Proverbially attentive to the slip and other, encrypted (not rhetorical, literary, or encoded) modes of residual representation, a psychoanalytic approach promises to help with what I consider the most interesting part of my work, authorizing a queer reading not because of thematics, but because of less obvious signals such as "surplus of meaning" and overbooking of the signifying system. At the same time, psychoanalytic models can be alienat-ing. Freud articulates the functioning of castration in its relationship to same-sex desire in a manner problematic for queer theory. That is why, for instance, in chapter 1, instead of putting the Fisher King narrative in the context of the Oedipus complex and fear of castration, I focus on the com-parison with the Mother of God mourning the death of God. The points I emphasize include the somatic and wordless expression of suffering, just one aspect of the perverted or, in Kristeva's terms, paranoid configuration of the hegemonic structures of power in the two narratives (*Stabat Mater* and Fisher King).

In reading Barthes, we must accept his "indecisive" relationship to psy-choanalytic theory. Andrew Brown notes that Barthes's relationship to the scientific discourse of psychoanalysis and to other master discourses of lit-erary theory (Marxism, structuralist narratology, etc.) was marked by "a cer-tain air of provisionality, as if it would not be long before he had found a better way of describing what it was he wanted to do" (Brown, *Roland Barthes*, p. 1).[3] He attributes to Barthes a tendency to incompletely, fluidly, provisionally construct, or to deconstruct terms and methods of his own work, "refusing to be imprisoned" by them (Brown, *Roland Barthes*, pp. 1–2). Barthes deflected criticism of his theoretical positions by insisting that he was a writer rather than a theorist. The distinction may be explained when we think of Barthes's comments, in the later decades of his life, on his work from the 1960s. When he returns to a text to clarify its objectives, Barthes replaces provisionality with subjectivity. When he reveals the scaf-folding of his work, a gesture of scholarship that (we would expect) objec-tivizes it, Barthes paradoxically further subjectivises it: autobiographical detail usurps the place of a generalization. This is the case of the Ruysbroeck quote, when in his 1975 comments on *The Pleasure of the Text* (1973), Barthes uncovers the genealogy of his thoughts on the surplus of pleasure in the text. He anchors it in a reading previously destined to remain private (Ruysbroeck's book on Barthes's night table). Instead of pushing his text toward an objective, scientific reformulation of his earlier thought, Barthes goes back, tying the earlier text to readings from which it sprung. But being a writer rather than a theorist does not imply lesser legibility. Barthes's step back, his personal introspection, brings him out, into the public sphere.

A paradox: the autobiographical detail, framed as an explanation, opens the possibility of a universal reading. This is also the case, I think, with Barthes's coming out in his writings. It can be compared with his frequent habit of glossing and referencing, either in the text itself or *post facto*. Such uncovering of the genealogy of Barthes's thought and situating of theory in a matrix that can be shared, a "scientific" interpretive gesture, is accomplished by the photographs that accompany the text of *Roland Barthes par Roland Barthes* (1975). Barthes offers the reader a peek at his notes, by photographing three note cards titled, "in bed," "outside," "at a work table." Each handwritten note in the photograph ostensibly only has an illustrative value. In fact, it has key significance. Under the pretext of offering random samples of writing, one photograph presents us with a facsimile of the particular manuscript fragment where "H." (of the printed versions) is spelled out in manuscript ("*Homosexualité*"). The initial "H." appears in the subtitle of one of the sections in "Additif au plaisir du texte" (Barthes, *Roland Barthes*) and in *Le Plaisir du texte*. In print, not only is "*déesse Homosexualité*" abbreviated to "H.," it is also diluted by being pared with "hashish," not a part of the manuscript entry. The photographed note is a purloined clue, perversely hidden in full view like Poe's "purloined letter," allowing us to decrypt the "H.," the hint. The author invites us to decrypt the message, inflected by its inclusion among family photographs, and thereby promoted to the status of sign. The series includes family pictures, portraits of young Barthes, and photographs of family home and town (Bayonne). Just as these likenesses are laden with social and ideological significance, so is the note, as "posed" as the pictures of Barthes's grandparents in the photographer's studio. One does not need a degree in French to know that, in 1975, homosexuality is not of the same order of desire as beauty, youth, wealth, and social standing—meanings carried by these other family photographs. The revelation of Barthes's sexuality is of a different kind from his revelation that one of his grandmothers belonged to the fashionable Parisian elite. Although both are narcissistic confessions, owning a fashionable grandmother is ironic. Ostentatiously owning an upper-class grandmother undermines the symbolic value of having one. Only under duress, and usually to inferiors, can the upper-class status be *donné à voir*, given to understand. On the other hand, owning same-sex preference is heroic, because silencing is the condition of its tolerance (*ça se savait*, it was known). The shared similarity is that silence is the condition of both upper-class privilege and the persecution of same-sex preference. In other terms, the "unspeakability" that defines the social functioning of both upper-class status and homosexuality works to very different ideological ends. That is why we have to distinguish between the values of these two revelations in order to understand both as equally thrilling, each in its way (ironic, heroic) defying the *petit bourgeois* order.

Because of the inflection it receives by being included in the family series, the presentation is not flat, as if to create a facsimile, a convention that we are reading the original text. The note is not a photographic copy that allows us a limited communion with the original text, but rather, like a tri-dimensional object in space, it invites us to pretend that we were caught rifling through odd bits of paper on Barthes's desk. The posing effectively anchors the cryptic (there is no commentary) bit of information in Barthes's personal life, but also in what we know as desiring, sexual beings.

The encrypted message comes in two parts: text and its match, brought to the table by the reader. Barthes's biography is a clue, but "by no means the only one, or nearly so important as, for instance, my relation with Ben or Robert," to paraphrase D.A. Miller, who describes two other, in many ways similar examples of Barthes's "wink."[4]

...I was preparing my first trip to Japan. Yet if I couldn't help taking Barthes's *Empire of Signs* as a point of departure (by no means the only one, or nearly so important as, for instance, my relation with Ben or Robert) this was mainly in the precise sense of *wanting to depart* from this text, from its armchair intellectual itinerary. My aggressive intention looked less to its proof in the course of beginning Japanese I had just completed, successfully enough to guarantee that unlike Barthes I wouldn't visit Japan altogether *sans paroles*, than in the Spartacus guide I had procured to help me explore the full extent of "gay Tokyo" permitted to fall under Western eyes...I gave... high priority in my travel preparations to memorizing the landmarks of Shinjuku Ni-chome featured on the Spartacus map. . . . Putting the edge on the sexual competence that I would feel as in Japanese however dubious I pronounced to myself the words for *type* (*taipu*), *cock* (*o-chinpo*), and *rubber* (*kondomu*), with some of the same exhilaration perhaps that Emma Bovary found in murmuring, "J'ai un amant, un amant," was my recollection of how impoverished Barthes's own practice of this lexicon [in the *Empire of Signs*, Barthes talks about the only significant travel lexicon—that of a rendez-vous] appeared to be: *maybe, possible, tired, I want to sleep* were the main pos-sibilities he registered—only *headache* was lacking, I felt, to complete the pathetic picture of "the homosexual" (for once the sterilized, sterilizing term was apt) who had in fact no sexuality, in any sense that counted had no sex. So I was startled into fury when, rereading the *Empire* just before my depar-ture, I saw that Barthes, in writing of those impromptu drawings by means of which the inhabitants of Tokyo give directions to strangers, illustrated the phenomenon with a sketch map of the same area of Shinjuku Ni-chome I had just committed to memory. *Siete voi qui?* I could have said with all the

astonished rage of Dante Alighieri when he found his mentor Brunetto
Latini in that West Village bar. (*Bringing Out Roland Barthes*, pp. 4–5)

Revealing the scaffolding of the final version of *The Pleasure of the Text*,
Barthes explains the difference he sometimes makes between pleasure and
jouissance: pleasure satisfies, *jouissance* surprises by surplus enjoyment:
"*jouissance* is not that which answers to desire (the satisfied), but what surprises, exceeds, reroutes, diverts it. One must turn to the mystics to find a
good formulation of that which can so deviate the subject" (Barthes, "Roland
Barthes," 3, p. 153).[5] He then quotes Ruysbroeck: "I call inebriation of the
mind that state where the fulfillment [*jouissance*] reaches beyond the possibilities which had been anticipated by desire" ("J'appelle l'ivresse de l'esprit
cet état où la jouissance dépasse les possibilités qu'avait entrevues le désir").[6]
Sometimes, as he admits, Barthes uses pleasure and *jouissance* interchangeably. As he either amplifies or erases the difference between them,
Barthes opens the *Pleasure of the Text* ironically, complaining that, due to the
vicissitutes of French language, his terminology is condemned to indeci-
sion, contradiction, ambiguity. I find it interesting that Barthes's commentators consistently read into the distinction between pleasure and *jouissance*
the issues that they consider most relevant to their own appreciation of
Barthes's thought, as if we all identified a hot spot where the formation of
meaning occurs.[7] For Steven Ungar, the discussion of *plaisir/jouissance*
spilled into a narrative of Barthes's teaching as an idealized model of
intellectual debate, while Michael Moriarty notes that *plaisir/jouissance*
work to affirm freedom from oppressive systems of culture, class and race:

> The text, like the erotic, suspends our sense of ourselves as unified subjects:
> we have no secure identity as receivers of a message, for there is no message;
> we cannot relate to its discourse, for we do not know who is speaking and
> are confronted with bottomless possibilities of irony; the multiplicity of the
> voices we hear multiplies our response eand divides our subjectivity; the text
> violates the symbolic barriers on which our culture, and therefore our place
> in it, depend. (Moriarty, *Roland Barthes*, p. 149)[8]

It is perhaps a testimony to human limitations in conceptualizing sensual events such as pleasure that the two definitions of *jouissance* evoked by
Barthes—postmodern and medieval/mystical; his own and Ruysbroeck's—
are interchangeable. I focus on Barthes not because the two definitions are
congruent, but because Barthes puts them together. In the true spirit of
Barthes—privileging the signifier—what encourages me to use Barthes in
discussing medieval texts and their operation is not just the congruence
between the medieval and the postmodern content of the thought (ultimate *jouissance* as surplus enjoyment), but more importantly, the process of

thinking, the mechanics of Barthes's text. His quoting practice is consonant with the medieval use of citations from *auctores*, philosophical, literary, or theological authorities, conferring the ultimate confirmation of the author's own thoughts. Barthes valorizes this practice. For him, the Middle Ages are far from barbaric. The true barbarism, he suggests, is the contemporary absence of self-awareness that results in endless repetitions. It allows some modern writers to consider themselves original while all they are doing is repeating stereotypes.[9] As a model opposed to that devalorized one, in "Entretien," Barthes speaks of a literary practice that would not consist in writing works but in a "perpetual commentary" on works already written. He assimilates medieval writing to contemporary writing, as a careful reading rooted in the intellectual tradition.

Barthes's invocation of homosexuality as the specific technique to achieve absolute pleasure of the text, in all its autobiographical, subjective framing in *Roland Barthes par Roland Barthes*, can be diverted to explain the explosion effect of medieval queer studies. I am not referring here to the metaphorical usage by Barthes of a typology of contemporary homoerotic practices (rendez-vous, drague, etc.) taken up by Barthes as emblems of literary practice. They have been noted by Barthes's scholars, from Diana Knight to Andrew Brown.[10] Rather, I want to ask a more general question: Why is queer theory so pertinent to deconstruction, and why has it become a significant way of reading medieval texts? What is the purpose of queer readings, other than, for instance, perversely outing nuns, not only against their communal will, but also against other modern readings with better cultural acceptance rates; to say nothing of the status of same-sex desire and subjectivity during the medieval period, constantly put into question? Linking his bodily experience to his reading practice ("the text of life, the life as text"), Barthes gives an answer that grants queer readings a text-based legitimacy. "Homosexuality" is for Barthes not only a "perversion," a pleasure, but also a pattern or a device, the very means to understanding that is guaranteed to procure *jouissance*, a means to transcendence:

> The power of *jouissance* from a perversion (in this case, the two H's: homosexuality and hashish) is always underestimated. The Law, the Doxa, the Science don't want to admit that perversion simply *makes one happy*; or, to be more precise, it produces a surplus: I am more sensitive, more perceptive, more talkative, better entertained, etc.; and in this *surplus* lies the difference (and therefore, the text of life, the life as text). Hence, it is a goddess, an invokable figure, a mode of intercession. (Barthes, "Roland Barthes," in *Oeuvres complètes* 3, p. 143)[11]

Barthes's use of the term "perversion" deserves an explanation. His use of the term "perversion" is as fluid and "indecisive" as his distinction between *plaisir* and *jouissance*. In my view, it falls into what Barthes himself calls his "indecisive" citation of analytical terminology. As he says: "[h]is rapport to psychoanalysis is not scrupulous (however, he cannot pride himself on any specific contestation, any refusal). It is an indecisive rapport." (Barthes, "Roland Barthes," in: *Oeuvres complètes* 3, p. 209).[12] Perversion as supreme pleasure, as surplus of pleasure, resonates with what Barthes says about difference (pp. 147–48), and his insistence on disseminating the binary opposition passive–active (pp. 196–97) as well as his insistence on plural homosexualities (p. 209). It seems clear that Barthes uses the word *perversion* simultaneously in its psychoanalytical sense—all sexual pleasure is perversion, all desire is a perverted need, because sexual pleasure (sucking for pleasure) perverts basic survival needs (suckling for sustenance); and in its popular acceptance of a transgressive sexual desire. To invest it with scientific precision, to take it back to Freud and Lacan and thereby to clarify it, is not what he intended.

At the close of *Le Plaisir du texte*, Barthes makes a typology of readerly pleasures and labels them all as sexual pleasures, and he only evokes the neurotic ones:

> We can imagine a typology of the pleasures of reading—or of the readers of pleasure; it would not be sociological, for pleasure is not an attribute of either product or production; it could only be psychoanalytic, linking the reading neurosis to the hallucinated form of the text. The fetishist would be matched with the divided-up text, the singling out of quotations, formulae, turns of phrase, with the pleasure of the word. The obsessive would experience the voluptuous release of the letter, of secondary, disconnected languages, of metalanguages (this class would include all the logophiles, linguists, semioticians, philologists: all those for whom language *returns*). A paranoiac would consume or produce complicated texts, stories developed like arguments, constructions posited like games, like secret constraints. As for the hysteric (so contrary to the obsessive), he would be the one who takes the text *for ready money*, who joins in the bottomless, truthless comedy of language, who is no longer the subject of any critical scrutiny and *throws himself* across the text (which is quite different from projecting himself into it). (Barthes, *The Pleasure of the Text*, p. 63)[13]

Privileging neurosis in the act of reading is linked to Barthes's definition of the writer. Barthes transforms a well-known royal *devise* ("prince ne daigne, empereur ne puis, roi suis") into "fou ne puis, sain ne daigne, névrosé je suis" [mad I cannot be, healthy I don't deign to be, I am neurotic] (Barthes, *Le Plaisir du texte*, p. 87). This privileging of neurosis is playful and serious at the same time. It plays on the popular acceptation of the deviant, the transgressive, the neurotic, the pervert, and it makes light of scientific psychoanalytic definitions by valorizing neurosis.[14] Deleuze and Guattari's critique of Freud adopts similar means to similar ends.

I now examine Barthes's "winks," encrypted hints, in the framework of psychoanalysis, and suggest parallels with medieval texts. Commenting on Barthes's use of the word "perversion"—what Barthes elsewhere calls writer's neurosis, and still elsewhere ultimate *jouissance*—Brown notes that in psychoanalytic theory, "[s]exuality is not something that may or may not become perverted, depending on the vicissitudes of the life of the psyche: it is always already perverted in so far as it is founded in the moment of mimicry and separation that begins in the process of anaclitic propping," the process whereby "an infantile sexual manifestation [for instance, suck-ing for pleasure] *"attaches itself to* [or 'props itself upon'; *entsteht in Anlehnung an*] one of the vital somatic functions" (i.e. sucking to feed) (Brown, *Roland Barthes*, p. 99). In Freud, desire is essentially a perverted need. This coupling of desire and perversion is emphasized by Lacanian distinction between dif-ferent stages of the development of a human being, first the "need" stage (pre-Symbolic, the Real) and then the "demand" and "desire" stage marked by two developments: entry into the imaginary and initiation into the Symbolic Order (language). If the first stage is that of the Mother and needs are satisfied because they are "real" (breast, milk), the second stage is that of the Father. The passage is initiated by the first instance of representation—a Mother showing the child its reflection in the mirror and commenting that the reflection in the mirror "is" the child. In actuality, the image in the mirror (the imaginary self) defers the child's self and makes it unattainable: it is the child, but better, more coherent, whole. Elsewhere, Lacan calls this imago an armor, an external skeleton, a prosthesis. The "mirror stage," or the development of the split subject (self and mirror image) is concomitant with the development of desire, initiation into language, and the institution of the Imaginary (no longer "needs" satisfied without language as in the realm of the "real").

I find it useful for legitimating my approach in this section that the dif-ference between need and desire is assimilated by Barthes to the relation that Ruysbroeck establishes between humanity and the Divine. In the con-text of Ruysbroeck in *Fragments d'un discours amoureux*, Barthes notes two gestures, "ideograms" that compose the narrative of the passage from need to desire and articulate the place of the phallus: "The discourse of Absence is a text with two ideograms: there are *the raised arms of Desire* and *the extended arms of Need*. I oscillate, I vacillate between the phallic image of raised arms and the baby image of extended arms" (Barthes, *Fragments d'un discours amoureux*, *"L'Absent,"* in *Oeuvres Complètes* 3, p. 472). It is as if Barthes reproduced the ambiguity that he maintains in the use of the terms pleasure and *jouissance*, in his use of Lacanian difference between desire and need. Kristeva's reflection that love is the fantasy of the (impossible) return to the pre-Symbolic, the maternal, an incest (chapter 1 in this book), anticipates what I read as the pathos of Barthes's image: vacillation, not a form of becoming, is the human condition.

Desires belong in the realm of the imaginary. The necessity to express desire motivates the child's long apprenticeship of the order of representation, the Symbolic Order of the Father. Lacan's mirror stage is the starting point of a narrative of socialization that combines initiation into language, split subjectivity, and the economy of lack that marks the passage from satisfiable needs (fusion with the Mother) to unattainable desires. Lacan's model of the chain of deferrals (or symbolizations) anchored in a fantasmatic nonessence (the Phallus), by definition unattainable (because nonexistent) explains in conjunction the uses of representation and the process of socialization and formation of an individual. Lacan's narrative of the process of symbolization further allows us to relate psychoanalysis to structuralist linguistics and fruitfully theorize its relationship to language. In *Literary Debate*, Denis Hollier and Jeffrey Mehlman have succintly pointed out the historical moment of interaction between the two theories—structuralist linguistics and psychoanalysis—a moment that, by all accounts, culminated in the mid-1960s.[15] As Hollier and Mehlman note, the excesses of the structuralist "unified theory" combining psychoanalysis and linguistics are resolved in poststructuralism:

> In structuralism's imperialist phase, efforts were made to articulate linguistic difference (à la Saussure) with sexual difference (à la Freud)—as though the castration complex managed to embody the structuralist lesson traumatically, indeed apocalyptically, in the flesh. One could no more attain psychical—or structuralist—maturity without coming to terms with the castration complex than Althusser's Marx could accede to *his* maturity without submission to the blade of a *coupure épistémologique*. (Indeed, the case can be made that one cut was a direct borrowing from the other.) Before long, however, it appeared that the investment in (castratory) difference was less threateningly liberating, as structuralism would have it, than merely inhibitory in its conventionality. The working through of that insight marks the transition from structuralism to post-structuralism. . . .(*Literary Debate*, p. 329)

The selection of texts following this historical vignette addresses the "shifting fate of a keystone concept:'castration.' " It includes, among others, Laplanche's digest of Freud (discussed below), and Deleuze and Guattari's *Anti-Oedipus*.[16] Deleuze and Guattari's intervention is brilliant in their intimate understanding of Freud's thought and irreverent in their willingness to contest Freud's fundamental idea. It addresses the popular definition of perversion (deviant sexuality), as well the psychoanalytical definition (all sexuality is a perversion of essential needs), which reminds me of Barthes's use of "perversion." Deleuze and Guattari remove castration from its central position in Freud's narrative of the child's socialization, and reposition it where Freud initially thought its place would be: as one of the many symbolic substitutions in an undifferentiated chain. After this geneticist/archivist move comes a paradox and a revolution: Deleuze and Guattari point out that fear of castration is not so much the central episode of a child's socialization, but rather the central operation of Freud's discourse on sexuality. They liken the operation of the castration complex in psychoanalysis to religious asceticism: "purely mythical. . .like the One in negative theology, it introduces lack into desire and causes exclusive series to emanate, to which it attributes a goal, and a path of resignation." Portraying fear of castration as part of an ascetic setup designed to elicit resignation, and likening Freudian and Lacanian psychoanalysis to theology is very effective. That comparison already lurks in the popular perception: the talking cure displacing the confessional practices of the Catholic Church, the analyst as a priest of the Psyche.[17] Deleuze and Guattari follow with their own desideratum, in a skillful narrative where their own model (desiring-machines) is presented as a historical origin, a "golden age" of desire coerced and preempted by the invasion of Freud's totalizing model:

> We must speak of "castration" in the same way we speak of oedipalization, whose crowning moment it is: castration designates the operation by which psychoanalysis castrates the unconscious, injects castration into the unconscious. Castration as a practical operation on the unconscious is achieved when the thousand break-flows of desiring-machines—all positive, all productive—are projected into the same mythical space, the unary stroke of the signifier. (cited in *Literary Debate*, p. 344)

Deleuze and Guattari successfully address the issue of sexual difference: Freud's decision not to theorize male and female socialization as symmetrical and equivalent, but as variations of the same (male) model. Freud firmly guards his specific form of Oedipus complex against interventions, for instance, those of Melanie Klein. No Electra complex is necessary, Freud explicitly says, to explain the socialization of an individual. As Deleuze and Guattari point out, this decision is linked to Freud's heteronormative definition of desire and sexuality. Their approach to the question is particularly direct. They observe a "fallacy" in Freud's logic, relevant to all further definitions and positionings: part (penis) becomes whole (phallus). Rooting the discussion of Freud's intransigence in the undeniable, self-evident physical reality of the body is a skillful move. Deleuze and Guattari point out the flawed logic that motivates Freud's decision, and they offer a very plausible explanation for it: Freud's limitations in imagining anything but heterosexuality as the norm:

> Freud had a concept at his disposal for stating this contrary notion—the concept of bisexuality; and it was not by chance that he was never able or never wanted to give this concept the analytical position and extension it required. . . .
>
> Here we have a properly analytical fallacy (which will be found again, to a considerable degree, in the theory of the signifier) that consists in passing from the detachable partial object [penis] to the position of a complete object as the thing detached (phallus). This passage implies a subject, defined as a fixed ego of one sex or the other, who necessarily experiences as a lack his subordination to the tyrannical complete object. This is perhaps no longer the case when the partial object is posited for itself on the body without organs, with—as its sole subject—not an "ego," but the drive that forms the desiring-machine along with it, and that enters into relationships of connection, disjunction, and conjunction with other partial objects, at the core of corresponding multiplicity whose every element can only be defined *positively*. (*Literary Debate*, p. 344)

If Deleuze and Guattari make a good case against Freud and for the recovery of polymorphous pleasures (for Freud, relegated to infancy), of infinitely gradated sexual differences (in the plural), of correspondingly multiple sexual pleasures and desires (for Freud, relegated to the status of regressions), it seems to me that the promise and the momentum of their thought has been absorbed into what Hollier and Mehlman, in their introduction, identify as "May '68 enthusiasm" (*Literary Debate*, p. 343). Just as May '68 intellectuals passed from revolutionary corps to the establishment, and the unique historical moment over which they presided became assimilated as just another entry in the chronicle of great expectations, Deleuze and Guattari's *Anti-Oedipus* occupies a place on the sidelines, not in the center of Freud-related approaches. The impact of their thought is diminished by its assimilation to theoretical relics of sexual liberation, because of the resistance (mixed with condescension or nostalgia) that the label "sexual liberation" frequently inspires. To me, it seems that the concept of desiring-machines has much wider applications than its "thematized" use in cyber-queer contexts. Deleuze and Guattari's thought presents an answer to some of the problems that arise in queer readings based on Freudian or Lacanian psychoanalysis, as even their critics point out:

> Freud, as a modernist thinker still committed to Enlightenment assumptions, stressed that the rational regulation of sexuality and desire was necessary to civilized life, despite the inevitable "discontents" that accompany civilization

as a result. Against such supposedly outmoded modernist assumptions, ludic (post)modern theory produces an atmosphere of sexual deregulation. . . . In this new space, desire is regarded as autonomous—unregulated and unencumbered. The shift is evident in the contrast between the model of necessary sexual regulation promoted by Freud in *Civilization and its Discontents* and the notion of sexual deregulation proposed by Gilles Deleuze and Félix Guattari. Deleuze and Guattari represent the deregulating process—in which desire becomes a space of "pure intensities" (*A Thousand Plateaus*, p. 4)—as a breakthrough beyond the Oedipus complex (that "grotesque triangle" [Anti-Oedipus, p. 171]), which colonizes the subject and restricts desire. Since the oedipal model is explicitly heterosexual, its supercession appeals particularly to many queer theorists, who take up the call for sexual deregulation. (Morton, "Birth of the Cyberqueer," pp. 370–71)[18]

Morton's 1995 critique of queer in particular and "ludic postmodernism" in general as socially and politically irresponsible culminates in his portrayal of "virtual, post-al spaces supposedly beyond historical consciousness where those who can afford it choose their reality," and where "postgay queerity and postleft political cyberpunk are the latest forms of bourgeois idealism" (Morton, "Birth of the Cyberqueer," p. 377). Time has proven Morton wrong: gay and lesbian thrive as personal and political categories, and cyberqueer is by no means the primary queer figure. But he was right about the reception of Deleuze and Guattari. His view of their work as "ludic"(which seems to be Morton's code word for "ethically or politically irresponsible") is shared, though perhaps undeserved.

I am interested in Barthes's *Pleasure of the Text* among other things because it is marked by queer hints, for instance, the semi-obscure reference to "the H. goddess." To understand the hint it is necessary to define its work, to assess the force of the prohibition against which it pushes, to describe the silencing imperative against which it displays its content. But these, as it were, constitute the hint on the outside. The key concepts inherent to the hint are anxiety and desire, and no one serves as a better guide through them than Freud and Laplanche. Laplanche focuses on the "crucial moment when the affect, cut off from the repressed primary representation, seeks to express itself on its own. And when it manifests itself in this way, cut off from its representation, it simultaneously loses the qualitative property of being this or that affect and becomes pure 'quantity,' or the aggression of the drive in its naked state, in the form of anxiety." This model allows us to focus on "the moment of desymbolized affect that falls between two contrasting moments in which the affect is bound to representations." This is the main point for Laplanche. The transition between the symbols in the process of successive symbolization is not seamless. There is a gap after one symbol is lost and another not yet acquired. It is into that interstice that anxiety introduces itself: "the moments of desymbolization in the transition from one symbol to another are absolutely essential and impossible to miss: the moment after a symbol is lost and before another one is found is the moment of anxiety, of that 'free-floating anxiety' which Freud sought to identify" (Laplanche, *Problématiques* 2, p. 341). First, Laplanche notes: "in this theory there is not just displacement from one representation to another. The representation has changed, to be sure, but the affect has also metamorphosed to the point where it is unrecognizable—from love of the father to fear of the horse." Freud's narrative of anxiety and desire is emblematized by two stories: the first, *fort-da*, of his nephew rolling out and reeling back a spool attached to a piece of string, reenacting the absence of his mother (anxiety) as the absence of the spool, in a safe way, since he is in full control, able to recall the absent by simply pulling the string. Freud's other example, the transformation of sexual desire for the father into anxiety about a horse, shows a similar operation at work. For Laplanche, this example is of great importance, because it shows that external danger (the domestic horse is a huge animal that can kill a man, let alone a child) is not the cause of anxiety. On the contrary, replacing desire for the father with fear of the horse circumscribes that fear, gives it limits, both in time and space, and makes it possible to bear: "once the anxiety-provoking animal is placed in the streets of Vienna, certain quite concrete steps can be taken to confine the anxiety to a particular time and place." Desire for the father is internal, an always present threat. The horse, on the other hand, is external, confined to a particular time and place, and can be avoided. Second, Laplanche points out that Freud's early work shows "anxiety. . .associated not with the repressed but with the forces of repression." Freud says: "It is anxiety that produces repression, not as I formerly thought repression that produces anxiety." That is, again, fundamental for Laplanche, even though in his later work Freud leans again toward the association between anxiety and external danger. Laplanche, on the other hand, insists that tying phobia to an external danger is a mistake. He is specific that such "behavioralist" or "rationalist" explanations of phobias are wrong. He believes that the key to understanding phobias is in acknowledging that it is the desire itself that is dangerous. Not the horse, but the desire for the father is the most fearsome; not an external, but an internal danger. Positing an external danger as the cause of anxiety evacuates the notion that Laplanche believes is central: "the notion of a primary internal danger of aggression by the drive which constantly threatens to transform itself into anxiety and which needs to be symbolized."

Then, Laplanche summarizes Freud's solutions concerning the relationship between drive and anxiety. The first is easy to follow. In the example of the horse, instead of becoming completely symbolized, anxiety is now tied to an external danger. Therefore, anxiety is reduced in time and space to the presence of that external danger, and possible to manage. Instead of a powerful internal danger, we have a relatively small, manageable external danger. Anxiety now plays another role as well: "a 'yellow light' that prevents a greater danger from arising." As Laplanche notes, anxiety functions as an index ("yellow light"), and therefore "finds itself on the side of the signifier" instead of, as Freud thought, on the side of the signified. That is the most interesting displacement, in terms of my application of Laplanche's explanation of phobias to reading episodes of castration in medieval romance. In the most reductive terms, this displacement from signified to signifier allows me to say that what is at stake in the episodes of genital wounding is not castration (that's a signifier), but same-sex desire (the signified). And, in its functioning as a "yellow light," the fear of castration can be replaced by its metaphor, heterosexual transgression (uxoriousness, philandering), or its metonymies, effeminacy, eunuchism, and other phenomena that transgress the virile norm (perfuming one's beard or curling one's hair, depilation). Metaphors and metonymies function as "a 'yellow light' that prevents a greater danger from arising": same-sex desire.

Another distinction needs to be emphasized as well. Laplanche is careful to note that anxiety is an index of desire ("yellow light"). The "yellow light" and other metaphors Laplanche uses ("signal," "mark") designate anxiety as an index (not a symbol), as part of a code (not a language)—as Laplanche says, on the side of signifier, not signified. This too has consequences for my application. If we say that castration in a text is not a symbol but rather an index, it means that castration does not need to function in the text on all the levels associated with the symbolic. It does not have to "make sense" in all the ways in which a symbol plugs into different levels of meaning. Its role as a signal, not symbol, may also mean that in the economy of the narrative, its presence is correspondingly limited. Since it is a signal and not a symbol, anxiety does not have to be essential to the narrative of desire (romance), quite the opposite: it may be secondary to the main plot. This hypothesis encourages me to look for castration (eunuchism, effeminacy, uxoriousness, philandering) as a signal of same-sex desire when it has a minor role in the narrative, as is frequently the case.

Characteristically, the hero is accused of same-sex preference by mistake or in bad faith. In the majority of cases, same-sex preference is bundled with condemnation. In the economy of the narrative, it is only a device, not a "real danger" (Lavinia's mother's invectives against Eneas); only a strategy to get to the truth, not the truth (the queen accusing Lanval of same-sex preference); only a mistaken supposition, not an actuality (Lavinia mistakenly thinking that Eneas does not love her and prefers men); only a way to save face, not the real reason (Conon de Bethune's lady rejected by her suitor, accusing him of same-sex preference). This persistent "false" positioning of same-sex preference in medieval romance and lyric poetry should not be mistaken for absence of same-sex preference. "Don't walk on the grass" signs do not advertise the fact that we, as a society, don't walk on the grass. The signs are there because kids will commonly do it, in spite of what their mothers have taught them.

If the fact that prohibitions document the occurrence of that which they prohibit is self-evident, psychoanalysis provides the tools to think through the complex relationship between anxiety and desire in literary representations. In Laplanche's discussion of Freud's different solutions to the problem of anxiety, we notice that Laplanche privileges the solutions where Freud relates anxiety directly to drive, and not indirectly to the punishment of the drive. Laplanche notes that the drive is as much for sexual pleasure as it is for anxiety. In other words, anxiety produces pleasure. The operative rule is no longer "if you seek pleasure, you will be castrated." Instead, "anxiety is described as a substitute for love." Laplanche's use of metaphor—anxiety is love's "other face"—recalls the Saussurian definition of the sign as two sides of the same piece of paper (the signified is the signifier's "other face"). Anxiety and desire are linked in a similar way. For Laplanche, the result is a double functioning of the "yellow light": "getting close to danger" and "getting close to pleasure." That is where we see the utility of Laplanche's distinction between "yellow light" as signifier and as signified: "Why does the subject cling to his symptom in this context? Not just because his symptom is a first line of defense against anxiety: the symptom is loved because of the anxiety it triggers, because this anxiety itself is associated with the drive, with pleasure" (cited in *Literary Debate*, p. 339).

The idea that "getting close to danger" feels like "getting close to pleasure" could well be the shortest definition of "narrative." *Perceval* and the texts that frame same-sex preference as an "unjust accusation" exhibit this close relationship between anxiety and pleasure, and one could say the same of any actualization of the heroic condition (the hero, by definition, gets in trouble, and therefore is in the position of anxiety associated with drive), of suspense, or of reader's omniscience: the reader knows how to solve the problems of the hero, but is outside of the story—at the same time close and infinitely far away. The texts that represent anxiety concerning castration and same-sex preference are no different. Perceval learns too late that he could have healed the Fisher King by asking a certain question. The missed opportunity for heroic actualization is like a drive, in that it is just out of reach and desirable. In Conon de Béthune, *Lanval*, *De nugis curialium*, and *Enéas*, same-sex preference is wrongly imputed to the hero. For the secondary character who articulates it, same-sex desire, bundled with condemnation, serves as a rationalization for having been rejected. It disguises the love object as a wrong love object (in each case, this is just a disguise), allowing the rejected character to redirect rejection from self to the other. In these "unjust accusation" narratives, the reader, who sides with the hero, is in the position of Perceval: unable to do anything but tantalizingly aware that the accusation is ill-founded, that it can be "repaired." The reader experiences anxiety on behalf of the hero who is in danger, at a close but irreducible distance from resolution.

After presenting the imbricated relationship of anxiety to desire, Laplanche focuses on "the problem of symbolization. . . .in the context of regression"—a rich subject, he observes—"and in terms of different levels of symbolization" (Laplanche, *Probématiques* 2, p. 339). Laplanche summarizes the importance for Freud of Otto Rank's view that all anxieties (e.g., the fear of castration), are "forms of camouflage," substitutes for birth trauma. As Laplanche observes, while Rank describes the relations between different anxieties as camouflage or simple substitution leading to the "common denominator," the ur-anxiety, that is "the primordial separation" experienced as the trauma of birth, Freud shows how anxieties, instead of simple substitution, are related by "elaboration or symbolization," and become "progressively richer." As a result of that progression, "affect and representation become increasingly independent of each other." This is very important for my argument, because it explains why hints of same-sex desire are independent, thematically and in other ways, from their signified. That is, the symbolization of same-sex desire need not have anything to do with same-sex desire. Subsequently, rather than for an overall thematic bent, it is productive to look for an affective bent, as I propose to do when I look at episodes that are oddly disjointed, seemingly unconnected, and in general share one characteristic only: they do not seem to fit the narrative economy. For me, these episodes express both to what extent same-sex desire is repressed, and on the other hand how impossible it is to erase the remainder of it. The traces that are most hermetic can be the most telling, but they also stretch the limits of credibility of my "cryptology," because the linking is not thematic, but instead heavily dependent on my interpretation.

Laplanche continues his description of the "chain of anxieties," which works like a chain of signifiers in the Lacanian model of apprenticeship in language and the Symbolic Order. The initial "anxiety situation" (birth) "is not experienced as a situation—it is a situation without representative content," and it anchors the "series of separations" in a reality that eludes representation. Laplanche then points out that the description of loss and its internalization in *The Problem of Anxiety* is completed in Freud's *Mourning and Melancholia*, where the loss leads to introjection, and the desire for the object turns into anxiety concerning the "shadow of the object" or, in Melanie Klein, "the bad object." Laplanche praises the elegance of Freud's model of anxiety, and now for the first time mentions that the origin of anxiety is "seemingly tangible. . .to the problem of the symbol" (p. 340).

It is a space where signifier and signified are fused ("symbol and symbolized, affect and representation, are coalesced as one"). Another tangibility emphasized by Laplanche between the operation of anxiety and symbolization concerns the status of the "symbolized thing," the affect or "X." It is, as Laplanche notes, "ultimately no more than a postulate" (p. 341). Finally, Laplanche insists on the moments of anxiety that correspond to "the moments of desymbolization. . . .after a symbol is lost and before another is found" (p. 341). Then, he observes the fundamental fact in Deleuze and Guattari's critique of Freud: castration, initially meant to be one symbolization among many, has become the ideal successful symbolization: "ineluctably, however, in the thought of both Freud and later analysts such as Lacan, this phase has tended to become the ultimate form of all psychic organization" (cited in *Literary Debate*, p. 341).

Laplanche's discussion of castration has the effect of highlighting its local (as opposed to universal) significance. Acceptance of castration is the end of the psychoanalytic cure, at least in theory: "If castration is not ignored by the unconscious, at least in the form of anxiety, in the core of some phantasms, it often seems that unconscious ignores the regulatory effects of castration which should theoretically lead to a perfect harmony, to a clear differentiation between the sexes, and to the 'right' to free exercise of sexuality" (Laplanche, *Problématiques* 2, p. 237).[19] If the full acceptance of castration as regulatory principle is the end of the cure, *Perceval* is the founding myth of an opposite regulatory system, where the dichotomy homo/hetero vanishes. In *Perceval*, castration is represented as a fault to be repaired. If we follow Laplanche's reading of Freud, the expected outcome of *this* foundation myth would be a blurring of the differentiation between the sexes, authorizing the erasure of differentiation based on the preference for one or the other sex, and the reestablishment of same-sex desire as an undifferentiated companion of opposite-sex desire.

I do not want to say that the medieval communal subject or its cultural icons are legible thanks to psychoanalysis, any more than I want to assimilate medieval subjectivity (if and how it exists) to the modern. On the contrary, I strongly suspect that the desire to become a medievalist is anchored in the fantasy that our texts will never "feel familiar." In subjective terms, I believe in all my hypotheses, like Barthes: "but I can always quote myself to signify an insistence, an obsession, since my own body is in question" (Barthes, *Oeuvres complètes* 3, p. 153). To those who would refuse me this authority and ask that I state my ethics in objective terms, I would reply that the question of the legitimacy of this conclusion is the same as the question of the legitimacy of queer readings of medieval texts, and the answer to both is theoretically unavailable because it is still fragmentary in practice. That does not delegitimize the practice, quite the contrary: it extends its mandate.

NOTES

Introduction   History of Desire, Desire for History

1. The miniatures (28 in all) seem to me unexceptional column-wide boxes dominated by blue, standard for manuscripts of this type. The programme is described by the editor: Jehan Maillart, *Le Roman du comte d'Anjou*, ed. Mario Roques (Paris: Champion, 1931), pp. 249–53. The scenes represent women consoling each other (the nurse consoling the young countess of Anjou), suffering together (nurse and countess fugitives in the forest), receiving shelter and care (arrival at the first widow's house; the countess's, then the count's encounter with the charitable bourgeoise of Etampes; joyful reception by the mistress of Hôtel Dieu), bidding farewell (departure from the first widow's house), patrons giving the poor women employment (the knight and his wife bidding the countess and her nurse to come to the castle), assisting in the happy ending (the mistress of Hôtel Dieu at the reunion of the spouses), receiving rewards (bourgeoise and mistress of Hôtel Dieu receive gold cups from the countess).

2. C. Stephen Jaeger, *Ennobling Love: In Search of a Lost Sensibility* (Philadelphia: University of Pennsylvania Press, 1999).

3. Max J. Exner, *The Question of Petting* (New York: Association Press, 1926). The title page lists the author's position as the director of the Department of Educational Measures of the American Social Hygiene Association, and notes: "Prepared and Distributed under the direction of The National Council of the Young Men's Christian Associations and the American Social Hygiene Association," and published "in response to an urgent demand."

4. See D.A. Miller, *Bringing Out Roland Barthes* (Berkeley: University of California Press, 1992), pp. 18–28. I would like to thank the Press Reader for pointing out this and a number of other references. Roland Barthes. *Oeuvres Complètes*. Ed. Eric Marty Paris: Seuil, 1993–95. 3 vols.

5. Judith Bennett, " 'Lesbian-Like' and the Social History of Lesbianisms," *Journal of the History of Sexuality* 9:1–2 (January/April 2000), pp. 1–24.

6. Allen J. Frantzen, *Before the Closet: Same-Sex Love from* Beowulf *to* Angels in America (Chicago: The University of Chicago Press, 1998).

7. John Boswell, *Same-Sex Unions in Pre-Modern Europe* (New York: Villard Books, 1994); Craig A. Williams, *Roman Homosexuality: Ideologies of Masculinity in Classical Antiquity* (Oxford: Oxford University Press, 1999).

Saara Lilja, *Homosexuality in Republican and Augustan Rome* (Helsinki, Finland: Societas Scientiarum Fennica, 1983); David M. Halperin, *How to do the History of Homosexuality* (Chicago: The University of Chicago Press, 2002); Amy Richlin, *The Garden of Priapus: Sexuality and Aggression in Roman Humor* (New Haven: Yale University Press, 1983). It is important to note mutual strong criticism of the other's approach in the case of David Halperin and Amy Richlin. See Halperin, *How to Do the History of Homosexuality*, n. 33, pp. 165–67.

8. Carolyn Dinshaw, *Getting Medieval: Sexualities and Communities, Pre- and Postmodern* (Durham and London: Duke University Press, 1999).

9. Josiah Blackmore and Gregory S. Hutcheson, eds., *Queer Iberia: Sexualities, Cultures, and Crossings from the Middle Ages to the Renaissance* (Durham : Duke University Press, 1999).

10. I want to thank Sven Erik Rose for his comments on the question of desire vs. acts, a paragraph that I borrow verbatim.

11. Jonathan Goldberg, *Sodometries: Renaissance Texts, Modern Sexualities* (Stanford: Stanford University Press, 1992).

12. Goldberg's description of the political crisis that brought down Piers Gaveston has some elements of this scenario.

13. Alan Bray, "Homosexuality and the Signs of Male Friendship in Elizabethan England," *History Workshop Journal* 29 (1990), pp. 1–19, and Cynthia Herrup, "The Patriarch at Home: The Trial of the 2nd Earl of Castlehaven for Rape and Sodomy," *History Workshop Journal* 41 (1996), pp. 1–18.

14. See Bennett, " 'Lesbian-Like,' " for a summary of criticisms and her answers concerning the use of the term.

15. Simon Gaunt, "From Epic to Romance: Gender and Sexuality in the Roman d'Eneas," *Romanic Review* 83:1 (January 1992), pp. 1–27.

16. Simon Gaunt, "Straight Minds/Queer Wishes in Old French Hagiography: La Vie de Sainte Euphrosine," *GLQ: A Journal of Lesbian and Gay Studies* 1:4 (1995), pp. 439–57.

17. Sahar Amer, "Lesbian sex and the Military: From Medical Arabic Tradition to French Literature," in Pamela Sheingorn and Francesca Canadé Sautman, *Same-Sex Love and Desire Among Women in the Middle Ages* (New-York: Palgrave, 2001), pp. 179–98.

18. Bennett's citation refers to Gerda Lerner, *The Creation of Feminist Consciousness* (Oxford: Clarendon Press. New York: Oxford University Press, 1993), p. 179; Jo Ann Kay McNamara, *Sisters in Arms: Catholic Nuns through Two Millenia* (Cambridge, Mass.: Harvard University Press, 1996) and, on the other hand, Ann Matter, "My Sister, My Spouse: Woman-Identified Women in Medieval Christianity," *Journal of Feminist Studies in Religion* 2:2 (1986), pp. 81–93, and Karma Lochrie, "Mystical Acts, Queer Tendencies," in *Constructing Medieval Sexuality*, ed. Karma Lochrie, Peggy McCracken, and James A. Schultz (Minneapolis: University of Minnesota Press, 1997), pp. 180–200.

19. SSHMA panel on queer theory at the International Medieval Congress in Kalamazoo, May 2001.

-->

20. Judith Butler. *Bodies That Matter: On the Discursive Limits of "Sex"* (New York: Routledge, 1993). Robert Sturges. *Chaucer's Pardoner and Gender Theory: Bodies of Discourse* (New York: Saint Martin's Press, 2000). Dinshaw, *Getting Medieval*, Glenn Burger, *Chaucer's Queer Nation* (Minneapolis: University of Minnesota Press, 2003), "Doing what comes Naturally: The Physician's Tale and the Pardoner," in *Masculinities in Chaucer: Approaches to Maleness in the Canterbury Tales and Troilus and Criseyde*, ed. Peter G. Beidler (Cambrige: D.S. Brewer, 1998), pp. 117–130, "Kissing the Pardoner," *PMLA* 107:5 (1992), pp. 1143–56, Vern L. Bullough, "Medical Masculinities and Modern Interpretations: The problem of the Pardoner," in *Conflicted Identities and Multiple Masculinities: Men in the Medieval West*, ed. Jacqueline Murray (New York: Garland, 1999), pp. 93–110, and Michael Calabrese, " 'Make a Mark That Shows': Orphean Song, Orphean Sexuality, and the Exile of Chaucer's Pardoner," *Viator* 24 (1993), pp. 269–86. Judith Butler's related notion of sedimention in *Bodies That Matter* has been exploited by Robert Sturges in *Chaucer's Pardoner.*
21. Mark D. Jordan, *The Invention of Sodomy in Christian Theology* (Chicago: University of Chicago Press, 1997).
22. Noah D. Guynn, "Eternal Flame: State Formation, Deviant Architecture, and the Monumentality of Same-Sex Eroticism in the Roman d'Eneas," *GLQ: A Journal of Lesbian and Gay Studies* 6:2 (2000), pp. 287–319.
23. David M. Halperin, "How to Do The History of Male Homosexuality," *GLQ: A Journal of Lesbian and Gay Studies* 6:1 (2000), pp. 87–123.
24. I want to acknowledge that putting power in question, an idea that a number of readers found exciting, was suggested by Jim Creech.
25. Bennett, "Lesbian-Like," n. 27, p. 11.

Chapter 1   Grail Narratives: Castration as a Thematic Site

1. All quotations from *Perceval* are from the Pléiade edition, Chrétien de Troyes, *Oeuvres Complètes*, ed. Daniel Poirion et al. (Paris: Gallimard, 1994). All translations are mine.
2. Maarten Jozef Vermaseren, *Cybele and Attis : The Myth and the Cult.* Trans. A.M.H. Lemmers (London : Thames and Hudson, 1977).
3. Quoted in: Joan Cadden, *Meaning of Sex Difference in the Middle Ages: Medicine, Science, and Culture* (Cambridge: Cambridge University Press, 1995), pp. 49–50.
4. All quotations of *City of God* are from: Saint Augustine, *The City of God Against the Pagans*, ed. and trans. George E. McCracken et al. (Loeb Classical Library. Cambridge, Mass.: Harvard University Press, 1966, 7 vols.). All quotations from Raoul de Presles's translation and gloss of Saint Augustine's *City of God* are from MS 9015 (. 1445), Bibliothèque Royale de Belgique, Brussels. In my transcription, expanded abbreviations are underlined, and paragraph marks, folios, and columns are indicated in parentheses. All translations are mine.
5. Chrétien de Troyes, *Perceval le Gallois: ou, Le conte du Graal. Chrétien de Troyes. Publié d'après les manuscrits originaux*, ed. Ch. Potvin (Geneva: Slatkine Reprints, 1977) (includes continuations by Gauthier de Denet and Manessier).

6. Please note that in my translation of Raoul de Presles, I privilege legibility over word-for-word accuracy (among others, I regularly render demonstrative pronouns as definite articles). For instance, the first sentence of the commentary quoted below, I translated as "In the 26th chapter, lord Saint Augustine shows how disgusting were the rites of the great Mother of Gods, especially one of her rituals which Varro and the others do not describe." Literally, the text reads: "In this 26th chapter lord Saint Augustine shows the filthiness of the rite which was done for this great mother of gods. Especially of one rite which was done for her of which Varro or another does not give any description/explanation."

7. Qui mout le vit sinple et plorant, / Et vit jusqu'au manton colant / L'eve qui des ialz li degote [Who saw him simple and weeping, and saw the water dripping from his eyes, flowing all the way to his chin] (ll. 6351–53).

8. Mark D. Jordan, *The Invention of Sodomy in Christian Theology* (Chicago: University of Chicago Press, 1997).

9. Arthur Groos, *Romancing the Grail: Genre, Science, and Quest in Wolfram's* Parzival (Ithaca: Cornell University Press, 1995), p. 148.

10. All quotes from Wolfram von Eschenbach are from *Parzival*, ed. Karl Lachman and Bernd Schirok (Berlin: Walter de Gruyter, 1999), for the German, and *Parzival*, trans. A.T. Hatto (Harmondsworth: Penguin, 1980), for the English.

11. Quoted in epigraph by Richard D. Mohr, *Gay Ideas: Outing and Other Controversies* (Boston: Beacon Press, 1992), p. 134.

12. Iacopone da Todi, *Laude*, ed. Franco Mancini (Rome: Giuseppe Laterza, 1974), pp. 339–41. For a treatment of the Virgin Mary in a medieval context, see Peggy McCracken, "Mothers in the Grail Quest: Desire, Pleasure, and Conception," *Arthuriana* 8:1 (1998): 35–48. McCracken refers to work by Atkinson, Pelican, Warner, Levi D'Ancona, and, more recently, Ashely and Sheingorn.

13. Mitchell Brown first pointed out to me that Perceval's encounter with the knights has homoerotic potential (in comments on an earlier version of this chapter). Mohr's discussion of the fascination with knights, medieval and modern, underscores the homoerotic potential of Perceval's early infatuation.

14. For instance, in L.T. Topsfield, *Chrétien de Troyes: A Study of the Arthurian Romances* (Cambridge: Cambridge University Press, 1981). See the discussion of Percevalian scholarship later in this chapter.

15. On the question of queer audience, see Robert Mills, " 'Whatever you do is a delight to me!' Masculinity, masochism, and queer play in representations of male martyrdom," *Exemplaria* 13:1 (2001). p. 1–37. Mills cites Gaunt's "queer wishes," and himself contributes "perverse optic" and "queer eye," among others, as labels of that position from which a queer reader speaks (p. 3). Mills also contributes to other issues raised in this chapter, castration, feminization, and "interpassivity."

16. The functioning of the Grail legend as a national legend is the focus of Sandra Hindman's examination of the manuscript tradition of *Perceval*. Sandra Hindman, *Sealed in Parchment: Rereadings of Knighthood in the Illuminated Manuscripts of Chrétien de Troyes* (Chicago: University of Chicago Press, 1994).

17. Howard R. Bloch, *Etymologies and Genealogies: A Literary Anthropology of the French Middle Ages* (Chicago: University of Chicago Press, 1983).

18. Julia Kristeva, *Révolution du langage poétique* (Paris: Seuil, 1974). *Révolution* appeared two years before the initial publication of "*Stabat Mater.*"

19. "Autour de Blanche de Castille (morte en 1252), la Vierge devient explicitement le centre de l'amour courtois, agglomérant les qualités de la femme désirée et celles de la sainte mère dans une totalité aussi accomplie qu'inaccessible. De quoi faire souffrir toute femme, faire rêver tout homme." (Kristeva, *Histoires d'amour*, p. 234) [Around the time of Blanche of Castile (who died in 1252), the Virgin explicitly became the focus of courtly love, thus gathering the attributes of the desired woman and of the holy mother in a totality as accomplished as it was inaccessible. Enough to make any woman suffer, any man dream] (Kristeva, *Tales of Love*, p. 245).

20. Elizabeth Badinter, *XY: De l'identité masculine* (Paris: Editions Odile Jacob, 1992). Translated as *XY: On Masculine Identity*, trans. Lydia Davis (New York: Columbia University Press: 1995).

21. Robert Mills's essay, mentioned above, gives an excellent account of some of the aspects of castration also mentioned here, and also touches on important issues which I do not develop, e.g., Žižek's "interpassivity," "the radically decentering process of identification by which one sustains a relationship with that which suffers" (Mills): "if the signifier is the form of 'being active through another,' the object is primordially that which suffers, endures it, for me, in my place: in short, that *enjoys* for me." Slavoj Žižek, *The Plague of Fantasies*, (London: Verso, 1997), pp. 112, 116; Mills, "Whatever you do. . .," n. 87 p. 36.

22. Robert S. Sturges, *Medieval Interpretation: Models of Reading in Literary Narrative, 1100–1500* (Carbondale: Southern Indiana University Press, 1991), provides a review of reader-oriented criticism, in Sturges's discussion of Chrétien de Troyes.

23. For a fuller list of these earlier interpretations, see Sturges, *Medieval Interpretation*, pp. 35–41; Bloch, *Etymology and Genealogy*, pp. 198–99; and, more recently, Michèle Vauthier, "The 'Roi Pescheor' and Iconographic Implications in the *Conte del Graal*," in *Word and Image in Arthurian Literature*, ed. Keith Busby (New York and London: Garland, 1996), pp. 320–21, and Brigitte Cazelles, *The Unholy Grail: A Social Reading of Chrétien de Troyes's Conte du Graal* (Stanford: Stanford University Press, 1996), pp. 151–55.

24. Because of my focus on Attis, I must mention Weston's study, *From Ritual to Romance* (Cambridge: The University Press, 1920). Her main argument connects the Grail legend to Mithraic cults. Attis figures prominently, since the rites of Cybele also originated in Asia Minor. Weston's study may be compared to James George Fraser's *Golden Bough* (1890) with which it shares the interest in comparative religion. Weston's male medievalist colleagues criticised her insistence on the castration myths. I would like to thank E. Jane Burns for this reference.

25. Maurice Delbouille, "Les hanches du Roi-Pêcheur et la génèse du *Conte del Graal*," in *Festschrift Walther von Wartburg zum 80. Geburstag. 18 Mai 1968* (Tübingen: Niemeyer, 1968), pp. 359–79.

26. Maurice Delbouille, "Réalité du château du Roi-Pêcheur dans le *Conte del Graal*," in *Mélanges offerts à René Crozet. . .à l'occasion de son 70 anniversaire,*

par ses amis, ses collègues, ses élèves. . .(Poitiers: Société d'Etudes Médiévales, 1966), pp. 903–913.

27. Jean Marx, *La Légende arthurienne et le Graal* (Paris: Presses Universitaires de France, 1952). Delbouille, "Les hanches," pp. 360–61, n.6.

28. Frappier, "Féerie du château du Roi–Pêcheur dans le conte du Graal," *Mélanges pour Jean Fourquet. 37 Essais de linguistique germanique et de littérature du moyen âge français et allemand*, ed. P. Valentin and G. Zink (Paris: Klincksieck, Munich: Hueber, 1969), p. 105.

29. Frappier, "La blessure du Roi Pêcheur dans le conte du Graal," in *Jean Misrahi Memorial Volume: Studies in Medieval Literature*, ed. Hans R. Runte, Henri Niedzielski, William L. Hendrickson, and Reinhard Kühn (Columbia, S.C.: French Literature Publications, 1977), p. 190.

30. The most extensive medieval texts on line and fly fishing are three relatively late, fifteenth-century treatises in English, pointing to the conclusion that only in the late Middle Ages did fishing become a topic of personal interest to the upper classes. Raising fish was a source of food and income on noble estates at least since Charlemagne, but the fishing grounds—*piscaturae*—were allotted to hired fishermen, rather than reserved for sport. Possibly because of its direct role in income production, fishing was not a royal entertainment. This conclusion is supported by the content and nature of the three manuscripts mentioned, all very utilitarian, as is evident in the production values of the English *Treatyse on Fishing with an Angle* (Beinecke Library MS 171). There may have been a more nuanced attitude toward fishing in the later fifteenth century, since Wynkyn de Worde saw fit to append the *Treatyse on Fishing*, preceded by a handsome woodcut picturing a fashionably dressed angler, to his printed edition of the Book of St. Albans, a treatise on hunting.

31. We have a depiction of such a one-legged hunter from a near-contemporary pavement mosaic in the cathedral of Lescar, dated to 1115–41, the bishopric of Guy de Loos.

32. Vauthier, "The 'Roi Pescheor,' " pp. 320–38.

33. K. J. Dover, *Greek Homosexuality* (London: Duckworth, 1978), mostly referring to poetry: charioteering and riding pp. 58–59, hunting pp. 58–59, and pp. 87–88.

34. Joan Cadden, *Meaning of Sex Difference in the Middle Ages: Medicine, Science, and Culture* (Cambridge: Cambridge University Press, 1995); Jacques Ferrand, *A Treatise on Lovesickness*, ed. and trans. Donald A. Beecher and Massimo Ciavolella (Syracuse: Syracuse University Press, 1990), pp. 230–31, and pp. 378–86, nn. 20–32.

35. Donald Maddox discusses this aspect in *The Arthurian Romances of Chrétien de Troyes: Once and Future Fictions* (Cambridge: Cambridge University Press, 1991), pp. 98–100.

36. Mary Frances Wack, *Lovesickness in the Middle Ages: The Viaticum and Its Commentaries* (Philadelphia: University of Pennsylvania Press, 1990), fig. 8.6, p. 164, discussion pp. 163–66.

37. Slavoj Žižek, *The Sublime Object of Ideology* (London: Verso, 1989), pp. 75–76.

38. Arthur Groos gives a thorough discussion of the cure: "Treating the Fisher King (*Parzival*, Book IX)," in *German Narrative Literature of the Twelfth and Thirteenth Centuries*, ed.Volker Honemann, Martin H. Jones, Adrian Stevens, and David Wells (Tübingen: Niemeyer, 1994), pp. 275–304; expanded in *Romancing the Grail*, pp. 144–69.

39. Variants: T "je, qui de duel grant dolor avoie" [I, who greatly suffered from grief], and U "je, qui de duel me mouroie" [I, who was dying of grief].

40. John Boswell, *Christianity, Social Tolerance, and Homosexuality* (Chicago: The University of Chicago Press, 1980). Recent discussions on the meaning of castration focus on Abelard as the major figure, including especially the cluster of articles in *Becoming Male in the Middle Ages*, ed. Jeffrey Jerome Cohen and Bonnie Wheeler, The New Middle Ages (New York: Garland, 1997), especially Martin Irvine, "Abelard and (Re)writing the Male Body: Castration, Identity, and Remasculinization," pp. 87–106; Bonnie Wheeler, "Originary Fantasies: Abelard's Castration and Confession," pp. 107–28; Yves Ferroul, "Abelard's Blissful Castration," pp. 129–49. See also Jo Ann McNamara, "The *Herrenfrage*: The Restructuring of the Gender System, 1050–1150," in *Medieval Masculinities: Regarding Men in the Middle Ages*, ed. Clare A. Lees, Medieval Cultures 7 (Minneapolis: University of Minnesota Press, 1994), pp. 3–29, esp. p. 16. On the meanings of castration and eunuchism, see recently Mathew S. Kuefler, "Castration and Eunuchism in the Middle Ages," in *Handbook of Medieval Sexuality*, ed.Vern L. Bullough and James A. Brundage (New York: Garland, 1996), pp. 279–306, and Elliot R. Wolfson, "Eunuchs Who Kept the Sabbath: Becoming Male and the Ascetic Ideal in Thirteenth-Century Jewish Secularism," in *Becoming Male*, ed. Cohen and Wheeler, pp. 151–85.

41. Julia Haig Gaisser, *Catullus and His Renaissance Readers* (Oxford: Clarendon Press. New York: Oxford University Press, 1993), pp. 16–23 and pp. 281–88, nn. 60–101. Gaisser comments on B. L. Ullman, "The Transmission of the Text of Catullus," in *Studi in onore di Luigi Castiglioni* 2 (Florence, 1960), pp. 1,027–1,057. Links to France include: in the ninth century, T (BN Lat. 8,071; called T from Jacques-Auguste de Thou, its sixteenth-century owner), a florilegium, the only extant early manuscript containing one poem by Catullus, and its sister manuscript,Vienna 277 (now incomplete and lacking Catullus), both "French in script" (p. 16).Vienna 277 has been linked with Tours. Ullman proposed that the exemplar of T and Vienna might have been from Tours, and was perhaps known to Gregory of Tours and Venantius Fortunatus. However, as Gaisser points out, if Fortunatus knew Catullus, he knew more than that one poem; the same is true of Heiricus of Auxerre, who uses rare Catulline expressions; and monk Hildmar, a Frenchman, perhaps from Corbie; Gaisser suggests he may have visited Verona from Brescia, where he resided in 841–45, and seen Catullus there. In the tenth century, Bishop Rather of Verona, who refers to Catullus in a sermon of 966 (he takes

Catullus as an example of an obscure poet), later lived in Lobbes, Aulne, and Haumont, and may have brought a copy of Catullus with him. This is the more likely because there may have been a copy of Catullus on hand in that area at that time: a copy of Priscian produced in the nearby Cologne, dated between the tenth and twelfth centuries, contains a correct quote from Catullus, corrupt in other Priscian manuscripts. The epigram celebrating the rediscovery of Catullus at the dawn of the fourteenth century mentions France in an obscure reference, although probably not in connection with the manuscript, but with the finder's patron: Frank Tenney, "Can Grande and Catullus," *American Journal of Philology* 48 (1927): 273–75, and Harry L. Levy, "Catullus and Cangrande della Scala," *Transactions of the American Philosophical Association* 99 (1968): 249–54. There are three extant fourteenth-century manuscripts of Catullus. A copy (A, now lost) of the rediscovered manuscript (V, also lost), was copied, giving O (fourteenth century, Oxford, Canon. Class. Lat. 30) and X (by Antonio da Legnano, now lost) which was then copied giving G in 1375 (again by Antonio da Legnano; Paris, BN Lat. 14,137; it came to BN from St-Germain-des-Près); and again before 1390, giving R (Vatican Library, Otton. Lat. 1829); that last manuscript, "corrected by [Coluccio] Salutati. . .became the ancestor of most fifteenth-century manuscripts," about thirty, in addition to excerpts in popular anthologies (Gaisser, Catullus, pp. 19–20).

42. The phrase occurs in William of Malmesbury, *De gestis regum Anglorum*, ii.159, in the context of a substitution in a bridal bed (describing the substitute).

43. Sharon Off Dunlap Smith, *Illustrations of Raoul de Praelles' Translation of St. Augustine's City of God Between 1375 and 1420* (Ph. D. Thesis, New York University, 1974), p. 19, n. 29.

44. Augustine uses *lex Voconia*, a law that prohibited naming women as successors, "even the only daughters," as an example of Roman iniquity and decadence. Of course, the laws of the Salian Franks, on which the French dynasty based their claim against England, had to be exempted from Augustine's condemnation of *lex Voconia*. Raoul de Presles does so explicitly, saying that *lex Voconia* and Augustine's remarks applied to private inheritance, as opposed to the dynastic (and therefore public) policy, and he quotes Waleys as the source of this interpretation, and Meyronnes as being in agreement with Waleys, in his *exposicion* [commentary] to Augustine 3:1; quoted in Jeanette Beer, "Patronage and the Translator: Raoul de Presles's *La cité de Dieu* and Calvin's *Institutio religionis Christianae*," in *Translation and the Transmission of Culture Between 1300 and 1600*, ed. Jeanette Beer and Kenneth Lloyd-Jones, *Studies in Medieval Culture* 35 (Kalamazoo: Medieval Institute Publications, 1995), pp. 105–106.

45. For a list of copies and editions of *La Cité de Dieu*, see Bossuat, *Raoul de Presles*, pp. 59–61. Smith, *Illustrations*, pp. 175–281, lists and fully annotates pre-1420 manuscripts.

46. Frédéric Lyna, *Les manuscrits à peintures de la Bibliothèque Royale de Belgique*, vol. 3, part 1 (Brussels: Bibliothèque Royale Albert Ier, 1984), p. 26.

47. Charity Cannon Willard, "Raoul de Presles's Translation of Saint Augustine's *De Civitate Dei*," in *Medieval Translators and Their Craft*, ed. Jeanette Beer, Studies in Medieval Culture 25 (Kalamazoo: Medieval Institute Publications, 1989), pp. 329–46, esp. pp. 341–42. Willard mentions the old manuscript number, as in Bossuat—at that time, either the two volumes were one, numbered 1155; or Bossuat's list counts books 1–10 as one copy of the whole, books 11–22 as another copy. On the copies owned by Jean de Berry, see Smith, *Illustrations*, p. 45, based on Delisle, *Recherches* 2, pp. 242–43, numbers 114–119. Willard is more cautious, stating that the duke had "at least three" copies, but she provides no further clarifications or references; Willard, "Raoul de Presles's Translation," p. 341.

Chapter 2   Dissection and Desire: Cross-Dressing and the Fashioning of Lesbian Identity

1. I want to thank William Paden for his valuable comments on this chapter, including on the translations of *Yde et Olive*, Claire Goldstein, who inspired the opening of the chapter, and the Reader for the press.

2. I thank Elisabeth Hodges for this example.

3. *Oxford English Dictionary, stock*: adj. 1.a: Kept regularly in stock for sale, as stock book, lot, model; stock-type. Ca. 1625 Fletcher, *Nice Valour*, V. iii: "For they begin already to engross it, / And make it a Stock-book."

4. Alistair J. Minnis, *Medieval Theory of Authorship: Scholastic Literary Attitudes in the Later Middle Ages* (London: Scholar Press, 1984).

5. Jacques Lacan, *Ecrits: A Selection*, trans. Bruce Fink (New York: W.W. Norton, 2002). Fink's translation also provides page numbers to the standard Seuil edition of Lacan's works, noted in square brackets here (Lacan, *Ecrits*, Paris: Seuil, 1999).

6. Robert Mills. "Whatever You Do Is a Delight to Me! Masculinity, Masochism, and Queer Play in Representations of Male Martyrdom," *Exemplaria* 13:1 (2001).

7. Eve Kosofsky Sedgwick, *Epistemology of the Closet* (London: Penguin, 1990), p. 140, quoted by Mills, " 'Whatever you do is a delight to me!'," n. 13, p. 6.

8. The citations are from Jacques Lacan, *Ecrits 2* (Paris: Seuil, 1971), pp. 151–91.

9. Judith M. Bennett, " 'Lesbian-Like' and the Social History of Lesbianisms," *Journal of the History of Sexuality* 9:1–2 (January/April 2000), n. 27, p. 11 [1–24]. David Halperin, "Forgetting Foucault: Acts, Identities, and the History of Sexuality," *Representations* 63 (1998), pp. 93–120. Anna Clark, "Anne Lister's Construction of Lesbian Identity," *Journal of the History of Sexuality* 7:1 (1996), p. 27 [23–50].

10. In her edition, Barbara Brewka refers to this romance as *Yde et Olive I* in order to distinguish it from *Yde et Olive II*, a different story with main characters also named Yde and Olive. This distinction is not necessary here, since I only refer to the first of the two texts. Therefore, I abbreviate throughout *Yde et Olive I* as *Yde et Olive*. See Barbara Brewka, *Esclarmonde, Clarisse et*

Florent, Yde et Olive I, Croissant, Yde et Olive II, Huon et les Geants: sequels to Huon de Bordeaux, as contained in Turin Ms. L.II.14: an edition (Ph.D. Diss., Vanderbilt University, 1977). See also Edmund Stengel, *Mittheilungen aus französischen Handshriften der Turiner Universitäts-Bibliothek, bereichert durch Auszüge anderer Bibliotheken, besonders der National-Bibliothek zu Paris* (Halle: Lippert, Marburg: Pfeil, 1873), and Max Schweigel, *Über die Chanson d'Esclarmonde, die Chanson de Clarisse et Florent und die Chanson d'Yde et Olive, drei Fortsetzungen des Chanson von Huon de Bordeaux,* Ausgaben und Abhandlungen 83 (Marburg: Elwert, 1889).

11. Sylvia Huot, *From Song to Book: The Poetics of Writing in Old French Lyric and Lyrical Narrative Poetry* (Ithaca: Cornell University Press, 1987), p. 3.

12. The earliest recorded case (1405), concerning Laurence and Jehanne of Bleury, is cited by Joan Cadden, *Meaning of Sex Difference in the Middle Ages: Medicine, Science, and Culture* (Cambridge: Cambridge University Press, 1995), p. 224, and by Jacqueline Murray, "Twice Marginal and Twice Invisible: Lesbians in the Middle Ages," in *Handbook of Medieval Sexuality*, ed. Vern L. Bullough and James A. Brundage (New York: Garland, 1996), pp. 191–222, esp. p. 202. Judith Bennett also mentions the case of two women charged in Rottweil, 1444; one woman drowned in Speier, 1477; and a case from Bruges, 1482–83, involving seven women who were executed (Bennett, " 'Lesbian-Like,' " n. 5, p. 3).

13. Francesca Canadé Sautman, "Invisible Women: Lesbian Working-Class Culture in France, 1880–1930," in *Homosexuality in Modern France*, ed. Jeffrey Merrick and Bryant T. Ragan, Jr. (New York: Oxford University Press, 1996), pp. 177–92.

14. For instance, Kathleen M. Blumreich. "Lesbian Desire in the Old French *Roman de Silence*," *Arthuriana* 7:2 (1997), pp. 47–62.

15. Glenn Burger, *Chaucer's Queer Nation* (Minneapolis: University of Minnesota Press, 2003), p. xviii. See also Dinshaw, *Getting Medieval.*

16. Works frequently cited in discussions of cross-dressing in a medievalist perspective include: Judith Butler, *Gender Trouble: Feminism and the Subversion of Identity* (New York: Routledge, 1990); Kathleen Biddick, "Gender, Bodies, Borders: Technologies of the Visible," *Speculum* 68:2 (April 1993), pp. 389–413; Sabrina P. Ramet, ed., *Gender Reversals and Gender Cultures: Anthropological and Historical Perspectives* (New York: Routledge, 1996); Diana Fuss, *Essentially Speaking: Feminism, Nature, and Difference* (New York: Routledge, 1989).

17. Keith Busby, " 'Plus acesmez qu'une popine': Male Cross-Dressing in Medieval French Narrative," in *Gender Transgressions: Crossing the Normative Barrier in Old French Literature*, ed. Karen J. Taylor (New York: Garland, 1998), pp. 45–59. Michelle Szkilnik. "The Grammar of the Sexes in Medieval French Romance," in *Gender Transgressions*, pp. 61–88.

18. Szkilnik notes that there exists no modern edition of *Valentin et Orson.* She bases her reading on the 1489 Lyons edition published by Jacques Maillard (three copies extant), and notes the episode of Pacolet in chapter XXXI.

19. Douin de Lavesne, *Trubert: Fabliau du XIIIe siècle*, ed. Guy Raynaud de Lage (Geneva: Droz, 1974).

20. This is still recognizable in Germanic languages, e.g., *kaninchen* (German), *kanin* (Swedish), *konÿn* (Dutch). I thank Sven Erik Rose for this comment.

21. Quoting Ambroise Paré, *Des monstres et prodiges* (Genève: Droz, 1971), p. 30.

22. Valerie R. Hotchkiss, *Clothes Make the Man: Female Cross-Dressing in Medieval Europe* (New York: Garland, 1996).

23. Marjorie B. Garber, *Vested Interests: Cross-Dressing and Cultural Anxiety*. (New York: Routledge, 1992).

24. *Parise la Duchesse* and *Aye d'Avignon* in the *Geste de Nanteuil*. For comments on *Tristan de Nanteuil*; *Esclarmonde, Clarisse et Florent, Yde et Olive*, see Francesca Canadé Sautman, "What Can They Possibly Do Together? Queer Epic Performances in *Tristan de Nanteuil*," in *Same Sex Love* ed. Sautman and Sheingorn pp. 199–232, at p. 202.

25. Szkilnik quotes Michèle Perret, "Travesties et transsexuelles: Yde, Silence, Grisandole, Blanchandine," *Romance Notes* (1985), pp. 25–35, and Christiane Marchello-Nizia, "Une utopie homosexuelle au quatorzième siècle: l'île sans femmes d'Agriano," *Stanford French Review* 14:1–2 (Spring–Fall 1990).

26. Elizabeth B. Keiser, *Courtly Desire and Medieval Homophobia: The Legitimation of Sexual Pleasure in Cleanness and Its Contexts* (Yale: Yale University Press, 1997), p. 159.

27. *Bérinus, Roman en prose du XIVe siècle*, ed. Robert Bossuat, 2 vols. (Paris: Société d'Anciens Textes Français, 1931–33).

28. Szkilnik, "The Grammar of the Sexes," n. 41, p. 84. Concerning the treatment of female transvestitism during an earlier period, Szkilnik refers the reader to Jacques Rossiaud, *Medieval Prostitution*, trans. L.G. Cochrane (Oxford: Blackwell, 1988), pp. 113 and 149.

29. Félix Guattari, "La valeur, la monnaie, le symbole," in *La jouissance et la loi*, trans. of: *Il Godimento e la legge*, ed. Aldo Verdiglione (Paris: Union Générale des Editions, 1976), pp. 290–98: "Tout fait social, comportemental, mythique, imaginaire, etc., pouvant être exprimé par le langage, on considérera qu'il est 'structuré comme un langage,' " p. 290.

30. For instance, continental Wace manuscripts are bound with romances, while Anglo-Normans combine them with chronicles, implying a different functioning of the same text. See Jean Blacker, "Will the Real Brut Please Stand Up? Wace's *Roman de Brut* in Anglo-Norman and Continental Manuscripts," *Text: An Interdisciplinary Journal of Textual Studies* 9 (1996), pp. 175–86.

31. D.C. Greetham, *Textual Scholarship* (New York: Garland, 1994), p. 69.

32. See Michel-André Bossy, "Cyclical Composition in Guiraut Riquier's Book of Poems," *Speculum* 66:2 (April 1991), pp. 277–93, and "Gender and Compilational Patterns in Troubadour Lyric: The Case of Manuscript N," with Nancy A. Jones, *French Forum* 21:3 (September 1996), pp. 261–80, among others.

33. See Christopher de Hamel, *Cutting up Manuscripts for Pleasure and Profit* (Charlottesville, Va.: Book Arts Press, 1996). I would like to thank

Christopher de Hamel for his very generous answer to my questions concerning cutouts, in his letter of April 27, 1999, where he directed me to the
following sources: Lucy Freeman Sandler, *Gothic Manuscripts, 1285–1385*
(London: New York: H. Miller Publishers; Oxford University Press, 1986), on
Alphonso Psalter, BL. Add. 24686, no. 1. In *Cutting up Manuscripts*, Christopher
de Hamel also mentions that twelfth-century miniatures from Bury
St. Edmunds are reused in an English Carthusian manuscript, specifically "in
the former Dyson Perrins manuscript described in G. Warner's *Descriptive
Catalogue* of that collection, 1920, no. 1, and the Sotheby's sale of 1 December 1959, lot 55" (Christopher de Hamel, letter, 27 April 1999). For Syon,
see Christopher de Hamel, *Syon Abbey, The Library of Bridgettine Nuns and
Their Peregrinations after the Reformation* (London: Roxburghe Club, 1991), p.
100. See also Joan Naughton's work on the Dominican nuns of Poissy
(example of a ca. 1400 manuscript reusing a thirteenth-century Bible). I
would also like to thank Jonathan Alexander who mentioned examples of
margins decorated by cutouts (in a conversation). See also his mention of
Syon Abbey and a "Cistercian collectarius decorated in Germany in the fifteenth century," in *Medieval Illuminators and Their Methods of Work* (New
Haven: Yale University Press, 1992). In his work on German nuns, Jeffrey
Hamburger also mentions several interesting examples, including the "pop-
up" books cited above. See Jeffrey F. Hamburger, *Nuns as Artists: The Visual
Culture of A Medieval Convent* (Berkeley: University of California Press, 1997).

34. I borrow this comparison from Angela Jane Weisl, " 'Quiting' Eve: Violence
    Against Women in the *Canterbury Tales*," in *Violence Against Women in Medieval
    Texts*, ed. Anna Roberts (University Presses of Florida: 1998), pp. 115–36.

35. I thank Sven Erik Rose for insisting on the social dimension of cross-dressing.

36. Renate Blumenfeld-Kosinski, *Reading Myth: Classical Mythology and Its Inter-
    pretations in Medieval French Literature* (Stanford: Stanford University Press,
    1997).

37. In articulating this narrative of evolution I followed Sandra Hindman's work
    on the role of Chrétien's *Graal* in emerging national French mythology.

38. Jane Chance, "Gender Subversion and Linguistic Castration in Fifteenth-
    Century Translations of Christine de Pizan," in *Violence Against Women*,
    pp. 161–94.

39. Judith Fetterly, "Introduction: On the Politics of Literature," in *The Resisting
    Reader, 1977*, rpt. In *Feminisms: An Anthology of Literary Theory and Criticism*,
    ed. Robyn W. Warhol and Diane Price Herndl (New Brunswick, N.J.:
    Rutgers University Press, 1991), pp. 492–501. Quoted by Jane Chance,
    "Gender Subversion," pp. 167, 172, 187.

40. François Villon, *Oeuvres poétiques*, ed. André Mary and Daniel Poirion (Paris:
    Flammarion, 1987).

41. A variation on the reading of carnivalesque gender reversals was proposed by
    Natalie Zemon Davis in a now venerable essay on "women on top," and later
    work in cultural studies, notably by Stallybrass and White, built on the
    conceptual frame she elaborated in that article: playful reversal as catalyst of

permanent change. It must be noted that Davis forges a fundamentally inno-
vative, not a strictly Bakhtinian reading. This optimistic reading must be contrasted with Bakhtin's pessimism about episodic reversals as factors of change.

42. Karma Lochrie, "Desiring Foucault," *Journal of Medieval and Early Modern
Studies* 27 (Winter 1997): 9. See also Karma Lochrie, *Covert Operations: The
Medieval Uses of Secrecy* (Philadelphia: University of Pennsylvania Press, 1999),
esp. pp. 14–24.

43. John Boswell, *Same-Sex Unions in Pre-Modern Europe* (New York: Villard
Books, 1994).

44. David M. Halperin has traced the evolution and influence of Foucault in his
work, most recently in *How to Do the History of Homosexuality*. In France, the
evolution of Foucault's thought is the subject of work by Didier Eribon,
most recently in *Réflexions sur la question gay*. Their approaches are different
on many counts, including disciplinary issues (one functions in the context
of American scholarship, the other is an essay). See also Michael Lucey's
comments in a preview of his translation of Eribon: Didier Eribon, "Michel
Foucault's Histories of Sexuality," foreword and trans. Michael Lucey, *GLQ:
A Journal of Lesbian and Gay Studies* 7:1 (2001), pp. 31–86, at p. 32, translator's
foreword. See also Sautman and Sheingorn, *Same Sex Love and Desire*, p. 6,
who refer to Dinshaw, *Getting Medieval*, pp. 1–54, and to James O'Higgins,
"Sexual Choice, Sexual Act: An Interview with Michel Foucault," trans.
James O'Higgins, *Salmagundi* 58:59 (Fall 1982–Winter 1983), pp. 10–24.

45. Simon Gaunt, "Straight Minds/'Queer' Wishes in Old French Hagiography:
La Vie de Sainte Euphrosine," *GLQ: A Journal of Lesbian and Gay Studies* 1:4
(1995), pp. 439–57.

46. Simon Gaunt, "From Epic to Romance: Gender and Sexuality in the *Roman
d'Eneas*," *Romanic Review* 83:1 (January 1992), pp. 1–27.

47. See the work of Robert L.A. Clark for the miracle play version (*Miracle de la
fille d'ung roy*), including Robert L.A. Clark and Claire Sponsler, "Queer Play:
The Cultural Work of Crossdressing in Medieval Drama," *New Literary History* 28:2 (1997), pp. 319–44. Robert Clark also directed me to Dianne Watt's
articles on the adaptations of *Yde et Olive*, including on the Middle English
Yde et Olive, part of *The Boke of Duke Huon of Burdeux* of John Bourchier,
2nd Baron Berners (1466/67–1533). See Dianne Watt, "Read My Lips: Clip-
pyng and Kyssyng in the Early Sixteenth Century," in *Queerly Phrased: Language, Gender, and Sexuality*, ed. and intro. Anna Livia and Kira Hall, fwd.
Edward Finegan, pp. 167–77; and Diane Watt, "Behaving Like a Man? Incest,
Lesbian Desire, and Gender Play in *Yde et Olive* and Its Adaptations," *Com-
parative Literature* 50:4 (Fall 1998), pp. 265–85. See Robert L.A. Clark. "A
Heroine's Sexual Itinerary: Incest, Transvestitism, and Same-Sex Marriage in
Yde et Olive," in *Gender Transgressions*, pp. 89–105.

48. Cited in Kristeva, "Stabat Mater" in *Histoires d'amour*, p. 229.

49. Pierre Guiraud, *Dictionnaire des Etymologies Obscures* (Paris: Payot, 1982),
pp. 58, 71, 93, 129. All lexical examples and translations are based on Adolf
Tobler and Erhard Lommatzsch, *Altfranzösisches Wörterbuch* (Berlin: Weidmann,

1925-), and Godefroi, *Dictionnaire de l'ancienne langue française et de tous ses dialectes du IXe au XVe siècles* (Paris: Librairie des Sciences et des Arts, 1936–38).

50. Ll. 7,026–7,030: Trestous li cors de joie li fourmie / Et dist em bas, c'on nel e[n]tenti mie: / 'Mes amis iert. Ains demain li voel dire. / Ains mais ne fui d'omme si entreprise, / S'est bien raisons et drois que je li die.'; ll. 7,046–7,047: La fille au roi l'a si fort enamé / Qu'ele li dist—ne li pot plus celer; ll. 7,087–7,089: 'Ore ai ma volenté. / N'ai pas mon tans en ce siecle gasté / Quant j'arai chou que tant ai desiré,' / As piés soin pere a a genous alé / Au redrecier a hautement crïé: 'Peres,' dist ele,' Or pensés du haster: / Tous jours me samble que il s'en doie aler.'

51. I would like to thank William Paden for correcting the translation of this line.

52. Marjorie B. Garber, *Vested Interests: Cross-Dressing and Cultural Anxiety* (New York: Routledge, 1992).

53. Kathryn Gravdal, "Confessing Incest: Legal Erasures and Literary Celebrations in Medieval France," *Comparative Literature Studies* 32 (1995): 290 [280–295].

54. My thanks to Claire Goldstein for this comment that I borrow *verbatim*.

55. The relationship between French and Arabic love conventions, vocabulary, and genres, although noted earlier, has only recently been explored from a queer perspective by scholars familiar with the Arabic tradition. See, e.g., two recent articles in the collection *Same Sex Love and Desire*, ed. Sheingorn and Sautman: Sahar Amer, "Lesbian Sex and the Military": and Fedwa Malti-Douglas, "Tribadism/Lesbianism and the Sexualized Body in Medieval Arabo-Islamic Narratives," pp. 123–41.

56. For instance, Angelica Rieger responds to Pierre Bec's statement that Bietris's canto may be a lesbian love song, by stating that it represents "the conventional, colloquial tone that was required by good manners between women": "Was Bieris de Romans Lesbian? Women's Relations with each other in the world of the troubadours." In William Paden, ed., *The Voice of the Trobairitz: Perspectives on the Women Troubadours* (Philadelphia: University of Pennsylvania Press, 1992), pp. 73–94, at p. 91. Cited in Matilda Tomaryn Bruckner, Laurie Shepard, and Sarah White, *The Voice of the Trobairitz* (Philadephia: University of Pennsylvania Press, 1989), p. 153. I thank William Paden for this reference.

Chapter 3   The Place of Homoerotic Motifs in the Medieval French Canon: Discontinuities and Displacements

1. *Enéas. Roman du 12e siècle*, ed. J.-J. Salvedra de Grave (Paris: Champion, 1929); Marie de France, *Les Lais de Marie de France*, ed., intro. and trans. Laurence Harf-Lancner (Paris: Le Livre de Poche, 1990); Christopher Baswell, "Men in the *Roman d'Eneas*: The Construction of Empire," in *Medieval Masculinities: Regarding Men in the Middle Ages*, ed. Claire Lees (Minneapolis: University of Minnesota Press, 1994), pp. 149–68; Simon Gaunt, "From Epic to Romance: Gender and Sexuality in the *Roman d'Eneas*," *Romanic Review* 83:1 (January 1992), pp. 1–27; Noah D. Guynn, "Eternal Flame: State Formation, Deviant Architecture, and the Monumentality of Same-Sex Eroticism in the

Roman d'Eneas," *GLQ: A Journal of Lesbian and Gay Studies* 6:2 (2000), pp. 287–319.

2. Walter Map, *Gualteri Mapes De nugis curialium distinctiones quinque*, ed. Thomas Wright (New York: AMS, 1968).

3. *Aucassin et Nicolete*, ed. and intro. Jean Dufournet (Paris: Flammarion, 1984); *Lancelot—Grail: The Old French Arthurian Vulgate and Post-Vulgate in Translation*, general ed. Norris J. Lacy, 5 vols. (New York and London: Garland, 1993); Guillaume de Lorris and Jehan de Meung, *Le Roman de la Rose*, ed. Armand Strubel (Paris: PUF, 1984).

4. Martha Powell Harley, "Narcissus, Hermaphroditus, and Attis: Ovidian Lovers at the Fontaine d'Amors in Guillaume de Lorris's *Roman de la Rose*," *PMLA* 101:3 (1986), pp. 324–37. Michael Camille, *The Medieval Art of Love: Objects and Subjects of Desire* (New York: Abrams, 1998); Pamela Sheingorn, "Charting the Field," in *Same Sex Love and Desire*, ed. Sautman and Sheingorn, pp. 1–48; Simon Gaunt, "Bel Acueil and the Improper Allegory of *the Romance of the Rose*," *New Medieval Literatures* 2 (1998), pp. 65–93; at p. 93; Ellen Friedrich, "When a Rose is not a Rose: Homoerotic emblems in the *Roman de la Rose*," in *Gender Transgressions*, ed. Taylor, pp. 21–43.

5. "To give Kelly his due, he does not neglect the consequences of Bel Acueil's gender for the allegory of the *Rose* and I shall return to his overall reading of the text as an allegory of sinful sexuality, but in assimilating Bel Acueil to 'Rose' [a girl named Rose] he simply discards the literal—what the text says—because it poses problems for his allegorical reading. And yet Jean de Meun strives to keep the literal at the front of the reader's mind. . .

    Is this conflict, generated by the 'problem' of Bel Acueil, simply in the eye of the modern beholder (as Fleming suggests), or were medieval readers sensible to it? . . .

    A number of textual features in the *Rose* create a tension between the ostensible allegory of a heterosexual seduction and a more literal homoerotic narrative. Moreover, if this is more marked in Jean de Meun's continuation than in Guillaume de Lorris's *Rose*, Jean merely develops a paradox that is already in evidence in Guilaume's text: Jean is hardly botching something that Guillaume did successfully. . . ." (Gaunt, "Bel Acueil," pp. 68–69).

6. Gaunt cites the following references: C.S. Lewis, *The Allegory of Love: A Study in Medieval Tradition* (Oxford: Oxford University Press, 1936), p. 155; John V. Fleming, *The Roman de la Rose: A Study in Allegory and Iconography* (Princeton: Princeton University Press, 1969), pp. 43–46; Alan M.F. Gunn, *The Mirror of Love: A Reinterpretation of the Romance of the Rose* (Lubbock, Tex.: Texas University Press, 1952), pp. 107–109; Douglas Kelly, *Internal Difference and Meanings in the Roman de la Rose* (Madison: University of Wisconsin Press, 1995), pp. 107–109; Heather M. Arden, *The Romance of the Rose* (Boston: Twayne Publishers, 1987), pp. 113–14, n. 8.; Michel Zink, "Bel-Acueil le travesti: du 'Roman de la Rose' de Guillaume de Lorris et Jean de Meun à 'Lucidor' de Hugo de Hoffmanstahl," *Littérature*, 47 (1982), pp. 31–40, at p. 34; Jean-Charles Payen, *La Rose et l'Utopie: Révolution sexuelle et communisme nostalgique chez Jean de Meung* (Paris: Editions sociales, 1976),

p. 18; Peter L. Allen, *The Art of Love: Amatory Fiction from Ovid to the Romance of the Rose* (Philadelphia: University of Pennsylvania Press, 1992), p. 92; David F. Hult, *Self-Fulfilling Prophecies: Readership and Authorship in the First Roman de la Rose* (Cambridge: Cambridge University Press, 1986), pp. 238–44; David Hult, "Language and Dismemberment: Abelard, Origen, and the *Romance of the Rose*," in Kevin Brownlee and Sylvia Huot, eds., *Rethinking the "Romance of the Rose": Text, Image, Reception* (Philadelphia: University of Pennsylvania Press, 1992), pp. 101–130; Sarah Kay, *The Romance of the Rose* (London: Grant and Cutler, 1995), p. 46.

7. Jo Ann Hoeppner Moran, "Literature and the Medieval Historian," *Medieval Perspectives* 10 (1995), pp. 49–66.

8. "That this play should extend even to the gender of the rose as love-object indicates just how fundamental play is to the *Rose*, given its ostensible heteronormativity" (Gaunt, "Bel Acueil," p. 72).

9. "If the *Rose* exemplifies a form of writing that enacts a repudiation of the 'straight,' then it may not be anachronistic—however unlikely it may seem— to claim Jean de Meun as a queer writer" (Gaunt, "Bel Acueil," p. 93). *Rose* simultaneously unhinges the hierarchy that separates homoeroticism from heterodoxy and that subordinates plain to metaphorical or allegorical writing: "despite its ostensible homophobia and heteronormativity, the *Rose* implicitly recognizes diverse forms of sexual pleasure while repudiating normative models of sexuality"(Gaunt, "Bel Acueil," p. 93).

10. "Ce ne sont certainement pas les passages qui nous paraissent à nous, en effet, peu faits pour des oreilles des femmes; au xiie siècle, ils ne choquaient pas autant, si l'on en juge pas le lai de *Lanval*, où Marie de France place dans la bouche de la reine la même accusation que, dans *Eneas*, la mère de Lavinie adresse à Enée (v. 8567 et s.)". J.-J. Salvedra de Grave, ed., *Eneas: Roman du 12e siècle*, 2 vols. (Paris: Champion, 1925 [vol. 1], 1929 [vol.2]).

11. Halperin, *How to do the History of Homosexuality*; Lilja, *Homosexuality in Republican and Augustan Rome*; Richlin, *The Garden of Priapus*; Williams, *Roman Homosexuality*.

12. *Wistasse* is quoted in Busby, " 'Plus acesmez qu'une popine': Male Cross-Dressing in Medieval French Narrative," In *Gender Transgressions: Crossing the Normative Barrier in Old French Literature*, ed. Karen J. Taylor (New York: Garland, 1998), pp. 45–59; Ad Putter, "Transvestite Knights in Medieval Life and Literature," in *Becoming Male in the Middle Ages*, p. 294, and Mills, " 'Whatever You Do,' " p. 20.

13. Dinshaw, *Getting Medieval*; Jordan, *The Invention of Sodomy*.

14. Lilja, *Homosexuality in Republican and Augustan Rome*.

15. "Quod pectus, quod crura tibi, quod bracchia vellis, / quod cincta est brevibus mentula tonsa pilis, / hoc praests, Labiene, tuae—quis nescit?—amicae, / cui praestas, culum quod, Labiene, pilas?" (Mart. 2.62) [Labienus, that you pluck the hairs from your chest, your legs, and your arms, and that your shaven dick is surrounded by short bristles—you offer this to your girlfriend; who does not know that? But, Labienus, to whom do you offer your depilated asshole?], cited by Williams, *Roman Homosexuality*, pp. 129–30.

16. Lancelot-Grail, ed. Lacy, p. 323: *The Story of Merlin*, chapter 35. References to the French text are to H. Oskar Sommer, *The Vulgate Version of the Arthurian Romances*, vols. 1–7 (Washington, D.C.: The Carnegie Institute, 1908–12), vol. 2, pp. 279–91.

17. *Cinaedus*, from Greek *kinaidos*, "dancer," is the most frequent designation that evokes a man's receptive role in sex in classical Latin. The primary sense of the word, an actor swinging the hips and playing the tambourine, "never died out" (Williams, *Roman Homosexuality*, pp.175–78, at p. 176). The word may draw on the link between being displayed on stage and being an object of desire, as well as on the tradition that made powerful men choose actors for lovers (e.g., Mecenas's lover Bathyllus; mentioned in Lilja).

18. The word is used both as a poetic meta-term (refrain, ornament, melody) and as a sort of onomatopeia (tra-la-la) in many refrains, especially in *pastourelles*, where its semantic over-determination is sometimes exploited (a *pastourelle* is a lyric poem describing an encounter between a knight and a shepherdess, usually a rape, and forms a subgenre of courtly love poetry in the North of France). Such is the case of the pastourelle 68 of the Chansonnier U where in each occurrence of the word *dorenlot*, a different section of the semantic field is being activated.

19. One notes, among others, the Old French *loriot*, a feminine headdress; *doreloter* in the sense of braiding or wrapping hair ("Adonc la belle Emmelot/ Desdolera son dorenlot," quoted by Tobler-Lommatzsch [then, the beautiful Emmelot unbraided her hairdo]). In seventeenth-century French, a *dorlotier* is a ribbon-and fringe-maker.

20. Scholars point to *Enéas* as the possible source for other occurrences of the motif of false attribution of same-sex preference. This link suggests that three of the four texts mentioned here (*Enéas*, Walter Map, Lanval, but not the probably later Conon de Bethune) belong to the same cultural milieu, the Plantagenet court.

21. Gaunt, "From Epic to Romance," and "Straight Minds/Queer Wishes in Old French Hagiography: *La Vie de Sainte Euphrosine*," *GLQ: A Journal of Lesbian and Gay Studies* 1:4 (1995), pp. 439–57.

22. On the functioning of *don* in the later period described in this chapter, at the Valois court, in the context of *étrennes*, New Year's gifts, see Brigitte Buettner's "Past presents: New Year's Gifts at the Valois Courts, ca. 1400," *The Art Bulletin* 83:4 (December 2001), pp. 598–625. Buettner quotes an often-cited-fifteenth-century English court document strictly defining gifting: the courtier-giver is instructed by the king to present a set amount of gold coins in a purse of a set value, and: "take the purse and the gold onto my Lord Chamberlain, then you must go down to the Jewell-house for a ticket to receive xxviii s. and vii.d. as a gift for your paines, and give vi d. there to the boy for your ticket; then go to Sir William Veall's office, and shew your ticket, and receive your xxviii s. vi d. Then go to the Jewell-House again, and take a peece of plate of xxx ounces weight, and marke it, and then in the afternoone you may go and fetch it away, and then give the Gentelman who delivers it to you xl s. in gold, and give to the box ii s. and to the porter vi d" (Buettner, "Past Presents," p. 619).

23. Lanval evokes his fidelity to the king, in terms which, in courtly lyrics, are interchangeably used for a vassal's service of his lord or a lover's devotion to his lady: "Lungement ai servi le rei, / Ne li voil pas mentir ma fei; / Ja pur vus ne pur vostre amur / Ne mesferai a mun seignur" (ll. 271–74) [I have long served the king, I will not belie my faith to him. I will never wrong him for you or for the love of you].

24. "Devant le rei est descendue, / Si ke de tuz iert bien veüe. / Sun mantel ad laissié chaeir, / Que meuz la peüssent veer. / Li reis, que mut fu enseignez, / Il s'est encuntre lui dresciez / Et tuit li autre l'enurerent" (ll. 603–609) [She descended before the king, so that everyone could see her. She let her cloak fall, so that they could see her better. The king, who was a man of taste, stood up for her, and all the others honored her].

25. Peggy McCracken, paper delivered at the International Medieval Conference at Kalamazoo, May 2002. The quotes that follow are from the abstract shared among the participants in the session.

26. "Tu descouvris ma poitrine assez blanche / Dont de mon sein les deux pommes pareilles / Veis a ton gré. . . "[you uncovered my white breast where you saw, at your pleasure, the two alike apples of my breasts]" ll. 42–44; composed before 1519 and included in 1532 in *l'Adolescence clémentine*, ed. Victor-Louis Saulnier (Paris: Bibliothèque de Cluny, 1958), pp. 67–73.

27. Overgrown limbs and flower-shaped body marks seem so aesthetically foreign that we see them no longer as part of the heroine's body, but as *membra disjecta*. They are ascribed to a particularly medieval literary aesthetic or associated to phenomena more anthropological than literary, closer to myth and folk story than to the genres where we would place them nowadays: literary fairy tale or surrealist novel. Feet play an important role in Adenet le Roi's *Berte au grand pied*, where they connote sexual impropriety, only to be redeemed in the end as the distinguishing trait and epithet of the eponymous queen Berte, an ancestress of the royal French dynasty. Hands are eroticized in romances related to the motif of the chopped-off hand, frequent in the story of the heroine's flight from incest. The heroine chops off her hand to prevent an incestuous marriage in Philippe de Beaumanoir's late-thirteenth-century *Manekine* (ca. 1270), and *Belle Helene de Constantinople*, a dynastic romance-cum-saints' legend popular both at the French and the Burgundian court.

28. Matthew Bardell, ed., *La Cort d'Amor: Critical Edition*. Research Monograph in French Studies 11. Oxford: Legenda (European Humanities Research Centre), 2002.

29. Ibid., p. 14. In Bardell's view, *La Cort d'Amor* is "a Court of Love governed by a reactionary male personification [Amor] in which 'female' views on love are challenged" (p. 15).

30. The passages in *Rose* that invite a queer reading include: the Lover at the fountain of Love, the dance and kiss of the two maidens (ll. 757–69), the relationship between Fair Welcome (Bel Acueil) and Lover (Amant), the relationship between Lover and God of Love (Amors), and the appearance of the love emblem, the rose, remarkably phallic.

31. That positioning is apparent in the illumination that Camille chooses to illustrate his point: the God of Love embracing the Lover in the walled Garden of Love, as ladies watch on from outside the walls.

32. Daniel Poirion, "Narcisse et Pygmalion dans le *Roman de la Rose*," in *Essays in Honor of Louis Francis Solano*, ed. Raymond J. Cormier and Urban T. Holmes (Chapel Hill: University of North Carolina Press, 1970), pp. 153–65.

33. Boswell, *Christianity*, pp. 213–14 and 243, cited by Friedrich, "When a Rose," p. 31.

34. Karl D. Uitti, " 'Cele [qui] doit estre Rose clamee' (Rose vv. 40–44): Guillaume's Intentionality," in *Rethinking the Romance of the Rose: Text, Image, Reception*, ed. Kevin Brownlee and Sylvia Huot (Philadelphia: University of Pennsylvania Press, 1992), pp. 39–64.

35. Important in the history of French literature, the continuations are now better known thanks to the excellent translation into English a decade ago by a team under the direction of Norris J. Lacy. As they magnify the story of Lancelot, the continuations bestow a spiritual meaning on Chrétien's legend. They conflate the *graal* and *tailloir* from the Fisher King episode with the vessels used in the Last Supper and crucifixion. Of these "spiritual continuations," the most famous is the first, Robert de Boron's, dating to the end of the twelfth century. About a generation later, the Vulgate version of the Arthurian cycle (ca. 1215–35), so called because of its popularity, gives the legend of Lancelot, the Grail, and King Arthur in five romances (*Estoire del saint Graal, Merlin, Lancelot Proper, La Queste del saint Graal*, and *La Mort Artu*). Soon afterward, still in the first half of the century, the Post-Vulgate version of the Cycle gives yet another version of the Arthurian legend. By omitting Lancelot Proper, and thus de-emphasizing the story of Lancelot and Guinevere, the Post-Vulgate version changes the profile of the story, continuing the shift of the Arthurian legend from courtly love to spiritual interests. See *Lancelot-Grail*, ed. Norris J. Lacy.

36. Gretchen Mieszkowski, "The Prose Lancelot's Galehot, Malory's Lavain, and the Queering of Late Medieval Literature," Arthuriana 5:1 (Spring 1995), pp. 21–51; see also Jean Markale, *Lancelot et la chevalerie arthurienne* (Paris: Imago, 1985), p. 80.

37. Christiane Marchello-Nizia, "Amour courtois, société masculine, et figures du pouvoir," *Annales* ESC 36 (1981), pp. 969–82. For a reading that resists Markale's and Marchello-Nizia's emphasis on homosexual potential of the male couple, see Reginald Hyatte, "Recoding Ideal Male Friendship as *Fine Amor* in the Prose Lancelot," *Neophilologus* 75:4 (1991), pp. 505–518.

38. Jill Gorman, presentation at the 2001 International Congress on Medieval Studies at Kalamazoo.

Conclusion

1. Guillaume de Ruysbroek (Rubroek, ca. 1220–ca.93) left a well-known account of his embassy to the Great Khan on behalf of Saint Louis (1253),

but it is Jan van Ruysbroeck, or van Rusbrock/van Ruusbroeck (1293–1381), Flemish mystic, sometimes called The Admirable, one of the first great Flemish prose writers and initiator of *devotio moderna*, who is quoted by Barthes, here and elsewhere (in *Fragments*, he figures as Rusbrock).

2. Jean Laplanche, Lecture of 20 May 1975, in *Literary Debate: Texts and Contexts*,. ed. Denis Hollier and Jeffrey Mehlman (New York: The New Press, 1999), pp. 336 [335–42]. Jean Laplanche, *Problématiques de l'angoisse 2: Castration, Symbolisations* (Paris: PUF, 1980).

3. Andrew Brown, *Roland Barthes: The Figures of Writing* (Oxford: Clarendon Press, 1992).

4. Miller's second example comes from Barthes's *Empire of Signs* (Berkeley: University of California Press, 1992):

5. All quotes in French of the *Plaisir du texte* are from Roland Barthes, *Le Plaisir du texte, précédé de Variations sur l'écriture*, preface Carlo Ossola, trans. Nadine Le Lirzin (Paris: Seuil, 2000): "Plaisir/jouissance: terminologiquement, cela vacille encore, j'achoppe, j'embrouille. De toute manière, il y aura toujours une marge d'indécision" (p. 85). "Plaisir du texte, texte de plaisir: ces expressions sont ambiguës parce qu'il n'y a pas de mot français pour courvrir à la fois le plaisir (le contentement) et la jouissance (l'évanouissement). Le mot 'plaisir' est donc ici (et sans pouvoir prévenir) tantôt extensif à la jouissance, tantôt il lui est opposé. . .Je suis contraint à cette ambiguïté.. . .je ne puis empêcher. . .je suis donc obligé de laisser aller l'énoncé de mon texte dans la contradiction" (p. 96).

6. The entry "Le paradoxe comme jouissance" in "Roland Barthes par Roland Barthes" reads:

> Additif au Plaisir du Texte: la jouissance, ce n'est pas ce qui répond au désir (le satisfait), mais ce qui le surprend, l'excède, le déroute, le dérive. Il faut se tourner vers les mystiques pour avoir une bonne formulation de ce qui peut faire ainsi dévier le sujet: Ruysbroek: 'J'appelle l'ivresse de l'esprit cet état où la jouissance dépasse les possibilités qu'avait entrevues le désir.'

> (Dans Le Plaisir du texte, la jouissance est déjà dite imprévisible, et le mot de Ruysbroeck est déjà cité; mais je puis toujours me citer pour signifier une insistance, une obsession, puisqu'il s'agit de mon corps.)
> *Roland Barthes par Roland Barthes*, Roland Barthes. *Oeuvres Complètes*, 3 (1974–80), ed. Eric Marty (Paris: Seuil, 1995), p. 143.

The importance of Ruysbroeck to marking the distinction between the terms is recognized, among others, by Carlo Ossola who, commenting on his translation of Barthes into Italian, quotes the same fragment (Barthes quoting Ruysbroeck on ultimate pleasure), and notes: "That is why I did not. . . render the word *jouissance* by *godimento*—'what *responds* to desire'—so as to attest the 'beyond desire,' the '*diletto*,' the '*dillezione*,' which is asked and given by the act of writing; writing always 'surrenders itself'. . .to vanquish us; the affectionate siege without surrender," playing on multiple meanings of French "*[se] rendre:*" surrender, render, give, restitute, surround (Barthes, *Le plaisir du texte*, p. 22). I am speculating that Ossola's use of *dilezzione* has something to do with dilation, opening up in pleasure. Similar difficulties arise in English. The simple translation of *jouissance* is *fulfillment* or *consummation* (primarily in a sexual sense) that implies corresponding to desire, not exceeding it. Unlike in Italian, *delight* seems chaste and learned, a Latin-based word where an Anglo-Saxon one is needed. In 1975, Richard Miller translates *jouissance* as *bliss*, and Miller's quandary is the very subject of Richard Howard's "Note on the Text," where Howard explains how Miller could not use coming, apologizes for the awkwardness of English, and complains about a lack of a "vocabulary of eroticism, an amorous discourse." Not following Miller's *bliss*, everyone prefers to maintain the French term, so that the French word now exists in English thought inflected by French theory. I follow that usage.

7. For instance, Steven Ungar, who is interested in the way Barthes's bodily presence humanizes his thought, opens his reflection on the pair *plaisir/jouissance* by commenting on Barthes's teaching. This inscribes the difference between the two terms into the central problematic of Ungar's book project, entitled: *Roland Barthes: Professor of Desire* (Lincoln: University of Nebraska Press, 1983), p. 119. In the opening of the chapter on the *Pleasure of the Text*, Ungar quotes Werner Danhauser's remarks on the body of the professor and the desire for knowledge: "Teaching is not only very personal, it is also very physical. . .when I teach somebody I teach some body" (Ungar, *Roland Barthes*, p. 113). Noting that Barthes's later works (including *Le Plaisir du texte*) are associated with his seminar at the Collège de France, Ungar implies that the body intervenes in a similar fashion in Barthes's pedagogy. Ungar tells us that Barthes was markedly more inclusive of the students than the French tradition requires (making it closer to the American, democratic mode of teaching). Ungar then assimilates the difference between *plaisir* and *jouissance* to the Platonic distinction between *philia* and *eros*, "friendly feeling and love." He concludes: "Writing on or about love in order to semiotize it is thus always to locate it on the side of the *plaisir* described in *The Pleasure of the Text* as a cultural and verbal phenomenon in contrast to the ineffable *jouissance*, commonly translated as 'bliss' but more directly rendered by [Stephen] Heath as orgasm" (Ungar, *Roland Barthes*, p. 119). This leads me to believe that for Ungar, pleasure is public and platonic and *jouissance* is private and lustful; and that *jouissance* needs to be redeemed by the import of love into lust. Ungar says that in the *Pleasure of the Text*, Barthes accomplishes that import of love into desire at a cultural juncture where sexual liberation may have worked to separate the two: "Barthes explores how to write about love at a moment when, from all indications, it is a labor of lust, nothing more than sex" (Ungar, *Roland Barthes*, p. 115). The work that Ungar assigns to Barthes's text, then, is to correct *jouissance*.

In his reading of *plaisir/jouissance*, Michael Moriarty emphasizes another aspect: Barthes's precautions against the infiltration of power into pleasure: Moriarty, *Roland Barthes* (Stanford: Stanford University Press, 1991), pp. 149–54. Moriarty writes in the British cultural studies tradition, and his book is intended as a general introduction to Barthes, patiently and clearly defining the terms. Moriarty's book is characteristic in its anticipation of a diverse readership and proactive inclusion of all constituencies. For instance, Moriarty addresses the question of gender-inclusive language in a brief note preceding the text. Moriarty's focus follows that trajectory. He notes that, in the discussion of pleasure and *jouissance*, Barthes raises the question of oppression that may mark same-sex desire just as it marks heterosexual desire. The oppression denounced by Barthes in the form of binaries such as passive/active sexual agency. These binary definitions of power, demobilized by the fluidity of the couple *plaisir/jouissance*, extend for Moriarty beyond sexual coupling and into such areas as subjectivity and equality.

8. The two bundles of interest—Ungar's interest in the body inflecting theory and reading, and Moriarty's interest in power and oppression—are connected by Ungar and Moriarty precisely to the questions of pleasure and *jouissance* in a text. The body (of the contemporary reader and of the medieval author and public) is always at stake in a queer reading, and the issues of power are of course paramount in a theoretical practice that frequently depends on Foucault's thought. For David Halperin, among others, power is the central preoccupation of an intellectual endeavor spanning decades. It is also one of the focal points of his newest book, *How to Do the History of Homosexuality*. On these three counts, Barthes appears as an important ally in thinking through queer theory.

9. Roland Barthes, "Entretien," in *Signs of the Times* (Cambridge: Cambridge University Press, 1971), rept. in *Oeuvres complètes*, vol. 2, p. 1,305; cited by Carlo Ossola, in Roland Barthes, *Le Plaisir du texte*, p. 9.

10. Diana Knight, "Roland Barthes: An Intertextual Figure," in *Intertextuality: Theories and Practices*, ed. Michael Worton and Judith Still (Manchester: Manchester University Press), pp. 92–107, esp. pp. 100–101.

11. "Le pouvoir de jouissance d'une perversion (en l'occurence celle des deux H: homosexualité et haschich) est toujours sous-estimé. La Loi, la Doxa, la Science ne veulent pas comprendre que la perversion, tout simplement, rend heureux; ou, pour préciser davantage, elle produit un plus: je suis plus sensible, plus perceptif, plus loquace, mieux distrait, etc. et dans ce plus vient se loger la différence (et partant, le texte de la vie, la vie comme texte). Dès lors, c'est une déesse, une figure invocable, une voie d'intercession" (Barthes, *Oeuvres complètes*, 3, p. 143).

12. The entry is entitled "*Rapport à la psychanalyse*," and its sole content is the quoted passage: "Son rapport à la psychanalyse n'est pas scrupuleux (sans qu'il puisse pourtant se prévaloir d'aucune contestation, d'aucun refus). C'est un rapport *indécis*."

13. Roland Barthes, *The Pleasure of the Text*, trans. Richard Miller, note on the text by Richard Howard (New York: Hill and Wang, 1975). *Le Plaisir du Texte*: "une typologie des plaisirs de lecture—ou des lecteurs de plaisir. . .engageant le rapport de la névrose lectrice à la forme hallucinée du texte. Le fétichiste s'accorderait au texte découpé, au morcellement des citations, des formules,

des frappes, au plaisir du mot. L'obsessionnel aurait la volupté de la lettre, des langages seconds, décrochés, des méta-langages (cette classe réunirait des logophiles, linguistes, sémioticiens, philologues: tous ceux pour qui le langage *revient*). Le paranoïaque consommerait ou produirait des textes retors, des histoires développées comme des raisonnements, des constructions posées comme des jeux, des contraintes secrètes. Quant à l'hystérique (si contraire à l'obsessionnel), il serait celui qui prend le texte *pour de l'argent comptant*, qui entre dans la comédie sans fond, sans vérité, du langage, qui n'est plus le sujet d'aucun regard critique et *se jette* à travers le texte (ce qui est tout autre chose que de s'y projeter)."

14. If Freudian thought was important to contemporary homosexual writers such as Genet who saw in Freud's model of socialization of the individual passing through the stage of same-sex desire an affirmation that same-sex desire is natural and common, experienced by all normal individuals, for the generations after Genet Freudian psychoanalysis played an opposite, negative role. While psychoanalysis naturalizes same-sex desire and erogenous nature of zones such as the mouth and the anus, it defines that desire and these other-than-genital ("polymorphous") erogenous zones as bound to a childlike stage, a stage that must be overcome to achieve adulthood and full social development. By that definition, "polymorphous pleasures" are "stuck" in the wrong phase of sexual development, not fully socialized or functional. Neurosis is valorized in the popular acceptance of the word—not a debilitating condition, a case to be cured, but an interesting quirkiness. Barthes taps into that popular use to valorize neurosis as the proper mental condition of writing and reading—and to valorize homosexuality as the ultimate form of writerly and readerly neurosis. Instead of a debilitating pathology, this neurosis is a condition of *jouissance*. The subtle, scotomized translation from popular acceptance of "neurosis" to homosexuality in particular, is distanced from but maintains a link with psychoanalysis. Unlike in psychoanalysis, neurosis and homosexuality are beneficial. Like in psychoanalysis, homosexuality and neurosis are interchangeable.

15. See, e.g., Annette Lavers, *Roland Barthes: Structuralism and After* (Cambridge, Mass: Harvard University Press, 1982). Lavers's book is usefully attentive in establishing chronologies and intellectual genealogies, inspiring confidence in her statement that the mid-1960s were a "watershed period"; n.2, p. 243, where she mentions a series of works published around 1966 by eminent structuralist linguists (Greimas's *Sémantique structurale*, Benveniste's *Problèmes de linguistique générale*, and the translations of Chomsky's works into French; and, only a couple of years earlier, Jakobson's *Essais de linguistique générale* (1963) and Saussure's astonishing *Anagrams* (1964)). As Lavers notes, 1966 also saw publication of other major works, such as Foucault's *Les mots et les choses*, Lacan's *Ecrits*, Laplanche and Pontalis's *Vocabulaire de la psychanalyse* (1967) which popularizes Freud and Lacan, and Althusser's two books on Marx (*Pour Marx* and, with Etienne Balibar and others, *Lire le Capital*). Lavers ends by mention of two other events: Cultural Revolution in China and the

manifesto by the Situationist International denouncing the West as "a Society of Spectacle."

16. Gilles Deleuze and Félix Guattari, *Anti-Oedipe* (Paris: Minuit, 1972). Translated as *Anti-Oedipus: Capitalism and Schizophrenia*, trans. Robert Hurley, Mark Seem, and Helen R. Lane (Minneapolis: University of Minnesota Press, 1983).

17. To say nothing of the use Lacan makes of the religion metaphor in "L'Excommunication," his inaugurating lecture at the Ecole Pratique des Hautes Etudes, where he resumes his seminar in 1964.

18. Donald Morton, "Birth of the Cyberqueer," *PMLA* 110:3 (May 1995): pp. 369–81.

19. Jean Laplanche, *Problématiques de l'angoisse 2: Castration, Symbolisations* (Paris: PUF, 1980).

INDEX

.